The Life
of Slang

The Life
of Slang

Julie Coleman

OXFORD
UNIVERSITY PRESS

OXFORD
UNIVERSITY PRESS

Great Clarendon Street, Oxford OX2 6DP

Oxford University Press is a department of the University of Oxford.
It furthers the University's objective of excellence in research, scholarship,
and education by publishing worldwide in

Oxford New York

Auckland Cape Town Dar es Salaam Hong Kong Karachi
Kuala Lumpur Madrid Melbourne Mexico City Nairobi
New Delhi Shanghai Taipei Toronto

With offices in

Argentina Austria Brazil Chile Czech Republic France Greece
Guatemala Hungary Italy Japan Poland Portugal Singapore
South Korea Switzerland Thailand Turkey Ukraine Vietnam

Oxford is a registered trade mark of Oxford University Press
in the UK and in certain other countries

Published in the United States
by Oxford University Press Inc., New York

British Library Cataloguing in Publication Data

Data available

Library of Congress Cataloging in Publication Data

Data available

Typeset by SPI Publisher Services, Pondicherry, India
Printed in Great Britain
on acid-free paper by
Clays Ltd, St Ives plc

ISBN 978-0-19-957199-4

1 3 5 7 9 10 8 6 4 2

For Paul, John, and Patrick ;-)

Contents

viii Contents

Preface

Slang is a subject that provokes strong emotions. Some people love slang and make sure they're always using the latest terms. Others hate it with a passion and look down their noses at people who use it. More complicated but equally strong feelings are evoked by incorrect and inappropriate slang use. If you use slang, you run the risk of being judged crass, uneducated, stupid, or hopelessly out of date, but the rewards are equally great: used correctly, slang will ease your entry into the social circles you want to mix in, increase your attractiveness to the opposite sex, and even save your life—or so the writers of slang dictionaries would have you believe.

This book is an account of slang used throughout the English-speaking world, from the earliest records to the latest tweet. You'll see throughout that slang has been stigmatized by association with the people who use it and that the people who use it have been stigmatized in their turn. If you want to put a group of people down, dismiss their language as slang. If you want to raise a group's status, claim that theirs is a rule-based language in its own right. During the Oakland Ebonics controversy in the 1990s, a California school board proposed to treat African American English as a separate language and to use funding for bilingual education to help African American children learn Standard English. Opponents rejected the notion that African American English was a language:

> These are kids that have had every opportunity to acclimate themselves to American society, and they have gotten themselves into this trap of

speaking this language – this slang really – that people can't understand.
Now we're going to legitimize it.

Standard language equals socialization and conformity; non-standard
language equals criminality and rebellion. No wonder slang-users are
scary.

The other side of the story is that if you don't understand my slang,
you're not in my gang. From this perspective, it's slang-users who
hold the power, and anyone who wants to communicate with them
effectively has to use slang. An article in the *Times Educational
Supplement* recently reported that British teachers were becoming
well versed in teenage slang:

> more than three-quarters of them say they know *vanilla checks* is slang for
> boring clothes, more than half know that *klingon* means a younger brother
> or sister and nearly half say they know that *phat* means great. . . . "expres-
> sive" answers given by pupils when writing about Shakespeare included
> "Macbeth, he is well wicked", "Macbeth was pure mental" and "Romeo was
> a numty, wasn't he?"

There are only two possible outcomes to the war between the Standard English Empire and the rebel alliance: either all slang is obliter-
ated and everyone speaks the same version of Standard English all
around the world (experts currently estimate that this will occur
approximately when hell freezes over), or we all adopt slang (which
would then become Standard English, creating an urgent need for
new slang terms). Although no resolution is possible, the conflict
between slang-lovers and -haters provides a fascinating perspective
on social and political change through the centuries, and that's what
this book is all about.

Endnotes
Ward Connerly (an African American Republican) is quoted dismissing African
American English as slang from Charles J. Fillmore, 'A Linguist Looks at the
Ebonics Debate', 161–9, in J. David Ramirez *et al.* (eds.), *Ebonics: The Urban
Education Debate*, 2nd edn (Clevedon/Buffalo/Toronto: Multilingual Matters,

2005), 167. David Rogers, 'We Know What U Mean, M8. Innit?', *TES*, 12 Dec. 2008, n.p. <http://www.tes.co.uk>, discussed British teachers' attitudes towards slang. My main dictionary sources are J. A. Simpson and E. S. C. Weiner (eds.), *OED Online*, 3rd edn (Oxford: Oxford University Press, 2000–) <http://www.oed.com>; Jonathon Green, *Green's Dictionary of Slang* (London: Chambers, 2010); Jonathan Lighter, *Historical Dictionary of American Slang* (New York: Random House, 1994–); and W. S. Ramson, *The Australian National Dictionary* (Melbourne: Oxford University Press, 1988) <http://203.166.81.53/and>. Internet searches were largely through Nexis <http://www.lexisnexis.com/uk/nexis>, Google Blog Search <http://blogsearch.google.com>, and (with caution) Google Books <http://books.google.com>. Entertaining and readable insights into the *OED*'s inclusion policies are available in Alex Games, *Balderdash and Piffle* (London: BBC Books, 2006), and Alex Horne, *Wordwatching* (London: Virgin Books, 2010).

1 What is Slang?

Slang in the ring

People have written many odd things about slang. They range from the carefully balanced to the rampantly polarized. The balanced ones we'll put aside for the moment, and only comment that there's been a great deal of detailed and careful research into how and why slang is used and how it's formed. But now for the polarization, which is much more interesting. Introducing, on one side of the ring: the champions of slang! They argue that slang is creative (*biff*), vibrant (*pow*), poetic (*kersplat*), and revolutionary (*ding ding*). It represents whatever is most real in the present moment; it's a badge of our loyalties and aspirations. But before we allow the umpire to raise the fist of slang triumphantly in the air, let's look in the opposite corner. There sit the champions of Standard English, legs crossed, arms folded. They're sniffily unimpressed with this whole silly undertaking. They're not even sure they're going to lower themselves by joining in with this ridiculous fight. But if they really must, they'll argue that slang is sloppy, vulgar, ugly, and trivial. Its users are either unedu-cated individuals who don't know any better, or educated ones who really should. The repetition of a narrow range of increasingly tiresome terms reveals limitations of vocabulary, imagination, and intelligence. By using Standard English, we can rise above our own petty and local concerns and communicate at once with an international English-speaking audience as well as with future generations. Choose your side.

The first part of this book provides a natural history of slang. Let's say slang is a frog (just humour me here): the first chapter describes what a frog is, the second looks at the spawning stage, the third considers factors conducive to further development (including, crucially, at least one other frog), the fourth looks at metamorphosis (the tadpole stage), and the fifth at the means by which frogs spread from pond to pond. I'm going to come back to this metaphor several times to try to make these distinctions clear. The second part provides an account of the history of English slang. Chapters in this section focus on slang in specific parts of the English-speaking world. The last two chapters, about mass media and IT slang, look at the history of slang since WWII. What there isn't so much of in this book is discussion of the way English is developing in parts of the world where it's either a minority language or a foreign language. Without a really thorough knowledge of the social and linguistic contexts, it's impossible to determine what is and isn't slang in these contexts, but it's to be hoped that people better qualified than me will write the books those subjects deserve.

Slang in the news

I'd like to start by looking at some newspaper stories about slang to identify why people get so worked up about it. The first extract is from a conversation, allegedly overheard by the writer, among a group of well-dressed teenage boys on a street corner in an Adelaide suburb in 1906:

> Things will be bally slow till next pay-day. I've done in nearly all my spond. Here, now; cheese it, or I'll lob one in your lug. Lend us a cigarette. Lend it; oh, no, I don't part. Look out, here's a bobby going to tell us to shove along. He's all right, I know him. You know the joker with the red nut. That's him.

The following words and phrases probably sounded slangy in this context, though they weren't always slang and some aren't any longer:

bally "very" (1899—)

do in "to spend completely" (1889-1977, chiefly Australia and NZ)

spond(s) "money" (a.1882—)

cheese it "to stop; to avoid" (1811—, originally thieves)

lob "to throw; to strike" (1847—, originally dialect)

lug "an ear" (1507—, originally Scottish)

lend "to give" (OE—)

part "to pay" (1864—)

bobby "a policeman" (1844—)

shove (along/up/out/off) "to depart" (1844—, originally US)

all right [to express approval] (1872—, now colloquial)

joker "a fellow; a character" (1810—, especially Australia and NZ)

nut "the head; hair" (1795—)

In this context, slang plays several functions for these youths: the first is to impress one another and any girls who might happen to be passing. Slang helps them to fit in with the group. The second is to exclude passers-by from their conversation, including the policeman and the eavesdropping journalist. Slang creates in-groups and out-groups and acts as an emblem of belonging. But the slang in this extract plays another function too: it provides the journalist and his readers with a focus for their anxieties about young people. Older people who complain about failures to obey linguistic rules often worry that deviant language is associated with deviant behaviour: that if impressionable young people become accustomed to words that challenge traditional values and perceptions, their world view will be distorted. Complaints about slang sometimes express concerns about declining civility and consideration: what could be more uncivil, after all, than excluding someone by using words you know they won't understand?

The next extract, originally from the *Detroit Free Post*, was re-printed in an Australian newspaper in 1892:

> The young man laid his cigarette down on the hall table while he went in to interview his father on the financial situation. After a few preliminaries he said:

> "By the way, pop, can I have a few 'stamps' to-day?"
> "Postage stamps?" inquired the father innocently.
> "No, sir," was the impatient reply; "I mean 'scads.'"
> "Scads, my son?" inquired the old gentleman in mild astonishment.

Requests for *stamps* "(paper) money" (1865-1905, US) and *scads* "money; (singular) a dollar" (1809-1959, originally US) having failed to produce the desired results, the son goes on to ask for *chink* (1573—), *dust* (1603—), *the ready* (1684—, from the adjectival use in *ready money*), *the stuff* (1766-1967), *tin* (1836-1961), *rocks* (1837-1977, US), *spondulicks* (1856—), *sugar* (1858—), and *soap* (1859-1894, US), all to no avail:

> "Won't you never catch on?" exclaimed the young man. "I want the 'duff', the 'wherewithal' don't you know; the 'rhino', the 'boodle', plain, ordinary every-day cash, pop, that's what I want."
> "Oh," exclaimed the father in a greatly relieved tone; "here's a quarter," and that's all the young man got.

The writer appears to run out of good slang synonyms at this stage, introducing *duff* "counterfeit money" (1781-1935), *the wherewithal* (1809—), *boodle* "(counterfeit) money; money used for bribery" (1822—, originally US), and *cash* (1596—), which may have sounded slangy in this period, but had once been in general use and is now colloquial. It isn't clear whether or how *rhino* "money" (1688-1935) is related to the animal (*rhinoceros a.*1398—, *rhino* 1870—). *Catch on* "to understand; to become aware of" (1882—, originally US) was also slang in this period.

As in the first extract, this example documents a problem in communicating between generations, but this young man is using slang to his father rather than his peers. In this imagined conversation, 'Pop' clearly understands more than he's letting on. Slang enables the young men of the first extract to rebel against their elders, but it also allows their elders to pretend not to understand, which enables them to complain about the youth of today without acknowledging that they were young once too.

The third extract, written by a British film-reviewer in 1919, looks at another area of linguistic uneasiness for many speakers of the English language:

> *Alias Mike Moran*, was particularly interesting for the way in which the English language was murdered in the sub-titles, which are so essential a part of the film. English audiences are beginning to get very tired of the continued use of American slang, much of which is unintelligible to them. It would be a great boon and a blessing if the phrasing could be drastically overhauled before the films from the United States are shown here. We could guess what the ex-convict hero meant when he complained that the Army had rejected him because he had been "in stir." But this was easy compared with such phrases as "Pipe the young sport and his skirt; a dead easy pick up," and "Nix, nix, Buddy, this guy's a friend of mine." One has a good deal to put up with nowadays, but surely this kind of thing is a needless infliction.

stir "prison" (1851–, originally UK)
pipe "to watch; to notice" (1838–, originally UK)
sport "a man; mate" (1885–, originally Australian)
skirt "a woman" (1562+1899–, originally UK)

dead "very" (1589–, originally UK)
pick-up "a robbery; a theft" (1846-1962, UK) or "a (potential) casual sexual partner" (1871–)
nix "no" (1862–, originally US)
buddy "a friend" (1788–, originally African American)

Slang creates frictions, misunderstandings, and pretended misunderstandings between nations as well as between generations. American/Australian/British people (delete as applicable) use incomprehensible slang on purpose just to be awkward. Why can't they talk properly? What we hate most of all, is when these alien forms are imported into our own national English. Actually, we all use some American (etc.) slang words ourselves, but those are fine. It's the new ones that are particularly irritating. Talk to even the most fluent slang-using teenager and you'll find that they look down on the slang used by their little brothers and sisters. If it's new and unfamiliar, most people won't like it.

In conflict with this resistance to difference is the ongoing fascination with the varieties of English spoken around the world. In 2005, cashing in on the success of a number of British films in the American market, British Airways created an online British–American dictionary that explained the meaning of words like *cheers* "goodbye" (1959—) or "thank you" (1976—), *laughing-gear* "mouth" (1964—), *peckish* "hungry" (1714—, now colloquial), *half-four* "four thirty",[1] *gen* "information; facts" (1940—, originally Services' slang), and *loo* defined as "restroom" (1932—, originally upper class). Let's make a conversation out of that lot, using some other terms we've already seen. Charles and David are in one of London's finest taverns:

> Charles: There you go. Get your laughing-gear round that, guv.
> David: Cheers mate. Down the hatch.
> Charles: Stone the crows, it's half-seven. I'm bally peckish.
> David: Where can we get a Ruby Murray round here, mate?
> Charles: I've got the gen if you've got the readies.
> David: I need the loo first. Won't be a mo.

Perhaps this sounds convincing if you're not a speaker of British English, but anybody who habitually spoke like this would be drinking alone because of their complete failure to understand the social rules governing the use of these terms. Another common function of slang, particularly in the media, is to caricature groups of speakers without regard to current (or any) reality.

In stark contrast, slang can also be used to symbolize truth and reality. This Canadian newspaper report recounts an address given, in 1918, by the poet and writer John Masefield, on the subject of 'The War and the Future':

---

[1]   *Half* before a number added half to it in nautical soundings (1809–*c*.1860), so that *half five* meant "five and a half fathoms", but the *Oxford English Dictionary* (*OED*) doesn't acknowledge its very general use in time keeping since the nineteenth century, whereby *half ten* means "ten thirty".

"It was the day after the landing, April 26," he said, "and an Australian captain was up the hill at Anzac. And an Australian major came to him, and said, 'Don't let your men fire to their front for the next half hour, because an Indian working party has just gone up and might be hit.' And the captain thought this odd, as he had seen no Indian working party. The major had the number 31 on his shoulder strap, and the captain thought this odd, as only eighteen battalions, from 1 to 18, had landed. And he said to the major, 'I say, are you fair dinkum?' (which means ... straight goods, on the level). And the major said 'Yes, I'm Major Fairdinkum.' So they shot him for a spy ... "

fair dinkum "honest; on the level" (1894–, usually Australian)

In this extract, to know and use slang is to be genuine, trustworthy, and reliable. Failure to use and understand slang appropriately can be fatal, literally in this context. This story wouldn't work if the interloper had tried to pass himself off as a British major: the guard couldn't have expected him to understand the slang used by his troops, and wouldn't have dared to address him using it. In an Australian context, slang is a potent symbol of equality and fraternity.

In Britain, slang has always been more closely tied up with ideas of social class than it is in other parts of the English-speaking world. Here a father recounts a dispute with a London cab-driver in 1868:

My son, who had just borrowed what he called "half a skid" of [sic] me, promptly took up the cudgels, or, in other words, the coarse language of the streets, and metaphorically smote that cabman hip and thigh. "Were we such a brace of fools," he asked with indignant fervour, "as to pay showful prices for riding in a blessed growler? Did the driver think to 'flummox' us by his lip, because he thought we weren't fly to him? He, the driver, must get up earlier and go to bed without getting buffy, which he hadn't done for a week of Sundays, before he found that little game would draw in the dibs. No more tight than we were, wasn't he?—(with great depth of meaning this)—then what made him so precious fishy about the gills, if he hadn't been out on the batter the night before?"

skid ?prefiguring *squid* "a pound" (1902–) *buffy* "drunk" (1853-1924)
shoful "fake; dishonest" (1846-*c*.1868) *game* "a plan" (*a*.1698–)
blessed "damned" (1806–) *dibs* "money" (1812-1984)
growler "a four-wheeled cab" (1865-1912) *tight* "drunk" (1830–)
flummox "to confuse; to trick" (1834–) *fishy* "seedy; hung-over" (1840-1882)
lip "impertinence" (1803–) *the gills* "the neck; the cheeks" (1566–)
fly "knowing" (1724–) *the batter* "a spree" (1837–)
get up early "to be alert" (1870–)

Slang is appropriate for this conversation not just because it allows the son to demonstrate that he's no wide-eyed innocent to be easily cheated. It's also fighting talk: the son uses slang to express his indignation verbally instead of physically. But, and it's the question his father asks the newspaper's readers, how did a well-brought-up and carefully educated young man come to know this slang?

Similarly nicely brought up is Sacha Baron Cohen, whose white would-be gangsta, Ali G, generated accusations of racism in Britain and the United States. *The Sun* dismissed these claims under the headline 'If you tinkin' Ali G is racis you can kiss me, batty boy':

> Dressed from head to toe in Tommy Hilfiger, he's the white boy from "da Staines Massive" who affects a black gangsta rapper accent to ask minor celebrities dumb questions... It would take a feeble-minded idiot or a pretty twisted political agenda to miss the gag.

Slang has long inhabited the area of friction between generations, nations, and social classes, but now it's particularly associated with ethnicity. Through fear of appearing racist or out of touch with the younger generation, Ali G's interviewees usually allowed his sexism, homophobia, and general ignorance to go unchallenged, expecting nothing better from him. His clothes and speech combined to create an impression of blackness at odds with the colour of his skin. The close association now felt between slang and ethnicity is a relatively recent phenomenon, dating from between the wars in the United States and exported around the world in more complex forms.

Slang in metaphors

Perhaps the best way to understand how people feel and have felt about slang is to look at some of the metaphors commonly used to describe it. The polarization of opinion is also apparent here, with most types of metaphor being used both for and against slang. When Edmund Spenser composed his allegorical epic, *The Faerie Queene*, in the 1590s, one of his aims was to demonstrate that beautiful poetry could be written without having to use fancy words from Greek and Latin. He looked back to earlier English poets for inspiration, describing Chaucer as a 'well of English undefiled' (spelling modernized). Now the Anglo-Saxons might have taken issue with that, but the idea that there is a liquid store of pure unspoilt English that can be drawn upon by speakers and writers is a common one, sometimes in allusion to this quotation. Sometimes slang is depicted as a torrent or a tide that carries speakers away. Sometimes it is less powerful, but just as dangerous: a counter-current to trap the unwary or a pollutant that seeps into English and dirties it. Liquid metaphors also describe slang in more positive terms, as a reservoir: a supply of fresh words to which Standard English can look in times of need.

The English language is also frequently referred to as a plant or a garden: it's a living thing that must be tended and nurtured to stop it reverting to its natural state. Slang terms are weeds that invade what should be the well-tended pastures of English. They are a burr sticking to the flower of English, or a fungus growing on the stem. Slang is a wild fruit grafted onto a tame stock: a source of new vitality, but only if properly controlled. More positively, slang terms are flowers from among which the English language plucks only the best for decoration.

Other writers prefer to depict the English language as a treasure (usually mentioning Shakespeare at some point): passed on to us by our ancestors as a common inheritance to be proud of, we have a duty to preserve it and pass it on in turn. Slang terms are coined as counterfeit currency. Those who use slang are characterized by the poverty of their language. Slang words are exotic treasures brought from abroad that may turn out to be worthless. Financial metaphors are also used more positively, with slang seen as a fresh contribution to the wealth of English.

The relationship between Standard English and slang is also presented in human terms. If a language is sufficiently virile, it can father its own slang terms. New words, like children, are evidence of virility, but illegitimate words are a stain on the family crest. Slang terms are low-born: illegitimate or orphan children without parentage. Born in the linguistic slums, these freakish and shifty individuals live outside the brotherhood of words, always trying to creep into use. Some, but only the most deserving, will succeed and be adopted, but only when they have proved themselves useful.

Slang is often depicted in masculine terms. It represents the recruiting grounds of the language, where those born without rank can impress their superiors and move up in the world. Slang is the adventurous element of speech: it seeks out treasures and excitement in strange places. Although English is sometimes depicted as the father of slang, it has also been described as a chaste female in need of protection from the virile manhood of its fickle suitor, slang. Slang is a slime-covered pebble littering the beach of purity: its use by young women casts doubt on their chastity.

The idea that English should be protected from slang is also presented in non-gendered metaphors. Slang and its users attack the English language: they are murderers of the language, delivering its death blow. They grip the heart of humanity or take the tongue in their clutches to enslave it. Slang is a fever of adolescence: a sign of immaturity that will pass without danger. On the other hand, slang is depicted as the lifeblood of language, a source of new vitality. The acceptance of a slang term is an instance of the survival of the fittest: it may have driven Standard English words from existence, but deservedly so. It was stronger, fitter, and better adapted to the changing environment.

Language is also commonly described in terms of clothing. To use Standard English in the appropriate setting is to be decently dressed for the occasion. Slang terms are bright colours and unusual fashions, novel and striking at first, but soon becoming threadbare and losing their charm. Some of these clothing images also play on associations between slang and licentiousness, in that bright colours and inappropriate dress have long been the stock in trade of the prostitute. They also imply that slang users are foolish, by depicting slang as the garish and foolish clothes of the jester.

Animal metaphors are less common, but slang users are compared to parrots, and their slang to the cries of animals: it's meaningless, conveying only a limited range of ideas to the listener, and represents mimicry rather than creativity. The language of an individual who overuses slang is as lifeless as a string of wet fish. More positively, English is like a snake that sheds its skin, finding new slang terms to match its new growth.

Least common of all, though still interesting, are the metaphors describing slang in terms of taste or in reference to machinery. These depict slang as a spice or a strong distillation, like whisky: good in small quantities, but requiring careful use. Slang is the escape valve in a train that releases pressure to prevent an explosion, but it's also the feeder that provides it with fuel. Slang is clearly a subject associated with heightened anxiety and strong feelings, but we still haven't pinned down exactly what it is.

Defining slang

Now you and I know what *slang* means. Of course we do. Why would I have written a book about it otherwise? Why would you have started reading it? But let's just check that we're using it in the same way.

The *OED* lists six different words spelt *slang*: four are nouns, one a verb, and one an adjective which is also used as an adverb. Although it's interesting that a type of cannon, a long narrow strip of land, and a watch chain have all also been called a *slang*, we can put those uses aside. *Slang* n^3 is the one we're mainly interested in, along with the adjective and verb related to it. The *OED* provides five definitions for *slang* n^3 that refer to language use, and another six that don't. Here are the five, which were first published in 1919, and may have been rewritten by the time this book comes out:

1. **a.** The special vocabulary used by any set of persons of a low or disreputable character; language of a low and vulgar type. (1756–)
   b. The special vocabulary or phraseology of a particular calling or profession; the cant or jargon of a certain class or period. (1801–)
   c. Language of a highly colloquial type, considered as below the level of standard educated speech, and consisting either of new words or of current words employed in some special sense. (1818–)
   d. Abuse, impertinence. (1805–)
2. Humbug, nonsense. (1762)

This is part of the reason why it is necessary to define what *slang* is before we get really stuck into the subject. *Slang* has been and is still used to refer to a wide variety of different types of language, not all of which are covered in these definitions. A book about all of them would have to cover a lot of ground and would end up not doing justice to any of it.

But for now let's stick with the *OED* definitions. The one my understanding of *slang* is closest to is 1c, but to make sense of it we need to look at what 'standard' and 'colloquial' mean. Standard English is the variety we learn to write in school because it's the most prestigious form (from the perspective of our teachers). It used to be the variety used in books and newspapers, but lots of writers now adopt a more informal tone and use a written form more similar to spoken language. There isn't an impermeable barrier around Standard English, though some commentators would like there to be: when informal words and phrases are used often enough, they can become an unremarkable and accepted part of the standard.

Most speakers of English don't use Standard English in everyday conversation. Someone who spoke like a book at all times would find it difficult to have a normal social or family life. How would they talk to their partner at intimate moments? Would they address their children only in the standard? Would they speak to their dog only in grammatically complete sentences? If they did, it's probable that the partner, the children, and quite possibly also the dog would drift away towards people that were... well... more fun. It's natural that we should alter our language according to where we are, what we're doing, and who we're talking to. Most people speak carefully when they're in formal situations, but in many informal situations a more relaxed style of speech makes a better impression. Normal speech is colloquial (from Latin *col-* "together" and *loqui* "to speak"). By speaking in colloquial English, we indicate that we are warm, friendly, approachable individuals who want to connect with other human beings on a personal level. We can understand slang to be 'highly colloquial' in the sense that it's further away from Standard English than colloquial language. It's acceptable in fewer places and used by fewer people.

Some types of English have enough peculiarities in grammar and word order to qualify as *registers* of English. If I were writing in an elevated poetic register, I mote elect t'employ strange words ne'er seen, and e'en their proper shape and order disarray. To write in a more colloquial register, I'll, like, use more contractions, and that. *Slang* isn't a register: slang is a label for individual uses of individual terms which are inserted into the appropriate slots in standard or colloquial English sentences. This means that it's often possible to guess at the meaning of an unfamiliar slang word from its context.

Some writers describe pronunciation, grammatical constructions, word order, and even spellings as *slang*, or use *slanguage* (1879—, originally jocular) to encompass all of these features. I'm sticking with the *OED* in using *slang* only with reference to words, though I'm willing to concede that pronunciation (and so on) can be *slangy*. Slang terms are usually used according to the grammatical rules of the standard language: almost all English slang plurals are formed by adding an -*s*, for example, and most slang past tenses by adding an -*ed*. When we use slang words, we don't put them in a different place in the sentence than we would their Standard English equivalents. It's unusual to find slang alternatives for words like *the, two, in*, or *because*, though they do occur. Far from considering *slang* as a language in its own right, some writers insist that a Standard English equivalent must exist before a term can be labelled as slang: that slang lies in the rejection of a more formal alternative. This position is supported by the fact that writers and dictionary-makers didn't pay much attention to the subject of slang until the eighteenth century, which is when written English became established in more or less the form that we now use it, but clearly slang-speakers talk about specific subjects in such detail that Standard English can't possibly supply all of the necessary synonyms.

My second problem with the *OED* definition is the emphasis on the novelty of slang. It's true that some slang enjoys only a brief period of use before it becomes entirely obsolete, but so do some Standard English and colloquial terms. For example, *obcaecate* "blind" (1568 +1579), *seplasiary* "a perfumer" (1650-1658), and *macaberesque* "macabre" (1876+1909) were all short-lived terms, but they weren't slang. By contrast, some slang terms have enjoyed a very long life, including *duds* "clothes" (*c*.1440—), *neck* "to swallow" (1518—), *stiff* "a corpse" (*c*.1790—), and *jerkwater* "insignificant" (1890—, US). Slang is short-lived in the same way that the sea turtle is short-lived: of the hundreds hatching on a beach, many won't even make it to the sea, but some will enjoy a longer life than many humans. There'll be more on turtles later.

Probably the most common fate for slang words that continue in use is that they become colloquial or even standard.[2] *Balmy* was slang

---

[2] If you're tempted to fling this book aside in disgust at my inclusion of terms that aren't slang in your usage, please think back to this. Lots of what was once slang isn't slang any more. Occasionally I've tried to indicate when a term moved from being slang to colloquial, but this is a perilous pastime. These dates are approximate and based on the evidence available to me. In the face of evidence to the contrary, I would revise these dates at once; in the face of unsupported assertion, I would shrug and say *whatever* (1973—, originally US).

when it was first documented in the sense "foolish; weak-minded" (1851—), but it's now colloquial in British English with the meaning "slightly crazy; eccentric" or "unlikely to succeed". It was originally derived from *balm* "an aromatic ointment", but is now more usually spelt *barmy* (1892—), under the influence of *barm* "the froth that forms on top of malt liquors". *Snide* "insinuating; sneering" (1859—) began as slang but is now found in wider conversational or even standard use. *Mortar-board* "a hat worn at graduation" (1854—) and *tip* "to give money in return for a service rendered" (1702—) were both slang when they were first used. *Snob* "an individual who despises others for their real or imagined inferiority" (1911—) developed from the sense "a social climber" (1848-1882), which in turn developed from the meaning "a vulgar or ostentatious person" (1838-1859) or "a lower-class person" (1831-1852). Its earliest uses were in the sense "a townsman" (*c.*1796-1865, Cambridge University), and "a shoemaker; a shoemaker's apprentice" (1781-1896). All of these senses were felt to be slang, but the current sense of *snob* is colloquial. *Bob* "five pence" (used with the sense "a shilling" 1772—) was recently used in an advert for McDonalds with the sense "a pound", probably from its use in contexts like *that'll save you a few bob*, in which it is used to refer to money in general. When speakers of British English complained, a spokesperson fell back on the excuse that non-standard words tend to change in meaning. Tsk! There'll be more on McDonalds later.

Some terms retain their slang status across long periods. *Pig* has been used with reference to police officers since the beginning of the nineteenth century (*c.*1800—), but it remains slang: it hasn't become standard or even colloquial in that sense. *Buck* "a dollar" (1856—) has enjoyed slang status in the United States for a century and a half, despite a fall-off in use at the beginning of the twentieth century. On the other hand, usages that were once perfectly unremarkable in Standard English can become restricted to informal language or slang. Examples include *tool* "the penis" (1553—), *lamps* "the eyes" (1590—, now dated), and *doll* "a woman, particularly an unintelligent one; an attractive woman" (1778—), all of which were once Standard English or even poetic.

Perhaps the OED definition of slang refers to language rather than words because it's quite unusual for a word to be found only in slang. Many slang terms develop from the standard language, in English at least, and Standard English words that include one or more slang senses are not at all uncommon. For example, wicked isn't slang when it's used with the sense "extremely bad; evil" (c.1275—), but the sense "extremely good; excellent" (1842—) is slang. Stoned has, over the centuries, been used to refer to individuals killed by stoning (1483), to male animals fortunate enough to have retained their testicles (1513-1694), and to fruit both with (1513—) and without (1728—) their stones, as well as with several other senses. None of these is slang. It wouldn't be correct to say that stoned is a slang word. However, when it's used to describe individuals incapacitated by alcohol or drugs (1951—), stoned is slang.

Sometimes there are only fine shades of meaning between standard, colloquial, and slang meanings. In British English, dodgy is standard with reference to a cunning individual who evades detection or capture (e.g. 'You'll never catch him. He's too dodgy for you'), colloquial with reference to something difficult, dangerous, or unreliable (e.g. 'This is dodgy weather for driving'), but slang with reference to something stolen or criminal ('The getaway car's dodgy, but it won't let you down'). Perhaps, then, we should talk about slang senses, rather than slang words.

In fact, even talking about slang senses isn't quite precise enough. The same sense of the same word may be slang for one speaker and not another. For example, hang a right or left "turn right/left" is colloquial in the United States (1966—), but slang in Britain. Brilliant "excellent" (1947—) may be colloquial in Britain, but it appears to be slang in the United States. But even statements like these are unreliable. Just because hang a right is slang in Britain at the moment, doesn't mean that it always will be. In 20 or 30 years time, it might have become part of normal colloquial English in Britain.

Rather than entering wider colloquial or even standard use, some slang terms become dated in the use of people belonging to a particular age group, sometimes to the great embarrassment of their children. These same terms might later change in status again. I can say with reasonable confidence that when I was a teenager during the early 1980s, I didn't use *cool* to express approbation ("fashionable; attractive" (1876—), "excellent" (1898—), "safe; unproblematic" (1951—)). It sounded to me, at that time, dated and absurdly American. The Fonz was *cool*, Snoopy was *cool*, and once I grew out of them, *coolness* wasn't something I aspired to. I cringed when I heard adults using it. Didn't they know how stupid they sounded? But it doesn't feel dated or American anymore: my students and my children use it, and so do I, though I try not to overdo it. *Groovy*, used as an adjective (1937—) or exclamation (1967—), seems to be somewhere along a similar path. They sounded dated when I was a teenager, and still sound dated to me, but they're being revived in British slang. It would be impossible to date these changes in status definitively: my own feeling that *cool* was uncool in the 1980s probably wasn't universal, even among British people my age. Perhaps I felt that *cool* was dated between 1980 and 1985 (I apologise for not making a note of the precise dates at the time), while other British people avoided it as early as 1975 or not until as late as 1985. Perhaps cooler people than me continued using *cool* the whole time, entirely unperturbed by anyone else's opinions. That is, after all, what being cool is all about.

Slang-users

This is, perhaps, an appropriate moment to say something about the people who use slang. Slang-users are sometimes dismissed as uneducated or unintelligent: they use slang because they have a limited vocabulary: they don't know any better words. This is, of course, *all my eye and Betty Martin* (1781—), *bosh* (1834—), *rot* (1846—), *tosh* (1892—), *crap* (1898—), *bullshit* (1915—), *bollocks* (1919—), and *pants* (1994—, UK). An individual whose slang vocabulary includes *banging, mega, sound as a pound, super cool, wicked,* and *wicked bad* undoubtedly also knows plenty of colloquial and standard words with the same meaning, like *good, great, fantastic, wonderful, excellent,* and *amazing,* several of which were slang themselves when they were first used. Someone who knew all of these terms would probably be able to select one appropriate to a given context without having to think about it. Slang doesn't drive other words from your head: it merely offers a range of alternatives that are more appropriate to less formal contexts. The slang-user may well have a wider vocabulary than their Standard-English-speaking critic. While it may be true that some unintelligent people use slang, there's no shortage of stupid people using Standard English.

According to the *OED* definition, slang often involves the use of established words in different ways, which implies that the first users of slang terms either didn't know the correct use of a word, or that they deliberately and creatively subverted its normal meaning and use. If the first explanation were correct, *prostrate* would be slang when it's used for *prostate* (1686—), *bona fides* (1845+1885, from Latin "good faith") would be slang when it's used as a plural (1942—), and *hopefully* would be slang when it is used in the sense "it is hoped" (1932—) instead of with the meaning "in a hopeful manner" (*c.*1639—). These aren't slang because we can't identify the social group they belong to, and since language just does change, there comes a point when even the most repressive judges have to stop calling changes in use wrong.

So is it the case that slang-users are particularly creative and innovative individuals, who mould language to their own ends and refuse to be restricted by convention? Well, no. Slang-users are no more innovative and creative than anyone else: they didn't come up with these usages, after all. The creators of slang terms are, by definition, creative, but the same could be said for creators of Standard English terms. Far more difficult than creating terms is getting other people to use them. This is another subject we're going to come back to.

The *OED* doesn't mention one important feature of the way *slang* is used today: its strong association with teenagers and young adults.

We go to school and then perhaps on to university with people of our own age. During this time we do most of our socializing with people our own age. For this reason, we tend to learn our slang from people our own age. This has probably contributed to the sense that slang has a limited shelf life, because teenagers will always seek to distinguish themselves not only from their parents, but also from their older (and younger) siblings and cousins. For example, attractive males are a common topic of conversation among teenage girls. A woman who was a teenager in the 1950s might have called an attractive man a *dreamboat* (1944—), but by the 1970s, when her own daughter was dating, the mother's peers would probably be the only ones still using that word, which would therefore have come to mean, for their daughters, "the type of man who would appeal to your mother". The daughter, in contrast, might be looking out for a *hunk* (1942—). It wouldn't matter that *hunk* is actually older than *dreamboat*. The important thing, in this context, is that it's not a term her mother uses.

It's only relatively recently, after WWII, that young people have been considered the main users and creators of slang. Before that point, only well-defined subgroups of young people were considered likely to be slang users. Public schoolboys and wealthy young men were written up as the most fluent slang users in nineteenth-century Britain (people at the top of the social scale rather than the bottom, it should be noted); the infantry were depicted as fluent slang users during WWI (at the bottom); with RAF officers apparently using the most during WWII (back up to the top again). These were all young men, but they weren't considered representative of young people or young men as a whole.

Slang, abuse, and swearing

We've distinguished slang from Standard English and colloquial language, but it's also necessary to define its lowest reaches. In 1888, an Australian newspaper reported a London courtroom judgement:

A plasterer who had saved £500 and therewith purchased two houses prosecuted a member of the Salvation Army for slander. At an army meeting at Uxbridge it was alleged that the defendant had suddenly startled the congregation by standing up and pointing at the plaintiff, saying:—"That man there has got two houses, and he has got them by roguery or thievery, or he has got them out of some broken down lawyer; and the moment he dies he will go straight to hell; he is regularly cast out from heaven"... Mr. Justice Manisty ruled that..."The words complained of were low, vulgar abuse—slang, and nothing else; but they did not impute any indictable offence, and therefore were not actionable. If everything of this kind were brought into court, there would be no end of actions for slander." This decision immensely widens the liberty of invective. It is no doubt a necessary liberty of speech to be able to predict the damnation of all and sundry, but it is odd that it is lawful publicly to accuse a man of acquiring property by thievery.

OED definition 1d reveals that *slang* has been used to refer to "abuse; impertinence". As in this example, however, a slanging match can take place entirely in Standard English. Many slang words are abusive, but many abusive words are not slang. For example, although I can insult you in slang by calling you a *twat* (1922—) or an *arsehole* (1949—), I can also insult you colloquially as a *cretin* (1933—) or *moron* (1917—), both of which once had precise medical meanings. Or I could use Standard English and call you a *fool* (*c*.1275—) or an *idiot* (*c*.1375—). Although a lot of insulting slang does exist, it isn't the meaning of a word that makes it slang.

Another group of words that are sometimes considered to be slang are swear words. *Swear word* is, in itself, harder to define than you might imagine, and a range of related terms are used with varying degrees of precision: *swearing, profanity, blasphemy, oaths, vulgarity, cussing*. There are at least two high-profile four-letter words that we might all agree are swear words, but the water becomes much murkier as soon as we move away from them. If I realized that I had accidentally left my children stranded in a car park, I would probably say 'Fuck!', and most people would agree that this is swearing. If, because

1 Defining swearing: Mark Parisi, 'Dam! Dam! Dam!'

I was with a delicate elderly relative, I said 'Bugger!' or 'Damn!' instead, these phrases would be playing exactly the same communicative and emotional function, but you might consider that one (or both) of them isn't swearing because it doesn't offend you. A definition of *swearing* based on explicitness or offensiveness is entirely subjective, so it's better to define swearing by its grammatical and communicative functions: *damn*, *bugger*, and *fuck* are all swearing when they're used in this way. Fortunately, we don't need to spend too much time agonizing over what is or isn't swearing, as long as it's understood that swearing isn't necessarily slang.

Bloody was once a shocking word. It was used largely by the working classes and caused their betters to shudder with horror. It was so shocking that after George Bernard Shaw had an actress utter it during one of his plays, the title of the play came to be used as a substitute for *bloody*: *not Pygmalion likely* (1914—). Really, it did! But although *bloody* is still used as a swear word, it would be hard to argue that it's now slang. Here's an account of a conversation with Robin Hobbs, a cricketer:

> While I was having a chat with Hobbsy a spectator came up and said: "Hello, Robin, do you think Essex will win today?"
> A droll Hobbs replied: "It will be a bloody good game if they do." Hobbs, 68, who played seven times for England, appeared for Essex between 1961–79.

Bloody isn't slang anymore in Britain, but it's still a swear word. Everyone knows it, and most people use it, particularly when they're trying not to be offensive. This would once have been unthinkable and, however unthinkable it may seem, *fuck* will eventually go the same way. Swearing and slang often occur together (like marijuana and tobacco), but it is still useful to distinguish between the two.

Identifying slang

It only remains to test your ability to identify what is and isn't slang. Here are some example sentences. Have a go at deciding whether or not they are slang before you read on:

1. They were tremendous.
2. Why don't you ring off?
3. He's awesome.

You didn't fall for that did you? They're not slang sentences because slang isn't a language. Would it be easier to answer, 'Which of these sentences includes slang?' Go on, have another look at them...

Actually, you'd be unwise to answer this question too. I haven't given you enough information. Whether these words are slang depends on the date and the context. In example 1, *tremendous* is colloquial now in the sense "extraordinarily good", but it was slang when it was first used in this way (1812—). Its rather less common original sense, "such as to excite trembling" (1632—), has never been slang. In example 2, *ring off* could be intended with the sense "to signal by the use of a bell that a telephone conversation has ended", which appears to have been slang during the 1880s, but had become an established technical sense by the end of the 1890s. In comparison, the meaning "to end a telephone call by replacing the receiver or pressing a button" would have been slang at around that time, though it's now an everyday colloquialism in Britain (with *hang up* more common in the United States). *Ring off* is also used with the sense "to stop talking" (1896-1953, Australian and New Zealand slang), usually as an imperative.

Awesome, in example 3, is Standard English if it means "full of awe" (1598—) or "inspiring awe" (1671—). The *OED* labels it as colloquial, originally and chiefly American, in the sense "remarkable; prodigious" (1920—). Only the sense "marvellous; great" (1975—) is labelled as slang. However, the *OED* labels the related interjection, used to express enthusiastic approval (1979—), as colloquial and originally American. I'd say it was still slang in British English.

The point is that it isn't possible to point at a word out of context and say 'that's slang'. Words don't have slanghood: there's no state of slangness inherent in a word or even in a sense of a word. It's only possible to identify an individual use of a word in a given context as slang. To work out whether these examples were slang or not, you'd have needed to know who was speaking, who they were speaking to, where they were, what they were doing, when they were speaking, and what they meant.

So can we turn to a slang dictionary and say 'whatever's in there is slang'? Unfortunately not, not really—the relationship between words in a dictionary and living slang is equivalent to the relationship between butterflies in a display case and butterflies in a garden. The words and senses listed in a dictionary have been pinned down at a particular moment in time. Even if they were correctly labelled, which is by no means always the case, there's no guarantee that the compiler understood the word *slang* as we are using it, and there's no guarantee that the label is still accurate.

You might wonder how it's possible to write a history of slang under these circumstances. How can we study slang we can't observe first-hand? On the whole, we have to rely on dictionaries and the slang used in plays and books, but it's important to remember that writers often use words with deliberate effect in creating characters and relationships. This isn't slang: it's a representation of slang, but it can seem so convincing that later writers are influenced by it. Like early European writers whose descriptions of the rhino and the oryx merged into the mythical unicorn, derivative slang writers sometimes produce something that is both far more pleasing than the original and also entirely false.

Conclusions

What should have become clear by now is not only that *slang* is a slippery word, but also that slang itself is slippery. Slang words change in meaning and status, but they may also have varied meanings and statuses at any one time. My speech is normal, and I'm sure yours is too: it's everyone else who speaks differently. This provides some explanation for the varied uses to which the word *slang* has been (and still is) put. It's often used either very loosely to mean "not Standard English" or more narrowly, but less helpfully, to mean "any feature of language I don't like". Many of the writers I'll quote throughout the course of this book use 'slang' in this way, to stigmatize the people who use it, and to some extent slang is in the eye of the beholder. For me, *slang* is a neutral term. It's identified by its social contexts and communicative functions. The next few chapters are going to explore why people use slang, where it comes from, and why.

Endnotes

Michael Adams, *Slang: The People's Poetry* (Oxford: Oxford University Press, 2009) offers a much more detailed answer to the question 'What is Slang?' American slang is well served by this and several other accessible and excellent books, including Tom Dalzell's *Flappers 2 Rappers: American Youth Slang* (Darby, PA: Diane Publishing, 1996). The conversation of the Adelaide hooligans was reported in 'Conversations in Slang', *The Advertiser* (Adelaide), 27 Jun. 1906, 8, and the conversation between a father and son is from 'Modern American Slang', *The Queenslander* (Brisbane), 11 Jun. 1892, 1134. *Alias Mike Moran* is reviewed in 'Need of a Slang Dictionary', *The Times* (London), 23 Jun. 1919, 18. The British Airways glossary was described in 'Multimedia News Release – Don't be 'Naff' – Learn to Use 'Chuffed', 'Laughing Gear', 'Half Four' and Dozens of other British Slang Words before your London Holiday', *PR Newswire US*, 4 May 2005. A spy masquerading as a major and a cheating cab-driver are described in 'Betrayed by Slang', *Alderson News*, 11 Apr. 1918, 3, and 'Slang', *Daily News*, 25 Sept. 1868, n.p. Also quoted are Ally Ross, 'If You Tinkin' Ali G is Racis You Can Kiss Me, Batty Boy', *The Sun*, 12 Jan. 2000, n.p.; Edmund Spenser, *The Faerie Queene* (London: William Ponsonbie, 1590), Book IV, Canto II; and Paul Weaver, and others, 'County Cricket Blog – as it Happened', *Guardian*, 20 Jul. 2010 <http://guardian.co.uk/sport/blog/2020/jul/20/country-cricket-live-blog>. Metaphors were collected from articles about slang accessed through Nexis, *British Newspapers 1600-1900* <http://www.bl.uk/eresources/newspapers/colindale2.html>; *Chronicling America: Historic American Newspapers* <http://chroniclingamerica.loc.gov>: National Library of Australia, *Australia Trove* <http://trove.nla.gov.au/newspaper>; *The Australian* <http://www.theaustralian.com.au>; and *The Times Digital Archive* <http://archive.timesonline.co.uk/tol/archive>. The list of slang expressions of approval is from a *Leicester Online Slang Glossary* compiled in 2009 by Julia Penfold <http://www.le.ac.uk/ee/glossaries>. A much longer and broader history of cool is provided in Dick Pountain and David Robbins, *Cool Rules: Anatomy of an Attitude* (London: Reaktion, 2000). The article 'Slang Not Slander', *The Queenslander* (Brisbane) 21 Apr. 1888, 628, which describes the acquittal of an over enthusiastic Salvation Armyist, cites the *Pall Mall Gazette* as its ultimate source.

2 Spawning

The usual place to begin the task of tracing the origins of a word (its etymology) is with the earliest available examples of its use. The word *tooth*, for instance, is used in lots of texts in Old English (OE), the language of the Anglo-Saxons and the direct ancestor of Modern English. Old Frisian and Old Saxon, languages spoken on the European mainland, were closely related to OE. The Old Frisian word for *tooth* was *toth* or *tond*; the Old Saxon was *tand*. Because there are similar forms in languages closely related to OE, we can deduce that the Anglo-Saxons probably brought the word *tooth* with them from the continent when they settled in Britain in the fifth century. *Tooth* is also related, more distantly, to Latin *dentem* and French *dent*. The differences between *tooth* and *dent* conform to patterns of change seen in many other words with similar histories, and this confirms our deductions about how the word *tooth* came to be in English. English acquired the word *dental* from Latin (or possibly French) in around 1599. Its earliest occurrences in English are in medical texts, and this suggests that it was originally a word used among learned men (learned women being rather scarce at the time). English acquired *dentist* from French in around 1759. In the earliest quotation for *dentist* in the *OED*, the word is described as a fancy French substitute for the perfectly good English *tooth drawer*. *Dandelion* is derived from the French *dent de lion* "lion's tooth", describing the jagged edges of its petals.

Now, knowing this much about the relationships between *tooth*, *dental*, *dentist*, and *dandelion*, you wouldn't be surprised to learn that the word *dent* "a hollow impression" belongs to the same word family. To understand how this meaning developed, you need only picture the dent left in a car as a bite mark, with the jagged edges of the metal representing teeth marks. Convinced? I hope not: the earliest recorded use of *dent* with the sense "an indentation" is from 1565 (before *dental* or *dentist*), and it can be traced back through closely related senses and through various spellings to the OE *dynt* "a stroke or blow with a weapon". *Dent* can't be related to *dentist* and *dental*. It was all very well as a theory, but the evidence didn't back it up.

So, if you want to trace the origins of a word, you look first at the earliest examples available and compare them with forms found in English and in likely source languages. Sometimes the context or the type of text gives you clues about where to look: for words in a scientific text from the seventeenth century, we might start with possible Latin roots, but for words in an Indian travelogue, we would probably start with Sanskrit or Hindi. The date of the earliest example would also influence which possible source languages we would look at, and common sense is very useful here. For instance, it would be hard to produce a convincing argument for the Native American origins of an English word that was used in the medieval period. Once you've located a likely source, you check that the form of the word fits in with what you know about changes in pronunciation and spelling from the history of other words borrowed from the same source language at the same time. Finally, you'd want there to be some similarity of meaning between the English word and the word you're suggesting as a source. Words aren't usually borrowed with a completely different sense. You can only be sure of an etymology if these types of evidence all coincide. Alternatively, you could rely on the conclusions of scholars who've already done all the work, and consult the *OED*, which is what I've done for the etymologies provided in this book wherever possible.[1]

Slang etymology

A text-based approach to etymology is all very well if you have lots of written examples of words in use, but it becomes rather more difficult when you're dealing with slang. Traditionally, slang tended to belong in speech. The earliest written examples of a word might date from ten, twenty, thirty (who knows how many?) years after its first use in conversation. In his *Dictionary of Slang and Unconventional English* (1937), Eric Partridge based his dates on the assumption that slang was always in circulation for a decade or more before it was written down: where he has a citation from 1880, he'll say the term has been in use since around 1870 or 1860 or even the middle of the nineteenth century. Beware of Partridge!

Another problem is that when you learn a word by hearing it rather than by seeing it written, you have to guess at the spelling, which is a shame, because spelling can provide useful confirmation of relationships between words. For example, even if we pronounce *forehead* to rhyme with *horrid*, as in the nursery rhyme, the spelling reminds us that it is the fore (front) part of the head.

When we learn a word by reading, we learn how to spell it. When we learn a Standard English word by hearing it, we can usually find out how to spell it by looking it up in a dictionary or asking a teacher, but with slang terms that might not be possible. This is fine, because you probably won't need to write them down in a forum where people will care about the spelling (though toilet-door readers can be very judgemental). There's often some variation in the written form of

---

[1] *OED* editors usually offer the results of their etymological research but not the workings out. Readers sometimes assume that the proposed etymology they believe in hasn't been considered, though it probably will have been. Discussion pages on *wikipedia* sometimes preserve arguments about etymology, and the ones for *big apple* and *fuck* offer an insight into the persistence of unproven etymological theories.

slang words before the spelling becomes stabilized. For example, in British English the word *prat* "an idiot" (1955—) is sometimes spelt <pratt> under the influence of the unrelated but unfortunate surname. *Prat* "a buttock; the buttocks" (1567—) was used in Britain until the nineteenth century, and survives in *pratfall* "a comedy fall" (1939—, originally theatrical). *Bloke* "a man" (1838—) was sometimes written <bloak> when it was first recorded, presumably by analogy with words like *oak* and *cloak*. While we are casting around for comparisons on which to base our spelling, it's easy to assume that a slang term is related to a similar sounding word. For example, when you hear the word *pot* "marijuana" (1938—), you might assume it's related to the Standard English term for containers in which plants are grown. This is going to influence the way you spell the sounds you've heard, but someone else, hearing those same sounds, particularly in an American accent, might assume that it should be spelt <pod> (recorded with the sense "marijuana" from 1952—) because it's derived from the pods of a plant. There's no evidence that *pot* "marijuana" is related to either of these words, and actually it's the buds that are harvested, not the pods, but assumptions underlying these spelling choices complicate the earliest evidence of the word's use in English.

The fact that it can be hard to determine the origins of slang words shouldn't stop us from trying. A great many slang words are derived from Standard English, and it's often possible to trace their development through closely related senses. For example, the adjective *gay* was adopted into English from French in the fourteenth century, and the *OED* records its use with a variety of senses in standard English and slang, including:

1. Noble, beautiful, excellent (*c*.1325-1802)
2. a. Bright or lively-looking, colourful (*a*.1375—)
   b. Showily dressed (*a*.1387—)
3. a. Carefree, light-hearted, merry (*c*.1400—)
4. a. Wanton; lascivious (*c*.1405-*a*.1450)
   b. Dedicated to pleasure, uninhibited, promiscuous (1597—)
   c. *euphemistic* (Of a woman) living by prostitution (?1795-1967)

    d. *originally US slang* (Of men, at first, then also women) homosexual (1941—)

    e. *slang* Foolish, stupid; socially inappropriate (1978—)

It's clear, particularly in a number of ambiguous examples since 1922, that the "homosexual" sense (4d) developed from the "dedicated to pleasure" sense (4b). Individuals dedicated to pleasure are likely to associate with those occupied in providing it, which explains the development of sense 4c. *Gay* people were those whose desire for sexual pleasure flew in the face of social acceptability and whose social gatherings were also characterized by their disregard for probity and convention. At the same time, many of the ambiguous examples refer to *gay* clothes and extravagant behaviour, and could therefore have

THE GREAT SOCIAL EVIL.

TIME:—Midnight. A Sketch not a Hundred Miles from the Haymarket.

Bella. "AH ! FANNY ! HOW LONG HAVE YOU BEEN *GAY* !"

2 Not so glad to be gay: John Leech, 'The Great Social Evil', *Punch*, 10 Jan. 1857, 114.

been influenced by the "showily dressed" sense (2b). In the early twentieth century, male prostitutes could be described as *gay* with reference to their sexuality (4d) and their profession (4c), as well as, perhaps, their behaviour (4b) and clothes (2b). The precise connotations intended by individual users in specific contexts can't be recaptured, let alone the interpretations made by individual hearers and readers, but the fact that it is so difficult to draw clear lines between these senses confirms beyond doubt that all these senses of *gay* are related to one another.

Slang created by changes in meaning

One of the commonest sources of slang is the figurative, extended, or narrowed use of Standard English terms. Often the difference between slang and standard senses will be fairly small. For example, *bowsprit* "nose" (1690-1935) makes perfect sense if you know that a ship's *bowsprit* is the bit that sticks out in front. The head is thicker than the neck, so it has been described as a *knob* (1725-1974); it's at the top of the body, like a *garret* (1788-1939); it's round and hard to break, like a *nut* (*a*.1790—). For the same reason, *knob* has also been used with the sense "the head of the penis" (1888/94—) and "the penis" (*c*.1910—), and these meanings appear to have ousted the "head" sense in British English. *Nut* has also been used to mean "(the head of) the penis" (1538—) as well as "a testicle" (1837/8—), this last usually in the plural, for obvious reasons. Similar comparisons underlie slang references to the anus as a *back door* (1592—), the penis as a *maypole* (1607-1788), and the hand as a *flipper* (1812—).

Although figurative applications of Standard English words create numerous slang uses, this isn't the only possible semantic development, by any means. Standard meanings are sometimes entirely reversed in slang usage. *Nasty* (1834—), *bad* (1880—), *mean* (1890—), and *ill* (1986—) are examples of negative terms that have been used to express enthusiastic approval. If speakers of Standard English disapprove, the slang-user will approve. Changes also occur in the opposite direction. Unreliable or unintelligent statements might still be met with an ironic *that's a good one* (1813—). If the slang-user approves, speakers of Standard English will disapprove. Having been used as a coded reference to homosexuality and become a symbol of the unapologetic assertion and acceptance of homosexuality, to the point that *gay* is probably now colloquial or even Standard English in its "homosexual" sense (4d), *gay* has since acquired newly negative connotations (4e).

Sometimes a change in the meaning of one word will produce changes in the meaning of associated terms. For example, instead of treating the reversal in meaning of *wicked*, *bad*, and the others as unrelated, we could consider them all as part of the same process:

{Standard English term of disapproval} → {slang term of approval}

Another example of linked changes in meaning arises in the overlap between words referring to royalty and homosexuality. Neither *queen* "a gay man" (1919—) nor *throne* "a lavatory" (1922—) was restricted to gay slang, but they opened the door to a range of related terms. Bruce Rodgers documented gay slang used across the United States, and particularly in San Francisco, in *The Queens' Vernacular* (1972). He listed *abdicate* "to leave a public toilet following the arrival of the police", *ball-gown* "a man's suit", *crown* "a tiara worn by a drag queen", *crown jewels* "the male genitals" (1971—), *enthroned* "sitting on a public toilet and cruising for sexual partners", *prince* "an attractive male homosexual", *princepessa* "a delicate, attention-seeking male homosexual", *queen of diamonds* "a male homosexual wearing jewellery", *queen of hearts* "a male homosexual heart-breaker", *regal* or *royal* "haughty", and *tiara* "any hat worn by a homosexual male." These terms might not have been frequent or widespread, but they demonstrate that any word undergoing semantic change has the potential to pull related terms in its wake, and that anyone who knows the more common terms will be in a position to interpret the rest.

Slang created by changes in function

Slang words sometimes arise from Standard English words used not in a new sense, but with a different grammatical function. For example, although the verb *ask* is Standard English in the sense "to make a request", *ask* is also used as a noun meaning "a request" (1987—, originally Australian sporting). The noun *beef* has given rise to several slang verbal senses, largely originating in American usage, including "to put more muscle into" (1860), "to add vigour or importance to" (1941—, usually with *up*), "to slaughter an animal for beef" (1869-1934), and "to complain" (1865—). Examples of grammatical creativity from my students' observations of contemporary slang include the use of the adjective *immense* as an interjection expressing approval (1771) and of the adjective *bad* used as a noun meaning "mistake; fault" (1986—, in phrases like *my bad*). Grammatical flexibility is common in Standard English as well as slang.

Usually words originate in their uninflected form, without endings, so that if we encountered the unfamiliar nouns *teacher* or *teaching*, or the adjective *teaching*, we would be on safe ground if we assumed that a verb, *teach*, also existed. When this assumption is mistaken, new words can be created by a process called back-formation. For example, the verb *burgle* (1872—) originated long after *burglary* (1532/3—) and *burglar* (1541—). *Pea* (1666—) arose from the assumption that the earlier form, *pease* (OE—, still found in titles of dishes, like *pease pudding*), was always plural. Slang and colloquial examples of back-formation include *flake* "an eccentric or crazy person" (1959—, chiefly US), apparently from *flaky* "eccentric; crazy" (1959—, chiefly US), *cross-dress* "to wear the clothes of the opposite sex" (1966—) from *cross-dressing* "transvestism" (1911—), and *emote* "to display the emotions" (1917—, originally US) from *emotion* "a feeling (of pleasure, fear, etc.)" (1808—).

Words can also be generated from proper nouns: from the names of people and places. Standard English examples include *sandwich* "a snack consisting of two slices of bread and a filling" (1762—), apparently named after the snacking fourth Earl of Sandwich. *Cheddar cheese* was first recorded in *a.*1661 with specific reference to a cheese produced in the town of Cheddar, but it's now more widely used for this type of cheese, no matter where it's made. Slang terms derived from specific personal and place names include *joseph* "a cloak" (1648-1861), named after the biblical owner of the technicolour dreamcoat, *Mae West* "an inflatable life jacket" (1940—), named after the large-breasted actress, and both *brummagem* (1637—, now infrequently used) and *brum* (1881-1966), meaning "counterfeit; fake" and derived from the name of the West Midlands city, Birmingham.

Proper nouns can also be used generically: we don't have to look for a specific male called *Jack* after whom the picture card was named in around 1675, nor for an individual female called *Dolly* who gave her name to the children's toy in around 1790. Slang terms derived from names include *betty* "a crowbar" (1648-1777), *oliver* "the moon" (1747-1928), and *jemmy* "a crowbar" (1808—, from a pet form for *James*).

Brand names are also sometimes used as words in their own right. *Hoover*, established as a proprietary name in 1927, has long been used to refer to vacuum cleaners generically. If you worry about whether it's possible to hoover with a Dyson, you might want to consider a career in corporate law. Losing control of a proprietary name can have serious financial implications, and McDonalds are notoriously vigorous in pursuing commercial and charitable concerns using the *Mc-* prefix. McDonalds asked the publishers of a Merriam–Webster Collegiate Dictionary to remove the definition *McJob* "a low-paying dead-end job" (1986—), on the grounds that it was insulting to their highly motivated and generously paid workforce. Slang adoptions of proprietary names include *hoover (up)* "to inhale (cocaine)" (1980/2—, originally US), *Special K* "ketamine" (1986—), and *nugget* "boot polish" (1903-1986, NZ and Australia, not slang in later use).

Slang created by changes in form

Standard English words can also be combined in irreverent and humorous ways to create slang synonyms. For example, the head has been described as the *knowledge box* (1785—), the mouth as the *cake-hole* (1943—), and a moustache as a *soup-strainer* (1867—). It is not uncommon for slang compounds and phrases to incorporate jokes and gratuitous insults. For instance, *Dutch oven* was used to refer to the mouth (1922) because Dutch people were stereotypically considered to be greedy eaters. Calling a small round steak and kidney pudding a *baby's head* (1905—) suggests a jocularly callous attitude towards infants, and it's particularly appropriate that this term apparently originated among public schoolboys whose younger siblings remained in the safety and warmth of their own homes. These terms assume a perspective shared between the speaker and listener. Calling a man a *skirt-chaser* (1926—) doesn't imply any particular admiration for him, but it may suggest an implicit agreement that women are interesting as objects rather than as individuals.

Occasionally, combining forms will take on a special meaning in slang words. For example, *-head* is used to create compounds meaning "an individual who over-indulges in [a substance]". It has produced terms like *pisshead* "an individual who drinks too much" (1946—, presumably based on the phrase *on the piss* "on a drinking spree" (1929—)), *acidhead* "a habitual user of LSD" (1965—), and *scaghead* "a heroin addict" (1996—, based on *scag* (also *skag*) "heroin" (1967—)). *Meathead* usually means "a stupid person" (1863—), but I've also heard it used with the sense "a (stupid) person who eats too much (or any) meat". The suffix *-age* appears to have little effect on the meaning of a word in current British slang usage, but it's added to create humorous connotations, particularly when it's employed in a grammatically flexible way. For example, *aceage* means the same thing as *ace* "excellent" (1934—) and *drinkage* (since at least 2002) means the same as *drink* or *drinking*, but always in reference to alcohol. *Tuneage* (since at least 2000) appears to mean "a good tune", so it may be that the suffix has positive connotations in its other uses. *Tard* (since at least 2000), created by back-formation from *retard* "a person suffering from delayed development or learning difficulties" (1909—) and "a stupid person" (1968—), has acquired the sense "an idiot" (2001—) in its own right in contemporary British slang. It's also given rise to forms like *fucktard* (since at least 2000) and *spacktard* (since at least 2004), both meaning "a complete idiot".

A suffix particularly productive at Rugby School and Oxford in the last decades of the nineteenth century was *-er* or *-ers*, which was usually used in combination with abbreviation to produce forms like *soccer* "association football" (1889—), *brekker(s)* "breakfast" (1889—), *rugger* "rugby football" (1893—), and *champers* "champagne" (1955—). Combined with abbreviation, *-ie* or *-y* suffixes are common in Australian colloquial language, producing forms like *tinnie* "a tin (or can) of beer" (1986—) and *barbie* "a barbecue" (1976—), which sound more slangy in other national contexts. Slang suffixes that are currently productive are *-io* (for example, *coolio* "cool" (since at least 2004) and *dealio* "deal" (since at least 2000), presumably from *daddy-o*), *-aroo* (*skankaroo* from *skank* "a potent type of marijuana" (2001—)), and *-aroonee* (*switcharoonee* "a switch; a swap" (since at least 2006)). The combining form *-ati*, modelled after *literati*, is currently popular in the media. Having first been used in *glitterati* "celebrities" (1946—), it now appears in the forms *bloggerati* "those who communicate in blogs" (since at least 2003) and *twitterati* "those who communicate via Twitter" (since at least 2007 with this meaning, but since at least 1989 with the sense "unintelligent talkative socialites"). *Glitterati, bloggerati,* and *twitterati* all imply that although the communicators may influence opinions on the subjects they discuss, they're not necessarily well-informed or worth listening to. More positively, the combining form *-(o)sphere*, based on words like *atmosphere* and *biosphere*, has given rise to *blogosphere* and *twittersphere* "blog/Twitter writers and readers and their intellectual environment" (1999—).

Slang prefixes also occur, but they appear to be less common. *Super-* is used to create Standard English terms as well, but some slang products include *superfatted* "very fat" (1927—), *super-cool* "very cool" (1967—), and *superfly* "very good; excellent" (1971—). Even less common are infixes, which are generally informal in English. Currently productive in slang is *-iz(n)-*, apparently used as an intensifier, in *biznatch* "bitch: an unpleasant person" (1997—, originally African American) and *shiznit* "shit" (1997—, originally African American and students). The combining form *-izzle* was popularized by Snoop Dogg, and is particularly found in *fo(r)shizzle* "for sure" (since at least 2001).

Slang created by abbreviation

Slang terms can also arise from various types of abbreviation of Standard English terms. The beginning of the word can be omitted, as in *za* for "pizza" (1968—) or *sup?* for "what's up?" (1981—); or the end of the word can be omitted, as in *Oz* for "Australia" (1908—), *dis* "to disrespect" (1980—), or *leg* or *ledge* (since at least 2007—) for *legend* "excellent" (1997—). These forms could be abbreviations of *legendary* or derived from the noun (*This party is a leg(end)*) or interjection (*Great party. Leg(end)!*). With slang etymologies like this, we should feel under less pressure to make a definitive decision than we might do in Standard English: different users may have derived the word in all three of these ways, and all three streams of derivation would have come together to reinforce the common usage. Sometimes pairs of words are abbreviated and combined in blends, such as *gaydar* "the ability to recognize a (fellow) homosexual" (1982—), *fugly* "fucking ugly" (1984—), and *blog* "a web log" (1999—). None of these processes is restricted to slang: clipping and blends produce colloquial and Standard English terms too, such as *pop(ular music)*, *telly(vision)*, *(tele)phone*, *(omni)bus*, *motel* (motor +hotel), *smog* (smoke+fog), and *emoticon* (*emote* or *emotion+icon*).

Two other forms of abbreviation became productive during the twentieth century: initialisms and, particularly after WWII, acronyms. Both consist of the initial letters of the phrase they represent, with the distinction being that initialisms, such as *BBC, CNN,* and *ABC,* are pronounced as a series of letters; while acronyms, like *AIDS (acquired immune deficiency syndrome), laser (light amplification by the stimulated emission of radiation),* and *WASP (white Anglo-Saxon Protestant)* are pronounced as words in their own right. As these examples show, Standard English words can also be produced in both ways. Some slang examples include *Naafi* (1927—, from *Navy, Army, and Air Force Institutes), JAP* (1969—, from *Jewish-American princess),* and *MILF* (1995—, from *Mother (Mom* or *Mum) I'd like to fuck). Lol* (1990—) provides a slang example of a

3 Crossed wires I: Mark Parisi, 'When You Type ROFL'.

word that can be either an initialism or an acronym. Short for *laughing out loud*, it originated in online communication but is now also used in speech, both as an initialism (spelt out) and as an acronym (rhyming with *doll*). In writing it usually means nothing more than, "I acknowledge your attempt at humour". In speech it can mean, "I consider your attempt at humour to have been embarrassingly unsuccessful".

Initialisms are pretty easy to spot, in speech at least, but some slang etymologists have a tendency to see acronyms where none exist. One of the best known examples is the derivation of *posh* "smart, stylish, genteel" (1914—) from the phrase *port out starboard home*, allegedly stamped on a superior class of passenger ticket to India to ensure that the holder enjoyed some respite from the sun on their voyages to and from India. Even before we start looking at the evidence, we would have to be wary of an acronym dating from before WWII and having nothing to do with WWI, because the earliest acronyms tended to originate in military contexts. Having no doubt received lots of confident assurances that the word is acronymic, the *OED* notes, rather impatiently, that although this 'popular explanation [is] still frequently repeated ... no evidence has been found for the existence of such tickets'. Similarly unconvincing etymologies have been presented, sometimes sincerely, for *fuck* (*filed under carnal knowledge*; *fornicate under consent of the king*), *swag* (*stuff we all get*), and *gay* (*good as you*; *good at yoga*; *got aids yet*), among others. Sometimes, as in the acronymic explanations for *gay* (please don't blame the messenger), the acronym is actually working the other way round: the word is broken down into its constituent letters and then a phrase is created to provide an insight into the meaning of the original word. Sometimes called *bacronyms*, these reverse acronyms are often intended to be humorous.

Slang created by changes in spelling

A relatively recent source of slang is typographical variation: the respelling of words to indicate that they are being used in a specific sense. This only works in written communication, but it can sometimes lead to changes in pronunciation when speakers wish to distinguish between two uses of a word. It's commonly used in advertising, as well as in text messaging, on social networking sites, and other online forums. In its simplest form, this typographical variation involves the insertion of a symbol to represent a sound (e.g. *m8* for "mate", *CU* for "see you"), but sometimes words are respelt to indicate that they're being used with a different emphasis. *Phat* "sexy, attractive; excellent, fashionable" (1963—) is probably derived from *fat*, but it's often respelt to avoid potential ambiguities. Rap artists often use respellings such as *-a* for *-er* (e.g. *nigga, gangsta*) and *-z* for *-s* (e.g. *boyz, gunz*) to express their rejection of conventional values. Sometimes the respelling does indicate a change in pronunciation. My students report the use of *choon* for "tune", specifically a good tune, *innit* for "isn't it", specifically when used as a tag question (*We're going to town, innit*) or interjection (A: *This is a great party.* B: *Innit!*) (1962—), and *tinternet*, coined or at least popularized by the comedian Peter Kay, for "the Internet", all apparently with little change in meaning.

Folk etymology

Changes in meaning or grammatical function, various forms of abbreviation, and respelling are the main ways that slang currently develops from existing words in Standard English, but these mechanisms don't account for all slang terms by any means. Sometimes a slang term has no clear relationship to, or only a fancied relationship with, existing Standard English words, and what often comes into operation here is a process already touched on, called folk etymology. Folk etymology produces accounts of the origins of words based on superficial similarities, like the association made between *pot* "marijuana" and Standard English *pot* and *pod*. Usually folk etymology is a more or less subconscious process: correct and incorrect etymologies can coexist perfectly happily, but sometimes misunderstandings about the origins of a word can cause changes in meaning. For example, the word *bedu* meant "a prayer" in OE, but because prayers were counted on rosaries, the term was transferred to the small round balls that were passed through the fingers as prayers were counted, which came to be known as *beads*. *Bare* is used both as an intensifier (*this is bare good* "this is very good") and as an adjective (*there are bare people here* "there are lots of people here") (1997—) in contemporary British slang. It isn't yet included in the *OED*, but *Green's Dictionary of Slang* traces it to a Barbadian use of *bare* as an adjective meaning "not many" (as in *barely enough*), also found in black British usage. Perhaps because it's ambiguous in contexts like *there are bare people here*, it's sometimes spelt <*bear*>. Similarly, *merk* "to kill or humiliate (someone)" (2002—) is sometimes spelt <murk> as if it were connected with *murky* "dark; unclear". *What a gwaan?* and *Wha'gwaan?* have been used as greetings among black British teenagers since 1986, according to Green, under the influence of West Indian usage. My students (mostly white) commonly record it as *wagwan* and sometimes abbreviate it to *wag*, leaving open the possibility that later users will develop theories about how this word can have developed from the verb *wag*. Over time, assumptions about the origins of these words may influence their meanings and usage. For example, if *bare* is understood to have positive connotations by association with teddy bears, it may come to be restricted in use as a cutesy intensifier only for positive adjectives, and be used in sentences like *this is bear good*, but not *this is bear bad*.

It isn't unusual for the origins of Standard English terms to be obscure or unknown. The origins of *awning, beagle, clever,* and *gravy* haven't been documented with any certainty, for instance. Because of the particular difficulties associated with slang etymology, we should resist the temptations of folk etymology and accept that 'origin unknown' is going to be a more common outcome for slang terms. Be particularly wary of good stories. You may have read that *slang* is related to the Old Norse *sleng-* and Modern English *sling*, because *slang* is thrown like a missile, but like many a good etymological anecdote, it isn't supported by the history of the two words. This and other theories are discussed in Liberman's *Analytic Dictionary of English Etymology*.

Folk etymology demonstrates that we think about the origins of words and phrases and about how they are related to one another without being prompted to do so. Before they learnt to read, my two sons often produced folk-etymological forms, including *cheekmonk* (for *chipmunk*, used to describe someone with too much food in their mouth), *hand-burger*, and *noodle in a haystack*. Luke Skywalker's shiny robotic friend was, for a while, referred to as *See-Through P.O.* These are the product of analytical thought about the origins and meanings of words, and the fact that they were produced by preschool children indicates how fundamental this desire to analyse meaning is. When we hear a word we don't know, we try to relate it to words we do know. The etymologies we come up with may be right or wrong, but it's only reference to the evidence that can determine this. Unfortunately, many people who write about the etymologies of slang words don't appreciate the importance of looking at the evidence, and prefer instead an exotic origin or a jolly good story. Don't be one of them: evaluate the evidence, not the theory. If there's only a theory, it probably isn't correct.

The influence of other words

It's possible, but unusual, for there to be two etymologies for a single word, either because it's impossible to distinguish between two closely related alternatives or because a process of folk etymology or assimilation has led two separate words to fall together. For example, grammarians now talk about the *mood* of verbs (indicative, subjunctive, imperative, interrogative), but the *OED* shows that this sense was originally part of the noun *mode* which was influenced by *mood* "a prevailing but temporary state of mind". A slang example of two words growing together is found in the term *shamus* "a watchman; a policeman" (1925—, US slang). In an extremely critical review of Eric Partridge's *Dictionary of the Underworld* (1949), Gershon Legman ridiculed his derivation of *shamus* from the Irish personal name *Seamus*, arguing instead that it is from the Hebrew word *shomus* "sexton; caretaker; night watchman". The *OED* provides both as possible sources, and there's no reason why two individuals in conversation couldn't understand one another perfectly despite interpreting the term differently:

> A: *Did you see that shomus?*
> B: *Who, Detective O'Malley?*
> A: *That's the one.*

Words that sound like tabooed words sometimes fall from use altogether instead of changing in meaning. For example, *coney* used to be the general term for "a rabbit" (*c*.1340-1885), but it may have been avoided after it became associated with *cunny* "the vagina" (1599—), allowing *rabbit* (*a*.1398—, in various forms) to become the dominant alternative. Similarly, the phrase *kick against the pricks* originally referred to animals risking punishment by resisting attempts to drive them with a *prick* "a goad or spur" (*c*.1225-1993). Once *prick* "a penis" (*c*.1555—) acquired the sense "a stupid or contemptible person" (1882—), it became possible to understand *kicking against the pricks* as referring to justifiable stubbornness. This extract is from a film review:

> Kristin Scott Thomas...has a major role as a former British au pair kicking against the pricks in haut-bourgeois Nîmes. The principal prick is her rich, insensitive husband...

What we can't know is how many speakers and writers now avoid using the phrase because they interpret *prick* with reference to its impolite senses, or how many hearers interpret it as obscene, and this is one way in which terms and phrases that were once widely used can become slang.

The failure to avoid words mistakenly associated with tabooed terms can have dire consequence. David Howard, head of the American Office of the Public Advocate, had to resign in 1999 after employees complained about his use of the word *niggardly* in conversation. They associated *niggard* "a parsimonious person" (*c*.1384—, in various forms) with the unrelated *nigger* (1574—). Although Howard was

rehired after investigations revealed that *niggardly* has no racial connotations, it's probable that he would have avoided using the word after
this incident, and his experience will have influenced other people too.
However secure you feel in your etymological knowledge, it's just not
worth using a word that's open to misunderstanding in this way, and
continuing to use a word once you've become aware it might offend
demonstrates a lack of concern for other people's feelings.

Slang loans

Of course, slang words aren't always generated from existing English
words. Some are borrowed from other languages, including *medico* "a
doctor; a medical student", from Italian or Spanish (1689—), and
kahuna "a skilled surfer" (1957—), from a Hawaiian word meaning "a
priest; wise man; expert" (1886-1948). My students report the use of
über, from the German preposition meaning "above", but employed
by them as an adjective: *this party is über/this is an über party.*[2]
Speakers of English have often derived slang from other languages
they've come into contact with, and soldiers have more opportunities
to travel than many other people. Some of the slang words picked up
by British soldiers through the years include *wallah* "a man", from a
Hindi suffix meaning "pertaining to or connected with" but used in
English compounds as if it were a noun meaning "man" (1785—),
and also as an independent word (1965—) referring to civil servants
or bureaucrats. *Bint* "a woman" (1855—) comes from an Arab term
meaning "daughter". From the French *il n'y en a plus* "there is no
more", British soldiers gained *napoo*, used as an interjection "all gone;
finished" (1915—), as a verb "to finish; to kill" (1915-1925), and an

---

[2] The *OED* lists a number of loans from German including *über* as a preposition or
prefix, but doesn't record its productive use in English. *Urban Dictionary* records
almost 500 words and phrases containing *uber*, although variable spelling contributes
to a great deal of repetition. They include *uberage* "greatness (the state of being *uber*)"
(since at least 2005), *ubergeek* "a computer nerd" (since at least 2001), and *uber hottie*
"an extremely attractive individual" (since at least 2005).

adjective "good for nothing; finished; dead" (1917—). American soldiers have also introduced slang terms from other languages. *Geronimo* (1941—) was first used as a battle cry from the name of an Apache chief. *Gungho* "enthusiastic; eager" (1942—) comes from the Chinese meaning "work together". *Banzai* "a reckless attack" (1945-*a*.1982) is derived from a Japanese celebratory cry meaning "ten thousand years". Hebrew has also contributed a number of slang terms to English, usually through the medium of Yiddish, including *meshuga* "crazy" (1885—), *schmuck* "a fool" (1892—), and possibly also *futz* "to mess around" (1929/30—).

Slang from sound

Most slang comes from adapting the use or form of existing words, but slang also creates entirely new words. Imitative (also called echoic and onomatopoeic) words often remain informal and sometimes humorous, even when they are widely used as direct representations of sounds like *clink* (*c*.1386—), *boom* (*c*.1440—), *quack* (1577—), *ping* (1835—), *woof* (1839—), and *bleep* (1953—). Slang terms created in this way or supported in their use by onomatopoeic associations include *zap* "to kill (with a gun)" (1942—), *yack* "to chatter inconsequentially" (1949—), and *barf* "to vomit" (1956—).

But where does slang come from?

It should be clear that none of these types of etymology is exclusive to slang. Standard English and slang both borrow words from other languages, reuse existing words with new grammatical functions or with slightly different meanings, abbreviate words, and produce blends, acronyms, and initialisms. There are compounds, combining forms, prefixes, and suffixes in Standard English. There are also onomatopoeic terms in Standard English. Most slang words are produced in ways that aren't particularly different from the ways Standard English words are produced.

There have, in fact, been very few mechanisms for producing new words that are exclusive to slang. Because they are so unusual, they tend to receive a disproportionate amount of attention, but their influence is pretty limited. The best known is rhyming slang, a form of wordplay originating in mid nineteenth-century London, in which standard (and sometimes slang) words are replaced by a rhyming phrase. For example, in rhyming slang *stairs* are referred to as *apples and pears* (1857—), one's *wife* is one's *trouble and strife* (1905—), and a *car* is a *jam-jar* (1930—). It's not uncommon that the rhyming element is omitted: someone behaving in a stupid or irritating fashion might be told that what they're saying is *cobblers (awls)* (1934—, from *balls* "nonsense" (1903—)): that they should use their *loaf (of bread)* "head" (1920—) or *stick it up their Khyber (Pass)* "arse: anus" (1916—). Despite the name, rhyming slang terms aren't always slang: *berk(ley/ shire) (hunt)* "cunt: a fool" (1936—) and *raspberry (tart)* "fart: a noise made by blowing with the tongue sticking out" (c.1880—) are widely used colloquialisms. Rhyming slang appears to have enjoyed some limited use among American criminals between the wars, but it remains reasonably productive in Britain, Australia, and New Zealand. Because the rhyming element is often deleted, it isn't hard to produce rhyming slang etymologies for terms that appear otherwise inexplicable, and so rhyming slang is another productive source of folk etymologies. For example, a manoeuvre in which a footballer kicks the ball between the legs of his opponent and then regains possession is called a *nutmeg* (1968—), and although it's often explained as rhyming slang for *leg*, there's no evidence to support this theory.

A few years before rhyming slang terms were first recorded, a social researcher named Henry Mayhew ventured into London's dingiest alleyways to document the lives of their poorest inhabitants. He published his findings in 1851, observing that market traders tended to reverse words to obscure their meanings in conversations that might be overheard by their customers. Back slang was always less productive than rhyming slang, and also less influential, probably because it's both easier to decode and generally less amusing. Some mundane examples include *neves* or *nevis* "seven" (1851 used adjectivally, 1901-1989 as a noun, particularly for "seven pounds" or "a seven-year sentence"), *slop* (1857-1879, from *ecilop* "police"), and *pennif* "a five-pound note" (1862+1891, from the slang term *finnip* "a five-pound note" (1839-1966)). *Yob* "a boy; a thug" (1859—) is the only widely used term to have originated in back slang.

Conclusions

The mechanisms involved in producing slang terms aren't generally different in kind from the mechanisms that produce Standard English terms, but a comparison between the two would probably reveal some differences in proportion. Far more slang than standard words are produced by abbreviation of various sorts, by blending, and by wordplay (such as onomatopoeia and rhyming slang). More slang than standard words have to be labelled 'origin unknown' or 'origin obscure'. With the minor exceptions of rhyming and back slang, slang terms are produced in exactly the same ways as Standard English words, and there's no reason why the few terms from rhyming slang and back slang that have found their way into wider usage shouldn't eventually become part of Standard English, at least on a national level.

Many playfully coined words don't catch on, and they are sometimes mistakenly labelled as slang because they don't belong to Standard English. What makes slang different from Standard English isn't its form or its origins, but its context and use: new words are just unfertilized spawn. They aren't slang yet. When spawn first appears in your pond, you can't tell whether it's going to develop into frogs, toads, or newts.[3] The chances are it won't develop at all if the conditions aren't right. It certainly won't develop if there's only one frog. Slang isn't slang until other people start using it.

---

[3] Toads and newts can be other types of word, if that works for you, but I don't want to push my luck with this metaphor. It's already a bit shaky—the frog parents are slang users rather than slang words.

Endnotes

Where tentative dates are given in this chapter, the words are drawn from my students' recent observations of their own slang (*Leicester Online Slang Glossaries*). It's unlikely that they're the first or only users, but these terms aren't documented in the dictionaries I've consulted, so the dates are based on Google blog searches (going back to 2000). The acronymic etymologies are largely from *Urban Dictionary* <http://www.urbandictionary.com>. Also cited were Anatoly Liberman's *Analytic Dictionary of English Etymology: An Introduction* (Minneapolis: University of Minnesota Press, 2008), 189–96, and Eric Partridge's *Dictionary of Slang and Unconventional English* (London: Routledge, 1937). McDonalds' objection to *McJob* is reported in <http://news.bbc.co.uk/1/hi/3255883.stm>. Adams, *Slang*, 82, 126, 166, talks in more detail about -*iz(n)*-, -*izzle*, and -*age*. I also referred to Bruce Rodgers' *The Queens' Vernacular: A Gay Lexicon* (San Francisco: Straight Arrow, 1972), Eric Partridge's *A Dictionary of the Underworld* (London: Routledge & Kegan Paul, 1949), and Gershon Legman's 'The Cant of Lexicography', *American Speech* 26 (1951), 130–7: (136–7). Michael Quinion's *Port Out Starboard Home* (London: Penguin, 2004) debunks numerous folk etymologies. The film review is from Philip French, 'Leaving', *The Observer*, 11 Jul. 2010, New Review, 26. Henry Mayhew presented his observations about back slang in *London Labour and the London Poor* (London: Woodfall, 1851).

3 Development

In this chapter I'll approach slang as a biologist might study a species of frog: by looking at the habitats it seems to thrive in. If those habitats have things in common, we can use them to identify the conditions that are most conducive to new words becoming slang.

Slang and creativity

New slang terms are often attributed to innovative and influential individuals or more generally to untutored poetic instinct. Inventing new terms is certainly a creative act, but it takes more than innovative creativity to qualify a term as slang. The invention of new words has long been a staple of magazine and newspaper competitions, and fledgling words can now be exposed to a worldwide audience through several websites dedicated to that purpose. For example, *Urban Dictionary* lists *prehab* "a clinic for patients who don't yet have an addiction", *stealth abs* "a fat stomach", and *snowpocalypse* "an inconveniently heavy fall of snow". No matter how creative an individual is, no matter how many words they create, and no matter how good those words are, they will only ever be witticisms unless other people start using them. I'm going to talk about individuals in the next chapter, but for now I want to concentrate on slang development as a group activity.

In this chapter, I'm using *slang development* to refer to the process by which a new word is created and becomes slang. I'm going to start with soldiers, because their situations represent most clearly the conditions that have traditionally contributed towards the development of slang, but I'll talk about other groups later in this chapter.[1] Developments in technology and the media have changed this traditional model, and I'll come on to this later too.

Military slang

Military conditions during WWI and WWII were particularly favourable to the development of new slang. During both conflicts, military forces had to train large numbers of conscripted civilians to obey orders without question, and to put their own needs, wishes, and safety after those of their battalion, ship, or regiment. This created the first condition conducive to slang development: a heightened desire for self-expression. Where all individuality is stripped away by uniforms, regulation haircuts, and the necessity of obeying orders without question, the desire to identify oneself as a separate human being becomes problematic. For individuals who haven't chosen their situation, this is particularly difficult. Refusing to conform in other ways isn't an option: a soldier who decides to customize his uniform or march out of step on principle will certainly be disciplined. But rebellious instincts can find relatively safe expression in the use of non-regulation language, such as (from WWII) *crud* "a real or imaginary disease" (1932–, originally US), *gremlin* "a mischievous creature who causes machinery to malfunction" (1941–, originally RAF), *skinhead* "a (newly recruited) member of the US marine corps" (1943–,

---

[1] All the groups discussed here were held to be conspicuously productive users of slang in their time. In each case, there are several contemporary dictionaries of their slang.

also meaning "a bald man" (1945—) and "a shaven right-wing yob" (1969—)), and *fuck-up* "an incompetent person; a misfit" (*c.*1945—).

Reduced to their number or last name, soldiers created new words for use among themselves: nicknames for each other and new labels for officers and for the objects and activities of military life. These terms allowed conscripted servicemen to grumble about food, equipment, and those in authority over them. They also offered the opportunity to use humour to enliven the dull routine of daily life. This illustrates the second condition conducive to slang development: slang speakers will usually be situated on the lower rungs of a hierarchy. In a military setting, all behaviour that's potentially threatening to the hierarchy is carefully monitored, and infringements of the rules are sometimes brutally punished, but slang offers the possibility for minor rebellion that won't usually meet with serious consequences. It can also be a reaction against having to learn and use new official terms. By inventing ridiculous terms of their own, soldiers were mocking the pomposity of official jargon[2] such as (from WWI) *debus* "to alight from a bus" (1915—), *human resources* "people" (1915—), *low-maintenance* "requiring little attention" (1916—), and *breakthrough* "an achievement that leads to a sudden increase in progress" (1918—).

However, plenty of individuals are situated towards the bottom of a hierarchy and denied self-expression, and they don't all become productive creators of slang. The third factor is that there must be a sense of group identity. Living under shared circumstances of inferiority and uniformity, individuals will use slang among themselves to heighten their sense of solidarity. Soldiers, for example, have a number of disparaging names for officers and military authorities, often alluding to elements of their uniform that set them apart from enlisted men. Names for officers include *swab* (1793-1850 in the

---

[2] *Jargon* is technical or professional language, with professional slang occupying the area between slang and jargon. Jargon terms tend to have precise and fixed meanings. Failure to use the correct jargon brings your expertise into question. Slang is more fluid in meaning and the use of a specific term is usually optional.

British navy, with reference to an officer's epaulettes), *chicken-guts* (1882—, US, now historical, with reference to gold trimmings or medals), *brass hat* (1893—, originally British army), *red tab* (1899—, in the British army), and *scrambled egg* (1943—, widely used with reference to gold braid or insignia and, by extension, to the officer himself). Terms like these contribute towards the development of solidarity between peers and undermine the hierarchy by drawing attention to the fact that officers are defined by their uniforms just as enlisted men are. Alluding to outer symbols of rank in this way asserts that they are only empty symbols: that all men are equal under their uniforms. The fourth condition, then, is that the oppressed group must have a sense that their situation is unfair or unreasonable, usually because they've experienced greater freedom in the past or hope to in the future. Oppressed groups at the bottom of hierarchies are denied their individuality in many settings, but the conditions for slang development are best where individuals collectively resist the forces acting upon them by means short of physical violence.

However, life under difficult conditions at the bottom of a hierarchy is rarely harmonious, and army slang also helped conscripted soldiers to negotiate differences between themselves, to the point of creating alternative hierarchies in which each branch of the service despised all the others. Slang allows enlisted men to say, 'I may be at the bottom of this pile, but at least I'm not in the army/navy/air force/ marines/office/kitchen (or wherever)'. Such terms include *flatfoot* "a sailor" (1835-1932) and "an infantryman" (1864—), *webfoot* "an infantryman" (1865-1928, US), *gravel-crusher* or *cruncher* "an infantryman" (1889—), *leatherneck* "a soldier" (1890-1916, UK) or "a marine" (1907—, US), *flyboy* "an airman" (1937—, US), and *brown job* "a member of the army" (1943—, RAF). Long serving soldiers use slang to express their disdain for raw recruits and other individuals who don't know the meaning of hard work. Slang terms serving these functions include *coffee-cooler* "a shirker; a soldier with an easy or safe assignment" (1862-1977, US), *dog-robber* "an officer's orderly" (1863—, US), and *boy scout* "an inexperienced soldier"

(1918-1929, US). These examples suggest that the alternative hierarchy works in tandem with the official one, but terms such as *old
soldier* "a shirker; one who avoids dangerous assignments" (1723—)
indicate that sometimes those who reach the top of the alternative
hierarchy are those who resist authority most skilfully. In contrast, a
soldier who seeks opportunities to impress his superiors is an *eager
beaver* (1943—, originally US). While the WWI *ace* was an airman
who'd brought down a specific (but varied) number of enemy planes
(1916—), *ace* was more often used sarcastically to mean "a clumsy or
stupid person" (1925—) during WWII, and this illustrates one way
that terms can vary in meaning according to the context. Members of
the infantry undoubtedly referred to themselves as *gravel-crushers*
and *flatfoots* in self-deprecation, but also to express pride in their
ability to withstand difficult conditions and hard work, unlike your
average *nancy boy* "a homosexual or effeminate man" (1927—) in the
navy/air force/administration (etc.).

Friction between individuals in a shared and uncomfortable situation is almost too universal to be worth mentioning, but for the
creation of slang to flourish it's necessary for friction within the
group to remain relatively minor. Conditions must militate against
the use of violence to settle personal difficulties. In a military setting,
this is because fights among the enlisted men will meet with severe
punishment, but it can also be motivated by self-preservation in other
ways: if one serviceman attacks another, there may be bystanders
who'll join in at the time or retaliate later. It's safer to find outlet for
irritation and resentment in the use of slang terms to an individual's
face or, even more prudently, behind his back.

A military setting, particularly under conditions of conscription,
will bring together people who wouldn't otherwise come into contact
with each another: individuals from different places, social classes,
educational levels, and ethnic groups. These disparate individuals will
speak differently, and the differences will give rise to humorous
teasing, or admiring imitation. Some individuals will try to lose
their distinctiveness, but others will want to stand out by using new

or unusual terms. If they're charismatic enough, or if the terms are witty enough, others might copy them.

All of the factors discussed so far are met in many workplaces: individuals with different backgrounds in a shared position at the bottom of the hierarchy (production line workers, for example, or shop assistants or people working in a call centre) are required to behave respectfully towards those above them, and to work towards a common goal that often conflicts with their individual wishes or desires. They're sometimes denied their individuality by being required to wear uniforms, or to engage with members of the public using an officially sanctioned script. They'll be punished if they rebel, usually by being sacked. There will also be frictions between these workers that can't be solved by a punch-up: one will work too hard, another not hard enough; one will laugh too loudly at the manager's jokes, another will fail to display the required levels of cheerfulness and cooperation; one will talk too much, another will breathe too loudly. Individuals in this type of setting usually choose to express their suppressed resentment, irritation, and anger by grumbling to workmates or, outside the workplace, to friends and family. If there are enough similarly minded work-mates, these emotions can also find expression through humour: through imitation, exaggeration, or practical jokes. A shop-worker who notices that a supervisor takes an undue number of breaks might joke to another that he's going to snort some more cocaine. By repetition this might become a standing joke, for a time, and acquire broader uses: *I'm just off to have a quick snort* might come to mean "I'm going to the toilet", for example, and *He's in the loo* might be said with a knowing wink, so that those in the know will pick up the implied meaning. What works against the transition from standing joke to slang in most workplaces is that workers come and go: they may move on to another position within the company or another job at any time, and they'll also usually socialize with other people outside the workplace. What they lack is what the conscripted soldiers had in abundance: a dense social network leading to a sense of belonging, isolation, and continuity.[3]

Slang develops best where the oppressed group is set apart from the outside world, restricted in their interactions by physical boundaries and regulations, and where at least some key individuals remain in that setting over periods of years rather than months. Slang also develops best where group identity is stronger, or at least more compelling, than external ties. Group identity is enhanced by pressure, which may result from the enforced position of inferiority, but other pressures may also contribute: particularly fear (of death, failure, rejection, and so on). In some situations it's acceptable to express fear directly, in words or tears, but in others direct emotional expression is interpreted as a sign of weakness and seen as a threat to the shared interests of the group. This is clearly the case within a military unit, where an individual who cried before a mission would not only make it harder for everyone else to ignore their own fears but also cause everyone to worry that their tearful comrade might let them down under pressure. Instead of expressing fear directly, individuals in situations like these use slang terms that both acknowledge and belittle their concerns, such as *fireworks* "bombardment; anti-aircraft fire" (1864—), *tin hat* "a steel helmet" (1903—, originally British, now usually historical), *whizz-bang* "a high-velocity German shell" (1915—, British, now usually historical), *grave* "a foxhole; a shallow trench" (1918-1930, US), and *flying coffin* "a dangerous aircraft" (1918—, US).

Although all of these conditions are met in the navy, not all of the terms used at sea qualify as slang. As early as the 1590s, in response to reports of the exploits of Sir Francis Drake, the shore-bound were offered the opportunity to learn the language of the sea with the help of reference books about naval life. These generally included non-standard terms only incidentally alongside more encyclopaedic information about knots, charts, and winds. The difference between the

---

[3] Doctors, the police, and restaurant staff are groups commonly identified as having well-developed professional slang. In each case, the long hours and high pressure make it difficult to maintain a social life outside work.

language used by conscripted soldiers and conscripted sailors during the two world wars is that many of the terms a new sailor had to learn had been in use for centuries. They were fixed in meaning and widely used throughout the hierarchy on board ship, including terms like *heads* "a ship's latrines" (1748—), *galley* "the kitchen on board a ship" (1750—), and *wardroom* "the room in which commissioned officers eat" (1758—), none of which is slang. There is naval slang, of course: there are terms that are used only below decks to resist the hierarchy and give vent to stress caused by frictions within and among the crew, such as (in the British navy) *rub* "a loan" (1914-1948), *ditch* "the sea" (1914-1942, used in the RAF later), and *wart* "a naval cadet" (1916-1962). The crucial difference between a military and naval setting is that the levels of isolation and continuity are set slightly too high in the navy: some terms that may have started out as slang ended up as jargon, with the result that when people talk about naval slang, they often find it difficult to distinguish between jargon and slang, or decide that the distinction isn't important.

Slang usually operates in rebellion against the standard form, but in a military setting it's in opposition with both Standard English and military jargon. Without a standard form of the language for comparison, it's impossible to say that a specific usage is non-standard. It's no coincidence, therefore, that publications dealing with non-standard English appeared at the same time that a standard written form was gradually becoming codified. A few books and pamphlets dating from the sixteenth and seventeenth centuries deal primarily with the language of beggars and thieves, as we'll see in Chapter 6, but the first dictionary attempting to restrict itself to what we now call slang was Grose's *Classical Dictionary of the Vulgar Tongue* (1785).[4]

---

[4] B. E.'s *New Dictionary of the Terms Ancient and Modern of the Canting Crew* (c.1698) is sometimes described as the first English slang dictionary. It included thieves' language and slang, but also jargon, dialect, colloquial language, and new words, and is better characterized as the first dictionary of non-standard English in general. These other types of non-standard language were still represented in Grose's dictionary, in smaller numbers, but a much larger proportion is slang.

Grose considered his dictionary to be the counterpart of and antidote to Samuel Johnson's hugely influential *Dictionary of the English Language* (1755). Johnson attempted to draw boundaries around Standard English: to make definitive rulings about what was in and what was out, and he generally omitted terms that he didn't consider good usage. This made it possible for Grose, and others, to concentrate on terms and senses implicitly designated as non-standard by their exclusion from more respectable dictionaries. Although less interesting than some of the other factors, this is probably the most central: without a recognized standard form of the language there can be no slang, though it isn't necessary to apply this rule to individual words.

In a military setting, slang also plays a variety of functions useful to those higher up the official hierarchy. It contributes towards the development of camaraderie, helps keep up morale, and provides a safe outlet for minor resentments. Because the officers have often passed through the same conditions as the enlisted men, they understand the importance of slang and therefore tend to turn a blind eye to its use, even when it functions as an act of petty rebellion. An officer who attempted to outlaw the use of slang would inevitably fail, and he'd make himself ridiculous in the process. However, it's possible to envisage a situation meeting all the other conditions we've identified, in which slang wouldn't flourish because the inventors or users of unofficial terms were so severely punished that the rebellion would cease to be a safe one: if using slang is punishable by death, you might as well try to escape instead.

The ideal conditions for slang

Focussing on military settings has allowed us to identify conditions that appear to support slang development:

- a standardized, official, or accepted form of the language which it exists within and rebels against

- a hierarchy
- a (real or perceived) threat to individuality and self-expression
- a sense of group identity at the bottom of the hierarchy
- an awareness or belief that conditions could be better
- frictions within the group that can only be expressed verbally
- linguistic variation within the group
- dense social networks
- continuity, but not too much
- fear (or some other form of pressure)
- some toleration of slang by those in authority.

Going back to our biological metaphor, we can hypothesize that these factors are the conditions that best ensure that frogspawn develops: they provide the ideal nutrients, oxygen levels, and water temperature for the development of slang. Now we need to test the theory.

Prison slang

If these conditions are indeed conducive to the development of slang, we'd expect to find them replicated in the conditions of other groups who've been identified as productive slang users. Prisoners clearly fit all of these conditions: some individuals occupy these physically isolated settings across considerable periods or come back repeatedly, but all prisoners will have had some taste of the greater freedoms of life outside the prison walls. Prison slang gives an advantage to established and habitual inmates by emphasizing their ability to understand and negotiate systems and hierarchies among officials and prisoners. A prison visitor in the United States found that the most influential prisoners, the ones at the top of the unofficial hierarchy, were the ones who used slang most, and that when a prisoner was addressed using prison slang he lost status if he wasn't able to use it in response. The external hierarchy is represented by prison staff, but although prisoners are to some extent united by their situation, there are also considerable frictions within the group that cannot prudently be expressed in outright violence. Instead, terms like *jacket* "a reputation for treacherous behaviour" (1963—, from the earlier sense "a personal file; a criminal record" (1937—), originally US military slang), *nonce* "a sex-offender; a paedophile" (1970—, UK), and *muppet* "a prisoner easily victimized by other inmates" (1988—, UK) are used. In this setting, it's probably interactions with other inmates that create the most fear, but individual prisoners might also worry about families, release dates, and the loyalty of those they care about: spouses, partners, accomplices outside of the prison, and associates within it. Personal identity is challenged by prison uniforms, regulation haircuts, physical restrictions, and strict discipline. Although the use of inflammatory language, particularly racist or homophobic terms, may be punishable in prisons, slang isn't intrinsically contrary to good discipline as long as it isn't used disrespectfully in the presence of prison officers.

Public school slang

So far so good: military and prison life both appear to support our theory of slang development. What happens in situations that don't fit the ideal conditions so neatly? The non-standard language of British public schoolboys was richly documented during the late nineteenth and early twentieth century. Some widely used terms, such as *fag* "a younger boy who performs duties for an older boy" (1785—, now usually historical (or ill-informed))[5] and *tuck* "food" (1835—), were used in many schools. Others were restricted to a single school, like *sock* "food" (1825—, Eton, now historical), *lout* "a common fellow" (1857, Rugby), *frowst* "a lie-in" (1880-1923, Harrow), and *sweater* "a servant" (1900+1973, Winchester).

Public schoolboys still exist, of course, and still use slang, but they're no longer as isolated or victimized (and victimizing) as once

---

[5] This developed from the sense "hard work, drudgery; fatigue" (1780—), from *fag* "to flag, droop, or decline" (1530-1878). It isn't related to *fag* "a (cheap) cigarette" (1888—) or *fag* "homosexual" (1921—, originally US).

they were and certainly wouldn't leap to mind as trend-leaders today, though they evidently did seem peculiarly innovative once. Nineteenth-century guidebooks for new boys presented non-standard terms alongside information about school customs and pastimes. In this unfamiliar and geographically isolated setting, boys who didn't behave appropriately were beaten by the masters and also by prefects occupying the top of the authorized hierarchy among the boys. Although the boys were united by their shared conditions, they were also in competition with one another to be top of the class, to be good at sports, to be more skilful in negotiating personal advantage, and to be better at fighting, or at least more belligerent. Boys who didn't conform would also meet with physical violence from their peers. The slow progression of boys through the school created continuity, so that terms could be passed on. Indeed, pride in school traditions was sometimes so fierce that school terms were used as a tool in enforced conformity. At Winchester College, for example, new boys were expected to learn the 'Notions' (a mixture of school slang, local lore, and age-old in-jokes) by rote. They were tested by the older boys, much as their knowledge of Greek or Latin might be tested in the classroom, but punished even more harshly if their responses weren't *up to (the) scratch* "up to a required standard" (1843—, originally sporting). The teachers knew about and tolerated this custom across several decades, and only restricted the violence involved after a scandal in the 1870s. Survival as a 'notion' doesn't prove continued slang usage, however.

Conditions in nineteenth-century public schools weren't entirely ideal for slang development. First, the distinction between those with official and unofficial authority was less clearly marked than in the army or prison. Prefects and sports captains were chosen by teachers, which meant that there was less friction between the two hierarchies. Secondly, school tradition sometimes created too much continuity. Slang is by its nature fluid: if the meanings and use of individual terms become too fixed, they develop into jargon rather than slang. Almost everyone who's ever compiled a list of public school slang has bemoaned its decline: complaining that current pupils no longer use the terms familiar from their own youth. These lost terms may well have been slang, but many public schools still include a list of 'slang terms' on their websites as a way of identifying traditions peculiar to each school. For example, the Eton College website indicates that *beak* "a master" (1888—, from the earlier meaning "a magistrate" (1749—)), *div* "a lesson" (apparently short for *division* "class"), *head man* "headmaster", and *slack bobs* "boys who neither row nor play cricket" (rowers are *wet bobs* (1865—), cricketers *dry bobs* (1844—)) are terms used among the boys. If conformity is still enforced and a new boy referring to a *lesson* or a *teacher* is ridiculed for his mistake, then we're looking at jargon rather than slang.

American college slang

American students provide another case study for slang development. Their slang includes *flunk (out)* "to fail an examination; to be dismissed from college for failing examinations" (1823—), *bone (up) (on)* "to study diligently" (1841—), *rushee* "a candidate for membership of a fraternity or sorority" (1916—), *mouse* "to neck; to pet" (1928-1999), *pizza face* "a person with facial acne" (1964—), and *brewski* "a beer" (1977—). As higher education enrolment rose in the US, colleges sought to distinguish themselves from one another in many of the same ways that public schools did: by clothing, sporting prowess, and language. Students' moral behaviour was once carefully monitored by college authorities, so the sense of hierarchy and repression would have been rather greater than it is for contemporary students. On the other hand, there was considerable pressure for conformity not just from those in authority, but also from other students. Moreover, just like their similarly privileged counterparts in Britain, many students at the most elite American institutions weren't the first member of their family to attend the university, which might have created just a little too much continuity. College slang didn't set into jargon in the way that some British public school

"That's like, so random!"

4   Student slang I: Rob Murray, 'That's Like, So Random'.

slang did, though. With the exception of students living in the most exclusive fraternity houses, the levels of isolation weren't high enough and the social networks weren't dense enough.

By the 1940s, it was becoming increasingly difficult to argue that college students were using slang in unique ways, let alone creating it. By the 1960s, there was no question that, with the exception of a few terms relating to courses and locations on campus, college and high-school students were now using slang in much the same way. What had happened in the intervening period was the gradual emergence of a now familiar figure: the teenager. For us, teenagers are probably archetypal slang users, but they don't appear to fit the conditions conducive to slang development. This is because slang isn't, despite what we may think, an integral part of being a teenager. Nineteenth-century public schoolboys may have used slang during their teenage years, but their contemporaries in factories and down mines were functioning in the adult world, drawing their non-standard terms from dialect, jargon, or (for some) professional slang. Nineteenth-century teenagers weren't a cohesive group in their own estimation or anyone else's. So how did teenagers come to be seen as a meaningful group, and why did they become such archetypal users of slang?

Teenage slang

One of the main factors in the development of the category of the 'teenager', from about the mid twentieth century, was the increase in school leaving ages: young people who would once have been able to earn money in the adult world were being controlled for longer by the restrictions of school life. This happened at a stage in their lives when they began to desire more freedom and greater powers of self-determination. Behaviour that would have been entirely normal at their age a century before became problematized (teenage pregnancies, smoking, drinking, etc.). Energy that would once have been exhausted by the demands of physical labour was expressed in frustration and rebellion. As living standards rose and families had more money to invest in their children's education, the pressure on teenagers to perform well at school increased at the same time in their lives that they were most concerned with achieving the approval of the unofficial hierarchy of their peers. Pressures from both hierarchies thus contribute to teenagers' anxieties, and often pull in different directions, as is demonstrated by the numerous slang terms for social and academic failures of various kinds, including *dropout* "a person who withdraws from a course of study" (1930—, now colloquial), *juvie* "a juvenile delinquent" (1930—, US), *drip* "a feeble or boring person" (1932—), *prick-teaser* "a flirtatious girl or woman" (1939—), *nerd* "a dull or unnecessarily diligent person" (1951—), *spaz* "a fool; an idiot" (1956—), *geek* "an intellectual or obsessive person" (1957—), and *slag* "a promiscuous girl or woman; a prostitute" (1958—). Conditions will be most productive of slang where schools are large enough to produce consistent social stratification by age. This creates the continuity necessary for the development of slang: teenagers will keep the same company across many years of schooling, and will operate within a social isolation that rivals the geographical isolation of soldiers and prisoners. Teenagers may occupy the same houses as their parents and irritating younger siblings, but they communicate primarily with their peers.

From the earliest days of 'the teenager', the concept was fuelled by commercial and media interest. Manufacturers and record producers recognized this new and susceptible market. Television and radio presenters wanted to be able to represent their audiences to advertisers as a well-defined group with disposable income and suggestible tastes. They were quick to use the latest slang so they could benefit by association with whatever was fashionable at the time. The influence of youth trends is now so dominant that we oldies might feel that we're the ones being oppressed, but you can bet that's not how teenagers feel. Expressions of approval and disapproval figure high in teenage slang, and there tends to be a rapid turnover, sometimes by recycling, as terms become dated by association with their maturing users. Terms with which teenagers have expressed their approval include, in chronological order: *bodacious* (1907—, originally US), *wizard* (1922—), *grouse* (1924—, originally Australia and New Zealand), *lush* (1928—, chiefly British), *righteous* (1930—, originally African American), *snazzy* (1931—, ?originally Australian), *fantastic* (1938—), *mad* (1941—, originally US), *supersonic* (1947—), *magic* (1956—), *fabulous* (1959—), *fab* (1959—), *ridiculous* (1959—, originally jazz), *safe* (1970—, originally South African; also used among criminals with the sense "reliable" (1846—)), *fabby* (1971—), *kwaii* (1974—, South African), *gnarly* (1978—, originally surfing), *death* (1979—, originally African American), *radical* (1979—, originally surfing), *awesome* (1979—, originally American, still slang in UK), *def* (1981—), *fabbo* (1984—, chiefly British and Australian), *sound*

(1988—, chiefly British and Irish, and used with the sense "reliable" since 1879), and *kicking* (1989—).[6]

Books, magazines, and films began to address teenagers as a group during the later twentieth century, and at times this sense of cohesion has been strong enough to overcome geographical distance altogether. Bill Hailey, Elvis Presley, and the Beatles, for instance, appealed to teenagers throughout the English-speaking world, as well as further afield, spreading slang as they went, including *gear* "excellent" (1951—, British), *rock and roll* [a type of music] (1954—, originally US), *see you later alligator* "get lost; goodbye" (1956—), *grotty* "unpleasant; nasty" (1964—, originally British). Common interests fuelled a sense of spiritual unity, although direct communication wasn't yet easily available. Hippies, in particular, felt themselves to be part of an international movement resisting the establishment. As a counterbalance to this globalization of youth culture, it has also become increasingly fractional. Teenagers have self-identified, and identified one another, as rockers, mods, punks, glam rockers, new romantics, skinheads, goths, emos, and gangstas, to name only a few of the many trends in music and fashion since the 1950s. Some teenagers choose to identify themselves by reference to a favourite television programme or sporting team, a preferred social activity or drug, or by participation in a particular sport: especially surfing or skateboarding. With the advent of the Internet, it's also possible for an individual who's entirely isolated geographically and socially to feel that they're part of a community of like-minded individuals. Online, within that group, slang will develop as surely as it does in physical proximity (see Chapter 11).

Military authorities have long recognized the useful functions played by slang. For example, the US War Department compiled a list of WWII slang even before the attack on Pearl Harbor made American participation unavoidable. This was designed to boost morale at home and in the forces, but also to provide a picture of the

---

[6] Other terms of approval have already been mentioned or will come up later on.

American troops as well fed, ethnically harmonious, and confident of victory. Similarly, advertisers and broadcasters have also become aware that by using slang to address teenagers (and, increasingly, also the rest of us), they can make their products seem newer and more appealing. For example, in *c*.1961, Vaseline Hair Tonic was advertised with a glossary and a competition to create new slang terms:

> You're hip in Teensville today if you're flip. And to be flip, Daddy-O, you've got to have the latest for your cha-cha-cha with the cats and chicks.

hip "in the know" (1904–)

-ville [in invented place names] (1843–)

flip "flippant; nonchalant" (1847–, originally US, usually negative)

daddy-o [as a term of address] (*c*.1935–)

cha-cha(-cha) [apparently referring to the ballroom dance] (1954–)

cat "a man (who is in the know)" (1931–)

chick "a young woman" (1899–)

Some slang terms originate in the media and advertising, and many more are popularized there. Advertisers and film makers began to cash in on the idea of 'the beat generation' at the end of the 1950s, for instance, and continued to employ beat language and stereotypes badly (as here) long after the trend-leaders had moved on. Despite the occasional ill-fated campaign against various aspects of teenage language, there's considerable toleration, celebration, and imitation of teenage language by the adult world. Advertising campaigns that have used slang include Fosters lager in the 1980s (*strewth, there's a bloke down there with no strides on!*), the British National Railway Museum in 2003 (*get down and dirty*), Rizla cigarette papers in 2003 (*twist and burn*), AT&T in 2007 (*idk my bff Rose*), and Nike in 2010 (*I don't leave anything in the chamber*).

Street slang

Contemporary American urban gang culture is another situation apparently conducive to slang development. Here the official hierarchy is represented by the educational and legal systems, by police and sometimes parents, as well as by the entire white establishment. The gang provides a highly structured unofficial hierarchy, and friction with rival gangs cements group identity further still. Although there's considerable pressure to conform within the group, gang members police their own individuality by responding aggressively to those who don't show them sufficient respect, and this is associated with fear of losing status or appearing weak, both of which are potentially dangerous. Differences within the group can be expressed almost as readily in violence as in words, and in this respect conditions are atypical for slang development. There's some social and geographical isolation, and gang membership produces some level of continuity, although the need to avoid detection when talking about drugs may provide a motivation towards continual innovation. However, what we think of as gang slang is several steps away from reality. People outside gang culture are exposed to its slang through music, film, and television. This tends to produce a higher level of stability of vocabulary and fixedness in meaning than you might expect to observe *on the street*, and terms used in *The Wire*, such as *police* "a police officer" (1839—), *re-up* "to replenish one's supply of drugs" (1975—), and *five-O* "a police officer" (1983—, from CBS's *Hawaii Five-O*), may no longer be in everyday use in the *hood* "a neighbourhood, particularly an inner-city area populated by African Americans" (1967—).

Slang dictionaries and personal identity

All of the groups discussed in this chapter were considered creative users of slang in their time. There are several (sometimes dozens) of contemporary slang glossaries for all of them. Popular dictionaries of current slang are produced for a variety of reasons:

- to promote greater understanding of the slang-using group
- to expose the dangers posed by the slang-using group

- to represent the dictionary-maker as belonging to the group whose slang they are documenting
- to imply or state directly that other people are outside that group
- to make money by responding to a current interest or anxiety.

Let me provide some examples. You're probably familiar with terms originating in gay slang, including *camp* "ostentatious; effeminate; homosexual" (1909—), *straight* "heterosexual" (1919—), *fag hag* "a heterosexual woman who associates with gay men" (1965—), and *breeder* "a heterosexual" (1979—, originally US). Since the 1970s, lots of gay slang has entered into more general usage, but this isn't what has motivated the writers of gay slang dictionaries. Glossaries of gay slang were first published in the late nineteenth century, usually by psychologists who'd found that understanding gay slang helped them to win the trust of their patients. A typewritten glossary of the 1950s, called *The Gay Girl's Guide to the Western World*, was designed to provide an insight into gay slang to those who hadn't yet ventured *out of the closet* (1963—, originally US). In a frank and extensive dictionary called *The Queens' Vernacular* (1972), already mentioned in the last chapter, Rodgers simultaneously celebrated the San Francisco gay scene and his own sexuality. In contrast, David Noebel's *The Homosexual Revolution* (1977) argues that Rodgers' list reinforces

Jude's description of homosexuals as "filthy dreamers" (Jude 1:7,8). It also confirms the fact that homosexuals do seduce and molest youth.

Noebel provided a glossary of gay slang based on selected and edited entries from Rodgers' dictionary to expose what he felt to be the dangers of tolerating homosexuality. More modern dictionaries, such as Paul Baker's *Fantabulosa* (2002), tend to emphasize the continuity of gay slang and appear to be motivated, at least in part, by a desire to bear witness to the existence of a stable gay community with its own history, traditions, and values. In each case, the motivations for documenting gay slang influence the types of terms recorded.

Rhyming slang dictionaries illustrate some of the other motivations for producing popular slang dictionaries. Many rhyming slang dictionaries are brief and haphazardly compiled. Their covers usually display icons of London (Tower Bridge; The Houses of Parliament; red double-decker buses; pearly kings and queens) or broader images of Englishness or Britishness (the flag of St George; the Union Jack). They're clearly aimed primarily at tourists, and provide a cheap and portable caricature of Cockney (or English, or British) life, ideal as a souvenir or gift. People buying these mini-dictionaries must understand that they're only intended as a bit of fun, but these publications can represent a valuable asset to a small publishing company: one pocket-sized rhyming-slang dictionary has been reprinted at least 34 times since 1971, without once having been revised or updated.

Other rhyming-slang dictionaries appear to be written for the in-group rather than for outsiders. Strictly speaking, these ought to address individuals from the East End of London, but migration from London hasn't stopped the descendants of Cockney barrow-boys claiming their heritage, nor those who aspire to be the descendants of Cockney barrow-boys. Actually, rhyming slang now appears to form part of a wider white working-class sense of self in England, and some rhyming-slang dictionaries address this broad English audience. They imply that Englishness is about more than just living in England or being born in England. Englishness is about having the shared values that come from a common English heritage, which is as eccentric, incomprehensible, and as difficult to acquire as rhyming slang. It is also usually masculine, and defines various types of people as outsiders, including *grass(hopper)* "copper: a policeman; an informer" (1893—), *four-by-two* "a Jew" (1921—), *brass (nail)* "tail: prostitute" (1934—), *bubble and squeak* "a Greek" (1938—), and *ginger (beer)* "a queer: a homosexual" (1956-1978). A few rhyming-slang terms from Australia and New Zealand function in a similar way, including *Jimmy Grant* "an immigrant" (1845-1968), *pom(egranite)>pommie* "immigrant; a British person" (1912—), *Moreton Bay (fig)* "fizgig: an informer; a busybody" (1953-1975), and *septic (tank)* "yank: an American" (1967—).

5 Slang play: Malcolm Poynter [untitled] from Ronnie Barker's *Fletcher's Book of Rhyming Slang* (London: Pan, 1979), 10.

Perhaps even more interesting are the slang dictionaries that haven't been produced. Where are the dictionaries of the slang used by sweatshop workers? Or by girls in boarding schools? Football hooligans? Skinheads? Paedophiles? These groups probably do use slang terms, and have probably originated some of their own. You could probably find some of their slang in general slang dictionaries, but no one has gone to the trouble of publishing a glossary concentrating on the slang of these groups in particular, on paper at least.[7] This is because no one has come forward to speak for these groups. No one has chosen to represent them as peculiarly creative users of slang. Equally, no one from outside the in-group has investigated whether they are or not. Probably we don't want to view these groups as intelligent, innovative, or creative. We don't want to see them as trend-setting and rebellious. Perhaps we'd rather not think about some of these groups or their language at all. We find slang only where it comes to our attention (i.e. we come into contact with slang users) or where we look for it. We look for slang only where we expect or want to find it: once a group has been identified as slang-creators, they tend to be credited with terms that other people came up with.

Conclusions

The term *slang* was originally condemnatory, and it sometimes still is, but through the course of the twentieth century, earlier in Australia and the United States, later in Britain, it came to be used in a more celebratory sense. Slang was once considered a sign of poor breeding or poor taste, but now it indicates that the speaker is fun-loving, youthful, and in touch with the latest trends. Although some adults try to discourage teenagers from using slang, plenty of others want to understand and adopt it. In a world that celebrates youth and novelty, slang now functions as a visible symbol of success or failure in keeping up with the times. The entertainment industries, the media, advertising, marketing, and the Internet have fundamentally changed the way that slang is created and spread, and the conditions identified in this chapter are no longer as central to slang development when

---

[7] I have to confess that I haven't looked for 'paedophile slang' because I didn't want to find it, but I can confirm that there were, at the time of writing, no online glossaries concentrating on the slang of the other groups.

newly created or adapted words can be introduced to millions of potential adopters more or less at the moment of their first use. There'll be more on these recent developments in Chapters 10 and 11.

Where slang is a product of a particular type of social setting, many terms will survive for only a short time: our frogspawn will develop only so far. Once circumstances change or individuals move on, it's likely that many of the terms they once needed will no longer be useful. But why do some slang terms survive? How do they move from one group to another until they are widely used around the world? This is the subject of the next two chapters, in which we'll see slang tadpoles developing into fully fledged frogs.

Endnotes

Wilfred Granville's *Sea Slang of the Twentieth Century* (London: Winchester, 1949) is an example of a dictionary that lists naval jargon and slang together. Contemporary naval terms are available in the *Sea Cadet Regulations* (2008) at <http://www.sccheadquarters.com>. The *Glossary of Eton Expressions* is at <http://www.etoncollege.com/glossary.aspx>. Bert Little's 'Prison Lingo: A Style of American English Slang', *Anthropological Linguistics* 24 (1982), 206–44, explains how slang is used in prison, and Tom Dalzell kindly gave me access to his copy of *Your Vaseline Hair Tonic Flip-Talk Contest Booklet* (New York: n.p., c.1961), n.p. Also mentioned are Samuel Johnson's *A Dictionary of the English Language* (London: J. & P. Knapton, 1755), Francis Grose's *A Classical Dictionary of the Vulgar Tongue* (London: Hooper, 1785), B. E.'s *A New Dictionary of the Terms Ancient and Modern of the Canting Crew* (London: W. Hawes, c.1698), the *Gay Girl's Guide to the U.S. and the Western World* (n.p., c.1955), Paul Baker's *Fantabulosa: A Dictionary of Polari and Gay Slang* (London: Continuum, 2002), and David A. Noebel's *The Homosexual Revolution* (Tulsa, OK: American Christian College, 1977). The title of 'most frequently reprinted rhyming slang dictionary' belongs to Jack Jones, *Rhyming Cockney Slang* (Bristol: Abson, 1971). Connie C. Eble's *Slang and Sociability: In-group Language among College Students* (Chapel Hill: North Carolina University Press, 1996) has much more to say on the development of American college slang.

4 Survival and Metamorphosis

The last chapter identified conditions favourable to the early stages of slang development. This chapter will ask why some slang tadpoles continue to develop, while so many others fail to thrive, leaving barely a trace behind. In other words, it's time to consider how the survival of the fittest operates in slang evolution. As in biological evolution, linguistic survival isn't governed by quality. People don't speak English around the world because it's better than other languages: they speak English because it was a home language or there were advantages to be gained from learning it later. Similarly, American slang (for example) hasn't spread around the world because it's objectively better than the alternatives, but because of the political, economic, and technological developments that made the United States a world power after WWI.

Slang used by American troops during WWI

We've seen that the two world wars presented ideal conditions for the development of new slang among the troops. This was particularly the case during WWI, when there were fewer opportunities for leave, especially for individuals stationed far from home. The mass media had little influence on WWI slang: films were still silent, gramophone players were expensive and heavy, and radio broadcasting didn't begin until shortly after the war. Music hall songs and acts did feature in the slang of trenches, but much of the military slang of this period was generated in the field.[1]

Some Americans joined the armed forces of other nations early in the war, and these scattered individuals adopted the slang and colloquial language used by their comrades. Although the United States had declared war on Germany in April 1917, it wasn't until the summer of 1918 that large numbers of American troops arrived in Europe. Nations involved in the conflict from the beginning had had considerably more time to develop new slang and to cement its use before the war was over. The American battalions of 1918 brought military and general American slang with them, and picked up existing terms from those who'd already adapted to their new and peculiar circumstances, including *Fritz(ie)* "a German; the Germans" (1914—), *windy* "(justifiably) frightened" (1916—), and *ack-ack* "anti-aircraft" (1917—). The invention of new terms was less necessary than it had been for British and Commonwealth forces, but new terms were created nonetheless. By 1919, the last American troops had returned to the United States. Back with their families and back in their jobs, they had little use for the slang terms they'd used abroad. Most of them no longer needed to talk about artillery shells and body lice, so their military slang terms fell from use, perhaps to be revived only nostalgically when returned soldiers bumped into one another and reminisced about their experiences orally or in print. American veterans may have bonded by remembering their common experiences through terms like *jam-can* "a field stove" (1918), *monkey* "tinned meat" (1918+1919, but used 1918-1983 in the longer form, *monkey meat*), and *Carnegie derby* "a steel helmet" (1918-1921, named after the Carnegie steel company). Terms like these are badges of experience and belonging, but once

---

[1] Slang terms in this section are from Lighter's 'The Slang of the American Expeditionary Forces in Europe'. For British WWI slang, see pp. 168–9 and 242–3.

they're only used with reference to a remembered environment, they're no longer living slang: they're just the fossilized remains of slang terms. Sometimes the terms that are remembered and preserved aren't the ones that were most widely spread or generally used.

Some veterans continued using some military slang in their everyday lives. Those who remained in military service inevitably continued using more of the slang they had learnt in the forces than those who moved into civilian life: in these more constant conditions, slang terms could be passed on through decades of military use and some received a new wave of exposure and use during WWII and in later conflicts. For example, metal identification disks worn around a soldier's neck were first called *dog tags* during WWI (1918—, originally US), and the term re-emerged among succeeding generations of conscripts. Other WWI slang that survived in military and naval use includes *foo-foo* "toiletries" (1918—) and *acting jack* "an acting corporal" (1917—). *By the numbers* "in a precise military fashion" (1918—) has spread into wider use since WWII.

A few civilian professions, such as the aviation industry, sought to recruit men with military experience because they particularly valued veterans' technological expertise and discipline. In these professions, terms originating in the war continued in use, such as *office* "an aeroplane's cockpit" (1917-1989) and *jenny* "an aeroplane used for training" (1924-1993). Some military slang continued in use among the police, such as *rookie* "a new recruit" (*c.*1880—, mainly US) and *looey* "a lieutenant" (1916—). Other terms are found in the slang of those who had more trouble adapting to civilian life, including gangsters, who found use for *typewriter* "machine gun" (1915-1979), and the homeless, who continued using *pogey bait* "sweets; candy" (1918—). Some WWI slang was able to stay alive in these contexts, but there was only room for terms that could adapt to their new circumstances. As in the physical process of evolution, only the fittest terms survived, and often it is mutation that makes this survival possible. For example, WWI soldiers who went *over the hill* (1917-1971) or *over the top* (1916—, historical in later use) were facing probable and immediate death, but civilians who are *over the hill* are merely past their best (1950—) while actions that are *over the top* are excessive or unreasonable (1935—). In their original context, these phrases weren't better than alternatives like *over the firing-step* or *over the sandbags*, but their survival indicates that they were fitter, in the evolutionary sense, for post-war use.

As we have seen, only a few American slang terms from WWI passed into more general use, often as a result of renewed exposure in later conflicts. Inexperienced new recruits were first described as *raggedy-assed* in 1918, and this use survives in military contexts, but civilians probably understand the term in the more general sense "inadequate; ragged". We all *sound off* occasionally about things that irritate or annoy us, perhaps without realising that the term originates with an order instructing a marching band to strike up a tune. The original sense dates from 1908; the figurative sense from 1918. When you call someone a *basket case* to imply that they can't cope with what life throws at them, do you have in mind its original sense "an individual who has lost all four limbs" (1919—)? Few of these WWI slang terms have retained their original sense unchanged: most survive only with a different, and often much more general, meaning. Without mutation, they couldn't have survived.

American slang after WWI

After all of the linguistic (and other) upheavals of WWI, you might think that it would be unnecessary to come up with any more new words for a while. After all the loss and destruction, many people did value continuity, but the proto-teenagers of the 1920s weren't interested in upholding tradition. Flappers and their less numerous male counterparts, largely just a little too young or a little too female to have been affected by the war directly, were nevertheless devoted to living life as though it might end at any moment. Glossaries of flapper slang appeared in several American newspapers during the early 1920s, many of them suspiciously similar. They begin by setting the scene:

Scene—A flapper's home at 1 A.M. Up-to-date member of the younger generation returning home from evening out, having left her "boy friend" at or near the door. Meets mother.

Mother—Well, dear, did you have a good time?

Flapper—Hot dog! It was the cat's pyjamas. Started perfectly blaah, though. Joe brought a strike-breaker, some tomato he turned sub-chaser for, 'cause his regular jane had given him the air. Jack had a flat-wheeler along who was a cellar-smeller. He got jammed. We struck a jazz-garden where a bunch of bun-dusters were necking it. Some wallie tried to horn in on our gang and we bloused. We crashed the gate at a swell joint like some finale-hoppers. We scandaled till one of the boys got beautifully shellacked, so we took the air.

Slang terms in this extract include:

flapper "a prostitute; a young woman who flouts convention" (1888–, now historical)

boyfriend "a woman's male escort or romantic partner" (1906–)

hot dog [an expression of approval] (1906, chiefly US)

cat's pyjamas "the peak of excellence" (1922–)

blah "disappointing; dull" (1922–)

strike-breaker [used with reference to industrial action] (1904–)

tomato "an attractive woman" (1922–)

sub-chaser [see below]

jane "a woman; a girlfriend" (1865–, chiefly US)

give the air "to dismiss; to jilt" (1900–)

flat-wheel(er) "a mean, poor, or unimpressive person" (1922-1929)

cellar-smeller "an individual who habitually drinks other people's alcohol" (1922)

jammed "drunk; stoned" (a.1856–)

strike "to arrive" (1798-1915, originally colonial)

jazz [a type of music] (1915–)

bunch "a group of people" (1622–)

bun-duster "a person who attends social functions but doesn't issue invitations in return" (1922)

neck (it) "to dance cheek to cheek; to engage in kissing or petting" (1842–)

wallie [see below]

horn in "to intrude; to butt in" (1909–, originally US)

gang "a group of people" (1632–)

blouse "to leave" (1922+1922)

crash the gate "to attend a party uninvited" (1919–)

swell "first rate; stylish" (1812–, originally UK)

joint "a place of resort, especially an opium den or speakeasy" (1821–, chiefly US)

finale-hopper "someone who arrives at the end of an event" (1922–, historical in later use)

scandal "to dance 'the Scandal'" (1922)

shellacked "drunk" (1922–)

Flappers were characterized by their disregard for convention and for the views of their elders. They thought for themselves, they dressed in shockingly revealing clothes that didn't restrict their movements, they cut their hair, smoked cigarettes, drank alcohol (despite Prohibition), and socialized without the inconvenience of chaperones whenever they could get away with it. They were, above all else, modern. Commentators observed them as individuals but wrote them up as a social movement. All of this behaviour was undoubtedly more striking among young women than young men, and young men were in short supply at this time, but it's a rare youth trend in which women are foregrounded, and this may be another way in which the war was being deliberately placed at a distance. Untouched by the war, unworried by financial restraints or economic portents, unrestricted by the demands of work or the conventions of the past, the flapper lived life to the full on behalf of all those who had to continue worrying. They also functioned, at this time, as a symbol of the folly of extending the vote to women. Their frivolity may have been endearing to some, but it was alarming to others.

It might be thought that newspapers presenting flappers' language would choose to foreground new terms even if better established words had continued in use, but many of the terms attributed to our flapper had already been in use for ten or fifteen years, and sometimes much longer.[2] Although these terms were by no means new, they were still novel enough or informal enough to strike a conservative mother or reader as modern, particularly in the mouths of middle-class young women. The flapper is being given credit for other people's inventiveness because it was modern for young ladies to be drinking, dancing, and using slang at all. Her use of slang is in keeping with the rest of her speech and with the way she lives her life. It is, above all, emphatic and exuberant. She uses intensifiers like *perfectly* and *beautifully* to celebrate experiences that aren't really

---

[2] Note that flappers aren't slang-developers, on the whole: they're slang-adopters (so they don't bring the conditions for slang development into question).

perfect or beautiful. She and her friends aren't forced to leave the party in disgrace, they *take the air*. A girl who socializes with someone else's boyfriend is a *strike-breaker*, in topical reference to the growing influence of the unions. The flapper abbreviates *because* to *'cause*, a form the *OED* describes as 'vulgar', and uses *some* repeatedly to emphasize her lack of interest in individuals who don't meet with her approval as well as her lack of concern for the consequences of her own actions. None of this was particularly modern, but its concentration in the speech of a well-to-do young woman addressing her mother would have been striking. But this isn't the genuine speech of a genuine flapper. This isn't social commentary: it's imaginative journalism.

It's clear that much of the flapper's speech was not as new as it might have sounded to newspaper readers of the time, but some of the slang in this extract does appear to have originated in this period. We can't be sure whether flappers were the originators of these terms, or whether they'd been in use unnoticed for several years before they were caught inadvertently in the trawler-net of media interest in flappers. Some are documented in use elsewhere, and a small number are still in use today. Of the slang terms included in this extract, *blouse, finale-hopper, flat-wheel(er), to crash the gate*,[3] *blah, shellacked, the cat's pyjamas*,[4] and *tomato* were all quite modern. It's possible that the British term *wally* "an unfashionable or inept person" represents continued use of the flapper term *wallie* "a goof with patent-leather hair", with the term apparently having crossed the Atlantic during the 1960s.

The language presented as belonging to these modern women shows very little overlap with WWI military slang. Of all the slang

---

[3] The form *gate-crasher* "one who crashes the gate" was first recorded in 1927; *gate-crashing* is recorded as a noun from the same year, and as an adjective from 1929. By 1931, *to gatecrash* had been created by back-formation.

[4] Other phrases referring to the peak of excellence that were also fashionable at the time include *the cat's whiskers* (1920—) and *the bee's knees* (1922—). *The dog's bollocks* (1949—) is rather later, and *the badger's nadgers* (2003—) is still relatively rare.

terms used in this scene, only *sub-chaser* could possibly be traced to military usage, having been used with the sense "a vessel which chases submarines" from 1918, though *sub* could also be understood as an abbreviation for *substitute* or *sub-deb* "a girl in her mid teens" (1917—, chiefly US) in this context. Flappers aren't so easily identified as enlisted men: they didn't form a group with regulations and agreed periods of membership, but the type of girl identified as a flapper during this period must have come into social contact with veterans of the war, men only a few years older than themselves. They must also have heard and read reports of wartime experience, but there's little sign of it in the language attributed to them. Perhaps the soldiers and flappers had so little in common that there just weren't any terms that were relevant to both of them. There weren't many jazz gardens in the trenches, after all. But it could be that the essence of flappers' modernity lay in their rejection of the war and everything associated with it. Not only must it never happen again, but it was also better not to dwell on it. Perhaps flappers and those who wrote about them were deliberately constructing a wall of solid frivolity to stand between themselves and any thought of the war.

Of these flapper terms, *bun-duster*, *cellar-smeller*, and *scandal* don't appear to have enjoyed wide usage. They all fall into the sections of the alphabet that haven't yet been updated in the *OED*, and if there's sufficient evidence of use some will undoubtedly be included in the completed third edition. But for some, there'll be no additional evidence of their use. Or, put another way, there will be no evidence of their use at all. This wouldn't be the only time journalists had talked up a trend.

The birth and death of slang

We've seen that it isn't a simple matter to identify when and where a slang word was created. Slang is characteristic of speech rather than writing (a statement not as true as it used to be, as we'll see in Chapter 11, but it certainly works for the flappers of the 1920s), but we're largely reliant on written sources for the slang of earlier periods. What spoken language we do have access to from this period is generally scripted: in films, plays, books, and songs we can get closer to the language of speech, but it's still a representation of speech rather than genuine spontaneous conversation. Many slang terms are used for a time without contemporaries commenting on them. It's only when they are used by individuals that the wider world is interested for other reasons, such as flappers, that slang terms are held up as examples of a current trend. Even in the best record we have of English words, the *OED*, and even in the sections of the alphabet that have been updated for the third edition, it's often possible to find earlier examples of use. But even if we could be certain that we'd found the earliest written example of a term, we still wouldn't know when it was first used in speech, and we've already seen that this issue is particularly pertinent for slang.

If identifying the birth of a slang term is hard, it's harder still to pin down its death. Veterans of WWI largely left its slang behind them. Where it wasn't relevant to civilian life, they didn't need it and so they didn't use it. Perhaps choosing not to use the slang of the war was part of putting the war behind them, but they could have used it if they'd wanted to. Terms remaining in their passive vocabularies could easily have been revived if circumstances had demanded it. Equally, when flappers grew up and settled down they probably had less use for the slang of dancing and drinking, but when it was their turn to be bemused by their children's lifestyles, they might have tried to engage with them by using the slang of their own youth. We have no evidence for this type of conversation. No journalist of the 1940s or 50s thought to document the slang of middle-aged middle-class mothers. What was interesting by then was the new slang of the new generation. In a creative representation of this exchange, it would be more effective to depict the mother's language conservatively to emphasize the distance between the generations. Like mothers, slang past its prime receives little attention.

The soldiers and flappers were close to one another chronologically, but they lived in different worlds. Their activities and interests were entirely different. It's little wonder that they had little slang in common. But do we see the same kind of slang loss where there's more similarity of context? For this purpose, let's have a look at the slang allegedly used by beats and hippies in the 1950s and 60s. Despite the decade that separates them, they have a similar world view and lifestyle, but does the similarity extend to their language?

Beat slang

Although there were a few earlier glossaries of beat language, the one in Lawrence Lipton's *The Holy Barbarians* (1959) is the earliest to document the slang of the beats from an internal perspective, and the beat slang terms listed in this section are all from Lipton's list. Lipton lived in Venice, California, which was decidedly where it was at, and he listed around 80 terms characteristic of his social group as part of an attempt to explain the beat perspective to the wider world. He doesn't claim that the beats originated these terms or that they were the only people to use them, but he does imply that it would be impossible to understand them without understanding their

6 Jazz slang: Charley Krebs, 'Wrong Axe' from the *Chicago Jazz Magazine*, April/ May 2005, 10.

language. Naturally the beats hadn't excised all well-established slang and colloquial terms from their vocabulary, but it's surprising how many terms that now sound definitively beatish had already been in use for some years and were in relatively widespread usage at the time. These include (from Lipton's list) *frantic* "frenzied; excited (usually in a bad way)" (1561—), *like* [as an interjection] (1778—, originally dialect), and *be nowhere* "to be out of one's depth" (1840—) or "to be insignificant or worthless" (1843—), both originally US.

Many terms attributed to the beats had been in use for some time in more specialized or restricted contexts. Jazz musicians and enthusiasts had been developing and changing their own slang terms for several decades, and the beats' association with jazz music and admiration for jazz musicians made it inevitable that they would adopt some of these terms, including some that originated outside the jazz world but largely in African American usage:

hot "excellent" (1866—)

ball "a good time" (1879—)

square "conventional; unappreciative of jazz" (1901—), only a slight shift from the sense "dependable; honourable; upright" (a.1644—)

gig "a professional musical engagement" (1908—)

cool "up to date; sophisticated" (1918—)

go "to be carried away by the pleasure of music; to make an effort" (1926-1974)

crazy "wild; exciting; excellent" (1927—)

be with it "to be informed or up to date" (1931—)

in the (or a) *groove* "enjoying music; enjoying anything" (1932-)

shack up "to cohabit" (1934—)

hipster "a cool and knowledgeable individual" (1940—)

fall out "to faint; to collapse" (1941—)

drug "exhausted; bored; depressed" (1946-1970)

gone "very excited or inspired; high on drugs" (1946—)

far out "excellent" (1954—)

funky "bluesy; emotional; fashionable" (1954—)

ax(e) "a musical instrument" (1955—)

Clearly the beats, like the flappers, were being given credit for the creativity of others: although many of these terms had been in use among black musicians for decades before, it was their use by white dropouts that was considered worthy of attention.

The beats also associated with users and sellers of drugs, and naturally they picked up some of the pre-existing vocabulary of this group, including *hype* "a drug-user; a hypodermic syringe" (1924—), *high* "exhilarated by the effects of drugs" (1931—), *connection* "a supplier of drugs" (1931—), and *hold* "to be in possession of drugs" (1935—). Drug-users shared many of the characteristics that contemporary commentators attributed to the beats, notably an unwillingness to wash or hold down a steady job. Whether or not beats were distinguishable from other drug-users at the time, there were clear reasons why these two groups might choose to *hang out* "to loiter; to consort" (1811—) together.

Terms originally found in the language of thieves and the homeless may also have become more general by the time the beats adopted them, but it isn't hard to envisage individuals passing from one of these milieu into another. For example, Lipton records that beats were using the terms *pad* "a house; a place to sleep" (1914—, originally in criminal slang) and *gimp* "a lame person; a lame leg; a limp" (1920—, originally in hobo and criminal slang). Similarly, since the beats rejected the values of wider society, it isn't surprising that some of the language of psychotherapy had slipped into their usage, such as *relate to* "to understand or have empathy with" (1947—).

Once the well-established terms have been accounted for, there are relatively few new terms in Lipton's list that could be attributed to the beats themselves. Of these, the only two to have entered wider usage are *turn on* "to introduce to drugs; to arouse sexually" (1955—)[5] and *ball* "to have sexual intercourse (with)" (1955—), which could be from *ball* "to have a good time" (1946—), *ball* "a testicle" (*a.*1325—), or a falling together of these two unrelated words.

---

[5] There's an isolated use in Henry James's *The Ambassadors* (1903), where it appears to mean "to inform; to confide in; to ask for assistance", which isn't quite the same thing.

Of the words in Lipton's glossary, only *work* "sexual intercourse" appears to have been restricted to this group. Analysing Lipton's terms demonstrates that although the beats may have spoken in a distinctive way, they were by no means as creative (in terms of slang production) or as *far out* as they were generally held to be at the time.

Hippy slang

A glossary of similar length was included in May Lay and Nancy Orban's *Hip Glossary of Hippie Language* (1967). Published in San Francisco only eight years later, it wasn't far removed from Lipton's list in time or space. It should come as no surprise, therefore, that it contains many of the same terms, some of which had been in use for a long time, including *cut out* "to move quickly; to leave" (1797—), *drag* "a bore" (1857—), and *to split* "to leave" (1865—). More numerous in Lay and Orban's hippy glossary are terms adopted by the beats from the jazz scene and from drug users, including some that had been in circulation for some time:

bust "to arrest" (1899/1900—, from the military sense "to demote" (1878—))

hep "in the know" (1904—)

spade "a black person; a black man" (1910—)

dealer "a supplier of drugs" (1928—)

fix "a dose of drugs" (1934—)

dig "to understand; to appreciate" (1934—, originally African American)

bread "money" (1935—)

square "someone who doesn't appreciate jazz; a conventional person" (1944—)

Perhaps some of the terms dating from the 1940s and 50s should be attributed to the creativity and influence of the beats, including:

benny "Benzedrine; a Benzedrine tablet" (1945—)

flip (out) "to go wild; to become insane" (1950—, also *flip one's wig* (1934—) and *flip one's lid* (1941—))

horse "heroin" (1950—)

the scene "a location or milieu in which like-minded fashionable people socialize" (1951—)

It shouldn't be surprising that a few terms used by African Americans but not exclusively associated with the jazz scene also found their way into the white counterculture in this period, though they're often used with a weakened or more general sense. *Soul*, for instance, is defined in the *OED* as referring to "the emotional or spiritual quality of Black American life and culture, manifested esp. in music" (1946—). Lay and Orban define it more generally as "a term used to describe that quality in a person most easily described in straight language as compassion; active and lively compassion; a

7 Hippy slang: From Ann Mathers's *The Hip Pocket Book* (New York: Aphrodite Press, 1967), 4.

being at one with the world and man". Similarly, *soul brother* (1959—), which the *OED* defines as "a fellow Black man" is weakened to "a friend" and *blood* "a Black person; a close friend" (1965—) is described as "a neutral word for a negro", though its original connotations were decidedly positive.

A few other terms in the hippy glossary appear to have developed from uses included in the beat list. Both glossaries listed *wig out* "to be overcome by emotion" (1955—), but the hippy list includes *wig* "the head; the brain; the mind" (1944-1980, US Black). *Swing*, "to be involved in the uninhibited fashionable scene" (1957—, often historical in later use) is included in the hippy list, while the beat glossary includes *swinging* "uninhibited" (*a.*1955—, often historical in later use). The hippy list documents the development of a new layer of meaning under the influence of the free-love movement of the 1960s, by also defining *swing* in the sense "to engage in promiscuous or group sex" (1964—).

Although most of the terms included in Lay and Orban's list hadn't been listed by Lipton as having been in use among the beats of the previous decade, they were by no means new. Several, such as *hashish* "dried leaves or resin from the cannabis plant" (1598—), *hookah* "a pipe that cools smoke by passing it through water" (1763—), *peyote* "a hallucinogenic drug made from the peyote cactus" (1849—), and *marijuana* "dried leaves or resin from the cannabis plant" (1874—) aren't slang at all. With the exception of *out of sight* "excellent" (1876—), *short* "a car" (1932—, used with the sense "a street car; a tram" from 1909), and *bug* "to annoy" (1947—, which appears to have originated in jazz or beat usage), these well-established terms illustrate the hippies' interests in politics, self-realization, and drugs:

blow "to smoke" (1773–)

where it's at "the true state of affairs; the place to be" (1854–)

head "a drug-user" (*a.*1911–)

papers "cigarette papers" (*c.*1911–)

the establishment "government; anyone in power" (1923–)

weed "marijuana" (1929–)

dyke "a lesbian" (1932–)

cope "to deal with a situation or problem" (1934–)

uptight "tense; anxious; inhibited" (1934–, but not common until 1966)

tea "marijuana" (1935–)

straight "conventional" (1941–)

the man "a drug-dealer" (1942–)

up "exhilarated by drugs; high" (1942–)

grass "marijuana" (1943–)

high "a drug-induced state of euphoria" (1944–)

hung up (on) "confused (about); preoccupied (with)" (1945–, originally jazz)

matchbox "a quantity of marijuana; a number of joints" (1946–)

hit "a dose of narcotics; a puff on a joint" (1951–)

score "the successful acquisition of drugs" (1951–), from the sense "the profits from a crime" (1914–, criminals), and more general uses

hang-up "difficulty; fixation" (1952–)

joint "a marijuana cigarette" (1952–, used with reference to hypodermic equipment since 1935 and normal cigarettes since 1942)

toke "to take a puff on a joint" (1952–)

psychedelic "mind-altering, especially in association with LSD" (1957–)

roach-holder "a cigarette holder" (1958–)

trip "a drug-induced hallucinogenic experience" (1959–)

lid "a measurement of marijuana, usually an ounce" (1961–)

bag "a preference or interest" (1962–, originally jazz)

meth "methamphetamine" (1963–)

The terms from the 1940s and 50s may have originated in beat usage, or have been borrowed from the beats by other drug-users, but Lipton didn't list them. Lipton also omitted *happening* "a performance; an exhibition; an event" (1959—) and *the underground* "a subculture" (1959—).

On the evidence of Lay and Orban's list, the hippies were more active slang-creators than Lipton's beats had been.[6] Although the two lists are approximately the same length, Lay and Orban identified 12 terms that had been in use for two years or less, largely relating to drug use and emotional states:

---

[6] It may just be that hippies had a stronger sense of group identity than the beats and put more effort into documenting their newness by enregistering their speech.

acid "LSD" (1965–)

blow one's mind "to induce hallucinations or pleasurable sensations" (1965–)

teeny bopper "a teenage follower of current trends" (1965–)

turn off "to repel; to inspire no interest" (1965–)

mellow yellow "banana skin prepared for smoking" (1966–)

narc "a narcotics officer" (1966–)

trip (out) "to experience drug-induced hallucination" (1966–)

be-in "a public gathering of hippies" (1967–), formed by analogy with Civil Rights *sit-ins* (1960–)

crash "to come down from a high" (1967–, apparently from *crash (out)* "to sleep, esp. for a single night or in an emergency" (1945–, originally Australian))

freak "a drug-user" (1967–)

key "a kilogramme of a drug" (1967–)

speed "amphetamine" (1967–)

Three of Lay and Orban's slang terms aren't attested elsewhere: *color-head* "an individual with a heightened interest in colour", *opiate* "a person under the influence of opium", and *super straight* "slightly unconventional".

Beats, hippies, and after

So what does all of this tell us about the beats and the hippies? It tells us that both groups were considered by their contemporaries (or themselves, at least) to be creative, modern, and unconventional. Although both groups acquired a great deal of their slang from elsewhere, they appear to have been credited with innovations that weren't theirs. It isn't clear whether our beat and hippy lexicographers knew that the terms they were documenting had originally been used by other groups: it is possible that they'd encountered them first amongst beats or hippies and assumed that these groups were the first users. On the other hand, it's also possible that some of these terms retained their associations with their earlier users, and that the beats and hippies were self-consciously associating themselves with oppressed and creative minorities. This second possibility brings us on to the reason why there was much more continuity between beat and hippy usage than there was between military and flapper slang.

Flappers wanted to distance themselves from the war generation, but the hippies admired the beats: they had a similar world view and similar ideas about what was and wasn't important. The continuity of vocabulary is a reflection of continuities in aspirations and philosophy, as well as in the life stories of some of the individuals involved.

There were differences, of course, between the beats and the hippies. The beats dropped out from society but were content to live alongside it, whereas many hippies sought to challenge and change the values and rules of mainstream society. New trends reacted against these ideals in their turn during the 1970s, particularly glam rock, punk, and disco. By the time I was a teenager, in the 1980s, calling someone a *hippy* "a person who is or attempts to be hip, now usually with reference to the late 1960s" (1952—) implied that they were unfashionably dressed and out of date. Far from being *hip*, a *hippy* was someone who'd failed to keep up with the latest trends. Individuals of our age or older who used terms like *far out* or *groovy* marked themselves as hippies by association and, for a time at least (in the circles I mixed in), these terms were only ever used ironically. If we described a party as *groovy* we meant not that it was "excellent", but that it was the kind of party that someone who might say *groovy* would think was excellent. To an adult, this might have sounded like a positive evaluation, but we knew it wasn't. So much information in one little word—no wonder slang survives! In other places and among other groups of people, these terms probably had entirely different connotations. Many of the terms used by the beats and the hippies were more firmly embedded in general American slang than they were in general British slang, and so they were more marked in British usage in the post-hippy period and perhaps more carefully avoided.

Slang Survival: Continued use

We've seen that there are various levels on which slang can survive. The first is that they continue in use with the same or a closely related sense. Many jazz terms, for example, were adopted by the beats and later by the hippies, often with only a slight widening in meaning. This will tend to happen where circumstances or attitudes remain relatively constant and where the new users of the slang terms are happy to be associated with the old users. The clothes and music may change, but as long as the underlying philosophy is similar, the slang terms can continue in use. We have also seen that once youth movements began to rebel against the ideals of the late 60s and 70s, much of the slang associated with that period began to fall from use.

Slang survival: Adaptation

The second level on which slang terms survive is best represented by the WWI terms still in general use. In circumstances that were completely different, and in a situation where many people were doing their best not to talk about or think about the war, these terms could survive only by adapting to their new conditions. Sometimes this survival was in much more restricted use, sometimes at the expense of a change in meaning, but it always comes about by chance rather than design. Adaptation for survival isn't a deliberate choice by the words or their users, any more than Darwin's wind-carried finches looked around their new island home and thought, 'Hmmm, I'm definitely going to need a bigger beak.'

Although changes in meaning are common at all levels of English, slang terms don't tend to experience the brakes of conservative usage and etymology. Individuals who object that *petrified* really means "turned to stone", or who object to the first vowel in *latte* rhyming with either *batty* or *farty* (with or without a glottal stop), are unlikely to extend the same careful reference to the etymological origins of slang terms. Such an individual is unlikely to argue that *chill* shouldn't be used to mean "to pass time idly" (1985—, originally US) because it really means "to calm down" (1979—, originally US). It's more likely that they'd either argue that these senses of *chill* should be avoided altogether, because they're slang, or that they'd be entirely unaware of them. Changes in slang usage occur more freely and without the disapproval that sometimes meets changes in Standard English.

Slang survival: Allusion

Slang terms can also survive in allusive use, often with ironic reference to their original meaning or users. Allusive use may be a temporary stage on the route to obsolescence, but it also offers the possibility of revival at a later stage. Similarly revivable are slang terms that are remembered rather than actively used. WWI veterans probably didn't entirely forget the slang of the war. Although most of these terms had little function in the post-war world, they remained available for use when required. Perhaps, meeting for the first time, decades after the conflict, they were still able to reminisce about the *Jack Johnsons* (1914-1962)[7] and *flaming onions* (1918-1943). Perhaps this use of a shared vocabulary drew old soldiers closer by coded reference to their unspeakable shared experience.

Slang survival: Representation

Slang survives in allusive use, where the original users refer back to their own usage, but it also survives in representations of usage. Because words like *fab* and *groovy* became so closely associated with the 1960s (although *groovy* had already been in use for several decades), they became easy shorthand for that decade not just among later youths of an ironic turn, but also for dramatic recreators of that period. In 1997, when Mike Myers wanted to parody British cinema of the 1960s, he had Austin Powers use slang that matched his clothes. After this point, people starting using words like *fab* and *groovy* third-hand: in ironic reference to a parody of 1960s usage, and these and other terms acquired a new lease of life as a consequence.

---

[7] This is from the name of an African American boxing champion nicknamed 'the big smoke' from *smoke* "a black person" (1902—, US).

Some of their current users are probably unaware of these terms' layered and complicated histories, and use them without any ironic intention.

Conclusions

For slang to survive, conditions have to remain similar or adaptation has to occur. Slang with no useful function won't survive in continued use, though it might survive in allusion or representation (bearing in mind that the existence of numerous synonyms doesn't render a slang term useless). It's possible for any word to be revived so long as some trace of its use remains on paper or in memory, and this makes it very dangerous to claim that a slang term has fallen from use. As we've seen, it can be difficult to identify first dates of use too, but focussing on slang terms and even on groups of users could distract us from the fact that neither could exist without individual slang-users. The next chapter considers the decisions made by individuals in choosing whether or not to use slang: it looks at the final stage of metamorphosis by which the tadpole becomes amphibious and is able to colonize other ponds.

Endnotes

The American WWI slang is from Jonathan Lighter's 'The Slang of the American Expeditionary Forces in Europe, 1917-1919: An Historical Glossary', *American Speech* 47 (1972), 5–142, with additional information from my main dictionary sources. I've quoted the scene between the flapper and her mother from 'Flapper Filology', *Philadelphia Evening Bulletin*, 8 Mar. 1922, 9, but it appeared in several other newspapers at around the same time. Lawrence Lipton's *The Holy Barbarians* (New York: Messner, 1959) and May Lay and Nancy Orban's *The Hip Glossary of Hippie Language* (San Francisco: [self-published], 1967) provided the beat and hippy slang.

5 The Spread of Slang

So far we've talked about how groups of people adapt slang already in existence or create their own slang for use in new circumstances. This chapter will focus on individuals' motivations for using slang. Under most normal circumstances, individuals aren't cut off from communication with those around them if they don't adopt new slang words. That's not how slang works—it's embedded within standard or colloquial language as an optional extra, so it's usually entirely possible to communicate clearly and effectively without it. It's normal for some individuals within a group to use a lot of slang, while other members of the same group will use little or none at all. Although slang development is favoured by the unusual circumstances set out in Chapter 3, in normal social interaction slang use more commonly arises from willing identification with a social subgroup. Most of us pick up and use slang in everyday conversation rather than in the enforced companionship of the barracks, prison cell, or school dormitory. We use slang in casual conversations in the places where we live, work, and socialize. Although we may wonder about the origins or meaning of a slang word or phrase when we first hear it, we quickly become used to it and sometimes adopt it ourselves. By these means, our slang tadpoles finally develop into frogs and become able to move far beyond their original pond.

Social grooming and individuality

Most slang words are optional substitutes for synonyms in Standard English. Usually whatever is said in slang could be expressed in Standard English. For example, here are some of the many responses to a video clip called 'BBC mistakes cab driver for IT-expert' on *YouTube*:

> Proper blagger...LOL, good one matey...this guy is a legend I reckon.
> hahahahahahaha!! what a ledge
> AHAHAHAA this is so EPIC !!!!AHAH
> rofl hes like its not me
> LOL this guy is sick
> This guy kicks ass.

The clip shows a man called Guy Goma, who was waiting for a job interview when he was mistakenly taken into a studio during a live broadcast and introduced as Guy Kewney, an IT expert. After his initial and amusingly apparent shock, Goma did his best to answer the questions put to him despite his lack of expertise. These responses to the clip all make the same basic points: that Goma made an impressive job of bluffing in a difficult situation and that the clip was very funny. Laughter is represented by *haha* (OE—), *ahah*, which may be a deliberate mistyping of *haha*, LOL (which we've already seen), and ROFL (*rolling on the floor laughing*, since at least 2000). We're told that Goma is a *ledge* and a *legend* (since at least 1997), and that he *kicks ass* (1977—, originally and chiefly US). He's *sick* "excellent" (1983—) and the clip is *epic* "significant; excellent" (since at least 2000). Another contributor took issue with the use of the word *sick*, interpreting it as criticism rather than a term of admiration (and assuming that the criticism was motivated by racism). To avoid such misunderstandings, the contributors could each have made their point more clearly by typing, 'I liked this man because his reaction to an awkward situation made me laugh.' So why didn't they? Well, once a few people had said this, there would be no point in repeating it in the same words, or adding a chorus of 'me too' and 'I agree'. Using slang makes it possible to say more or less the same thing in a variety of ways. Saying the same thing in a variety of ways is less about communicating meaning than about building and maintaining relationships. It contributes to the social grooming function played by conversation, in the same way that greetings, compliments, and observations about the weather do, but slang helps us to express ourselves as individuals at the same time. In the responses to this clip, slang also conveys a far more exuberant sense of admiration and humour than Standard English can. Finally, using slang allows the contributors to distance themselves from the authority figure in this situation (the BBC interviewer) and to identify with Goma or at least to signal that they're admiring him rather than laughing at him.

Codes and hidden hierarchies

Often, by choosing to use a slang term in preference to a Standard English synonym, we're providing information about ourselves and about our relationships and interests. Let's take a more traditional situation for slang use: face-to-face conversation. Unfortunately, examples aren't so readily available, and rather than resort to literary representations or film clips, I've made up my own using current slang terms documented by my students. These conversations include more slang than you'd be likely to find in real life.

A white male student—let's call him Jack—pushes his way over to a friend in a student bar in Leicester and shouts, 'Sam, mate. I'm *so* crunk!', probably assuming that Sam will understand what he means. The meanings of *crunk* include "excellent; exciting; excited, especially as a result of listening to (hip hop or rap) music; intoxicated with drink or drugs; obnoxious" (1995—), and several of these senses work reasonably well in this context, where the right kind of DJ is playing the right kind of music. Many contributors to *Urban Dictionary* consider it to be a blend of *crazy* and *drunk*, and use it specifically with reference to a state of exhilaration brought about by alcohol or drugs rather than music. The *OED* offers this as a possible etymology, along with a derivation from an otherwise unattested strong past participle of *crank*: the DJ *cranks* up the music, the music is *cranked*, the audience is *crunk*. *Urban* lexicographers who mention either etymology generally do so to affirm the correctness of their understanding of the meaning of the term and to demonstrate that anyone who uses it differently is wrong.

In fact, even if Sam had never heard the word before, Jack's body language and facial expression, along with the context, would probably have enabled him to make a pretty good guess at its meaning. The meaning of *crunk* is less important than its interpersonal function. Because *crunk* tends to be used in the context of hip hop and rap music, it confirms that Jack likes and understands the music and the cultural trends that go along with it. To claim this identification, Jack probably has to work harder as a white British student than if he were a Black youth from inner London, let alone a genuine urban African American. But Jack isn't just saying, 'I find rap music exhilarating'; he's assuming that Sam does as well. If Sam does, he'll probably be familiar with *crunk* and his response will confirm his appreciation and cement the bond between them. If he doesn't, but he's reasonably socially adept, he'll probably pretend that he knows the word for now. Perhaps he'll look it up on *Urban Dictionary*, but it's more likely that he'll forget about it until next time he hears or reads it, and that a combination of the contexts in which he comes across the term will help him to refine his understanding of its meaning. Jack may intend *crunk* to mean "exhilarated by hip hop" and Sam may hear the slurring in Jack's voice and decide that it must mean "drunk". If the next time Sam hears the word *crunk*, "drunk" still works as its meaning, and if enough other people make the same misinterpretation and use the word accordingly, the word will have that new meaning for some people, and resistance is futile.

If, instead of bluffing, Sam were to ask what *crunk* meant, Jack would either be amused by Sam's innocence (if he were an exchange student or had had an unusually repressive upbringing, for example), or he would conclude that there must be some good reason why Sam doesn't have many friends. But Sam won't ask. For all he knows, everyone who's anyone knows what *crunk* means. Asking its meaning would reveal that he's out of touch and out of fashion. It might expose him to prolonged and damaging mockery, or it might just mean that the conversation with Jack fizzles out into awkwardness. Using slang can operate as a kind of password: either you know what I'm saying or you're not my kind of person. Fortunately, for now, Sam only has to pretend to recognize the password when Jack uses it.

After agreeing that Jack is *crunk*, probably by using a rather non-specific interjection, such as *yeah* or *safe*, and apparently getting away with it, Sam asks, 'Have you got any weed, man?' Jack replies, 'I'm down to my last bifta, mate' ("a (large) joint; a hand-rolled cigarette" (1936—)). Sam and Jack both smoke marijuana and feel entirely secure in acknowledging this to one another, though they may not have had any prior knowledge of one another's habits.[1] Indeed, Sam's use of *man* (1568—) functions as an apology for asking the question, if it turns out that an apology is necessary. If Jack were a law-abiding abstainer, a reply of 'sorry man' or 'sorry *mate*' (1500—) would have diffused a potentially awkward situation by signalling that, despite Jack's inability to provide the requested substance, the assumed state of friendliness wasn't unfounded.[2]

By using *bifta* in his reply, Jack is not only confirming Sam's assumption that he doesn't disapprove of marijuana use, but is also

---

[1]   This is a useful moment to point out that real students in real universities are far too busy studying to go to bars, and if anyone offered them a joint they would certainly not inhale.

[2]   Terms like *man*, *mate*, and *brother* (1912—, originally African American) imply common membership of a group, and they can backfire if the person addressed resents the implied bond. They can also sound condescending when the claimed equality is undermined by other indications of unequal wealth or status.

indicating that he smokes it himself. In situations like these, slang terms can be used in a form of one-upmanship, and by producing a similarly specialized term in response, Sam would be able to demonstrate that he can equal Jack's expertise and knowledge. It's unlikely that any of this is deliberate or conscious, but whatever Sam's response, he and Jack will both leave this conversation with a sense of each other's relative experience in pot-smoking and also of the likelihood of being able to *blag* "to obtain for free" (1934—) some from one another in future.

Shared assumptions and implicit judgements

Having established their common ground, Sam and Jack have a beer. After a while, Jack notices a girl who's trying to catch Sam's eye. 'Hey man,' he says, 'you've scored.' Sam looks around. 'Over there,' says Jack, 'the hottie by the door. She's gagging for it'. 'Shit,' says Sam. 'What?' 'I copped off with her last week and the skank's changed her status to "it's complicated".' 'You got yourself a stalker, bro.' A Standard English version of this conversation might run:

> Jack: Sam, that woman appears to be interested in you ... The attractive one by the door. She seems to be on the look out for a sexual partner.
> Sam: Oh no!
> Jack: What?
> Sam: I had sexual intercourse with her last week and the promiscuous young lady has changed her Facebook status to indicate that she is in some kind of relationship.
> Jack: I acknowledge the awkwardness of the situation in which you find yourself. You appear, inadvertently, to have become the object of her affections.

Again, slang isn't being used merely to convey factual content. There's an additional level of meaning that the Standard English translation can't represent: the shared assumptions and values communicated by the original. Both versions reveal Jack's assumption that Sam is heterosexual, but the slang one indicates that Jack is too, or at least wants Sam to believe he is: by calling the woman (let's call her Amy) a *hottie* (1913—, originally Australian), he isn't just signalling that she's attractive, but also that he finds her attractive. Although this acknowledges Sam's success in attracting Amy's attention, Jack's slang also implies that his own previous experience enables him to identify Amy's interest in Sam. By using *score* (1959—), Jack may also be indicating a healthy heterosexual interest in sport. Thus he reasserts his own virility in a situation that looks set to undermine it. There are lots of slang synonyms for "to have sexual intercourse", including many that emphasize the act of penetration, depicting the woman as a passive recipient and downplaying emotional involvement. By saying that he *copped off with* (1940—) Amy (an American might once have said he *copped* her *off* (1899-1976)), Sam is signalling that a casual and purely physical connection took place between them and that it was inappropriate for her to assume that this represented the beginning of a meaningful relationship. Describing Amy as a *skank* (1964—, originally US) allows Sam to suggest that there's no reason for him to worry about Amy's feelings because she sleeps around a lot and should understand that she has no reason and no right to expect any further involvement.[3] He assumes that Jack will agree with this interpretation of their sexual encounter, and Jack acknowledges their shared values by describing Amy as a *stalker* (1947—), which was originally used with reference to celebrities' criminally obsessive fans but is now used in the much weaker sense "anyone, especially a spurned lover, who harbours unwelcome affections". Jack uses slang to confirm that, in his view, Sam's interpretation of events is the only reasonable and correct one. This dissipates any doubts Sam might have had

---

[3] Let's not complicate matters by speculating about whether Sam calls Amy a *skank* because he is disgusted by her promiscuity or his own. Do you really want me to have to make up a therapist as well?

about his own behaviour and responsibilities, and also about whether it's going to be any fun hanging out with Jack.

Closed doors

Later, Sam leaves with Amy and Jack staggers off on his own. He's drunk and tired: disappointed that Sam scored and he didn't. The last thing he needs is for his Dad to be waiting up for him, beer in hand:

> **Dad:** Jack! Waaazzuup?
> **Jack:** (Grunts)
> **Dad:** Good gig?
> **Jack:** Yeah, whatever.
> **Dad:** Thought you'd be off bonking some totty by now. When I was your age...
> **Jack:** I'm wrecked Dad. Gotta get some kip.
> **Dad:** Ok son, good night.
> **Jack:** Laters.

In this conversation Jack doesn't say much because he doesn't want to engage in conversation with his Dad (we'll call him Ian). Ian's doing all the work in this conversation—trying to bond with his son by offering up topics of conversation and using slang to create the shared intimacy and assumptions that Jack and Sam were able to create earlier in the evening. Unfortunately, Ian isn't a very up-to-date or fluent user of slang. *Wazzup* was used in a successful advertising campaign by Budweiser for several years from around 1999 with the sense "what's going on?; what are you doing?", and although Jack may be too young to remember the adverts, he probably recognizes the allusion. He's probably heard it in more recent comedy shows and cartoons, used by characters who don't realize they're embarrassingly out of touch. *Wazzup* is still used, but without the lengthening of the vowel. It's now more clearly a greeting that, like *how do you do*, doesn't require any answer other than its own repetition. In other words, in response to *wazzup*, Jack would generally say *wazzup*. Here

"I've got my hat on back-to-front, I'm wearing a silly pair of trousers, I've got a ring through my nose but I still can't communicate with him."

8 Youth slang: Adey Bryant, 'I've Got My Hat on Back-to-front, but I Still Can't Communicate With Him'.

he answers only with a grunt, which isn't an encouraging response however you interpret it. Unperturbed, Ian asks about the *gig*, using the word as Jack would use it and as he did during his own youth (though in his day a DJ wouldn't have counted as a live performer). Jack resents the implied shared experience and despises Ian for trying to ingratiate himself.

Ian tries again to assert their commonality by showing that he's aware that picking up women is one of the possible goals of a night out. Unfortunately, he employs *totty* "a girl or woman, especially a promiscuous one" (1890—) in a slightly different way than Jack would, by using it to refer to a single woman instead of to women collectively. Jack might refer to an individual woman as *a bit of totty* or *a piece of totty* (in a post-feminist ironic sort of way, if he's challenged), but *hottie* is a more likely alternative. Similarly, by using *bonk* "to have sexual intercourse (with)" (1975—), Ian intends to signal that he's easy-going and open-minded, but his use of this old-fashioned slang term confirms Jack's impression that actually Ian doesn't know what he's talking about. Kinder than your average son, Jack comes up with an excuse for avoiding talking to his Dad, with the usefully ambiguous confession that he is *wrecked* "drunk; under the influence of drugs" (1967/8—) and in need of some *kip* "sleep" (1879—). When Ian reverts to Standard English, he's rewarded with a friendly *laters* "see you later" (1999—).

In this conversation, slang plays a different social function. Instead of drawing the speakers closer together, it drives them further apart. Although Ian once had a social life rather like Jack's, and although he may share many of the same underlying values, he doesn't have the fluent command of current youth slang that he needs to signal this. Instead, by using out-of-date slang, he confirms the distance between them. In fact, as I'm sure you've realised, if Ian had been able to use the same slang as Jack with great fluency, the distance between them would have been confirmed anyway. An adult using youth slang is either ridiculous or *creepy* "repugnant; sycophantic" (1883—) so Ian can't win: because he's the one trying to use slang to win approval, it's Jack who decides the terms on which that approval can (or, more probably, can't) be won.

Fitting in and winning approval

Students have often been identified as particularly fluent and creative users of slang, perhaps partly because they've always been readily available to academics wanting to study slang use. Actually, students generally arrive at university with an extensive vocabulary of slang terms at their command. Let's go back to Amy, a typical first year, who's sitting in the shared kitchen in her halls of residence the morning after. She moved to Leicester from Northamptonshire, not far away, and found herself sharing a flat with students from various parts of the UK. Amy and her flatmates have a number of terms in common, but they each brought a few unusual or local slang terms with them from home. In this conversation Amy is talking to Liz, from Scotland, and Laura, from Yorkshire:

> Liz: Amy, I'm scoobied. Why did you let that twanger near your fud again?
> Laura: You wuss!
> Amy: That's harsh. I think he's lush.
> Liz: You're a pikey sweatbag.
> Amy: Fair sneech, but it takes one to know one, Mrs Sweatbag.
> Laura: Liz, can I borrow some shrap until the weekend?
> Liz: I haven't got any. Have you Amy?
> Amy: Nope. No wonga till payday.

Because these three have lived together for some months, some mixing of slang terms has already occurred. Laura has picked up *wuss* "a weak or ineffectual person" (1976—, originally US) from Liz, Liz has picked up *twanger* "an odd or eccentric person" from Amy, and Amy uses Liz's *wonga* "money" (1984—). Amy and Liz aren't as friendly with Laura as they are with each another, so they haven't picked up any of her slang. Here, for example, they use *wonga* in preference to Laura's *shrap* (short for *shrapnel* "small change" (1919—, originally Australian and New Zealand military slang)). As in the conversation between Jack and his Dad, the slang user is the one trying to win approval. Laura tries to create a shared bond by using the other girls' slang, but Amy and Liz have the power to decide whether or not to return the compliment by reciprocating. In the same way that these girls might be influenced by one another's clothes or hair, they'll only emulate the slang of those they admire.

Laura may be tolerated as a third party in this friendship, but the girls' collective use of slang signals her marginal position.

Status and knowledge

Laura's younger sister, Mia, is seventeen and in her last year at school. Because they both went to the same school, the sisters share many slang terms in common, but not all. Back at home at the weekend, the following conversation takes place between Laura, Mia, and Mia's friend Charlie:

> **Mia:** You got any shrap?
> **Laura:** Nope. Completely out of wonga.
> **Charlie:** Me too.
> **Laura:** What are you doing tonight?
> **Charlie:** Going down the Tavern.
> **Mia:** Looking for Dan the man?
> **Charlie:** OMG! No way. He's like totally gay.
> **Mia:** Lol!

Laura has decided that *shrap* isn't as cool as *wonga* and signals this to Mia by using her new slang term instead. Charlie doesn't repeat either term, but perhaps later on she'll use *wonga* and see how people react. In conversation between themselves, Charlie and Mia use the Internet abbreviations *OMG* "Oh my God" (1917+1994—) and *lol*, and also *gay* in the sense "lame; unfashionable; unappealing". Because Laura's slightly older than the other two, she doesn't use *gay* in this sense and she doesn't use *OMG* or *lol* in speech, nor do her friends at home or university. Because these terms aren't used by the people Laura admires, she thinks they sound childish. Like any older sibling, her first instinct is to tell Mia why she's wrong, but she has to decide whether it's a good idea to do this while Charlie is around. Laura holds her tongue for now because being in a minority undermines her big-sisterly authority.

Whether Laura expresses her disapproval now or later, it's highly unlikely that Charlie and Mia will stop using the offending terms. Although they like Laura and accept that she has marginally more experience of the world, she can't challenge the influence of their peers. If all their friends use *OMG, lol,* and *gay* as they do, they'll decide that it's Laura who's wrong. She's hanging around with the wrong kind of people; she's come over all *la-di-da* "affected; pretentious" (1861—) since she went to university; she's completely out of touch with what's really important. In fact, Mia may begin to use these terms more when Laura's around, purely to irritate her:

> **Mia:** OMG, you can't go out wearing that!
> **Laura:** Why?
> **Mia:** Because it's bare gay.
> **Laura:** Bare gay! You sound so stupid.
> **Mia:** You would say that.
> **Laura:** Why?
> **Mia:** Gay.
> **Laura:** Yeah, right. Like you even know anyone gay.
> **Mia:** Yeah. Well you're gay, innit.

Perturbed by her sister's criticism, Mia goes on Facebook to record her feelings. Charlie is available to chat:

> **Mia:** my sisters so gay!!
> **Charlie:** lol. why?
> **Mia:** shes always dissing me
> **Charlie:** douchebag! you should frape her!
> **Mia:** rofl!! – Laura is a douchebag.
> **Charlie:** lush!
> **Mia:** gtgpc l8rs ;) xxx

In this exchange, Mia requests reassurance from Charlie, who dismisses Laura as a *douchebag* "an unattractive or boring person" (1950—, originally US), and advises Mia to make malicious changes to Laura's Facebook page. Putting aside its trivialization of sexual violence, *frape*, a blend of *Facebook* and *rape* (since at least 2007—), offers a usefully brief way of expressing something that could only be expressed by a longer phrase in Standard English. Like many people, Charlie and Mia have terms for approval (*lush*) and disapproval (*gay*) that they use habitually. When they've been used so often that they start to lose their force, newer terms will begin to be used alongside them to express stronger degrees of approval. Alongside *lol* and *rofl*, Mia and Charlie use abbreviations that they either couldn't or wouldn't represent in speech: representations of the phrase, 'got to go, parent(s) coming/calling', and of *laters*, which we've already seen in Jack's usage.

Reasons for using slang

In his book *Slang: Today and Yesterday* (first published in 1933), Eric Partridge listed 17 reasons for using slang, and when people refer back to this list they usually say that he was being more pedantic than was strictly necessary. Hah! Call that pedantic? So far, we've seen that the people who used slang to respond to the BBC clip were doing so to:

1. express their individuality
2. express themselves more vividly than can be easily done in Standard English
3. express emotion
4. create humour.

We've also seen that Sam and Jack used slang to:

5. identify themselves as a member of a group (which may be a social group, but also an age group or interest group)
6. fit in with the people around them (which may be a well-defined group or merely the selection of individuals who happen to be there at the time)
7. test whether someone else is also a member of the group
8. identify hierarchies within the group

9. express shared attitudes and values (and thus create temporary group membership)
10. imply or refer back to shared experience
11. deny or distance emotion.

In the conversations between Jack and his Dad, slang was also used to:

12. communicate with deliberate ambiguity (so that the hearer can choose their own interpretation)
13. identify someone as not being a member of the group.

Among Amy and her flatmates, slang was used to:

14. try to win entry to the in-group
15. exclude someone from membership of the group
16. appear cool to people outside the group.

In Amy's conversation with Mia and Charlie, slang also functioned to:

17. reject someone else's values or attitudes
18. shock or offend
19. rebel
20. irritate
21. communicate secretly (so that one hearer understands and another doesn't).

In the Facebook exchange between Mia and Charlie, slang was used because:

22. it's easier in some way (usually quicker)
23. everyone else uses it
24. it has become a habit or mannerism
25. there isn't a word that means the same thing in Standard English
26. although there is a synonym in Standard English, the slang-user doesn't know it.

I've subdivided some of these reasons more than Partridge did, but this doesn't entirely account for the difference in number. Partridge doesn't mention the creation of hierarchies, the use of slang to shock, offend, rebel, irritate, or to communicate with deliberate ambiguity, and he doesn't acknowledge any of the less positive reasons for using slang (23–26). On the other hand, Partridge has a few reasons I've omitted, which he numbers as follows:

7. To enrich the language. (This deliberateness is rare save among the well-educated, Cockneys forming the most notable exception; it is literary rather than spontaneous.)

8. To lend an air of solidity, concreteness, to the abstract; of earthiness to the idealistic; of immediacy and appositeness to the remote. (In the cultured the effort is usually premeditated, while in the uncultured it is almost always unconscious when it is not rather subconscious.)

10. To speak or write down to an inferior, or to amuse a superior public; or merely to be on a colloquial level with either one's audience or one's subject matter.

These reveal some striking differences between Partridge's assumptions and mine, and those differences are a result of changes in the status and use of slang since the early twentieth century. Partridge assumes that uncultured people use slang without thinking about it, and that when cultured people use slang it's conscious and probably also condescending. My assumption is that slang is concerned more with power relationships than with culture (it was probably harder to distinguish between the two in Partridge's day). Slang users now hold the power in many conversations, and 'cultured' people will often work hard to gain their approval.

Reasons or functions?

Lists like this imply that users of slang are deliberately employing it for these purposes. Here's the conversation between Jack and Ian, rewritten to represent the thinking processes that this would involve:

Dad: Jack! [thinks: I'm slightly drunk and rather lonely. I need to make an effort to ingratiate myself with my son by implying that we both like beer and are interested in one another's activities. Making reference to that popular beer commercial will be a useful way of doing this.]

Jack: [thinks: Dad is trying to win my approval by making reference to a really old beer commercial. I know what the expected reply is, but I'm too tired to make an effort right now and I don't want to talk about my evening with someone who so obviously can't even begin to understand how I feel.]

While it may sometimes be true that individuals use slang self-consciously to create certain effects, it is probable that most of the time slang isn't being used self-consciously. Slang is often just a way of expressing emotions:

Dad: [feels: drunkenly affectionate]
Jack: [feels: tired and unsociable]

Although the person hearing a slang term may conclude that the slang-user is cool or rebellious or humorous, the slang-user may be using the same term they usually would: the same term that everyone in their group of friends would also use. In other words, although slang appears to function as a mark of rebelliousness and non-conformity, and may be created by nonconformists, it's often adopted most enthusiastically by the most diligent conformists. In use, slang is often much more about fitting in than rebelling. It's about saying the same thing as the rest of the group rather than about saying something new.

Equally, although slang can be used for many reasons, most of these functions could also be fulfilled by Standard English. You can be funny, rebellious, friendly, aloof, stylish, and many other things in Standard English, but where Standard English lets you down is that it changes only slowly. This means that individuals who are less funny, rebellious (and so on) can achieve the same results merely by imitation. The main thing that sets slang apart from Standard English is its chronological and contextual specificity. Last year the really cool people were saying that they were *crunk*; this year the people aspiring to be cool are saying it; next year, if not before, the really cool people will have stopped saying it; and by the year after it will have become a word whose use identifies you as a hopeless *wannabe* (1979—, originally US). This doesn't mean that the term itself will be short-lived, just that its social meanings might be. Like a code—incomprehensible to those who aren't in the know—slang represents a complex layer of social coding in conversation. Like any good code, it changes often. Unfortunately, there's no enigma machine to help us in decoding it. You can look up a slang term online or in a dictionary, but understanding its meaning is only half of the information you'll need to use it properly. If you haven't picked it up by its use in social situations, you'll probably never be able to use it really convincingly. Best not to try, hey?

Slang creation and use

Think back to the championship bout in Chapter 1: the champions of slang and Standard English were slugging it out and I avoided declaring which side I was on. Actually, it was an unfair fight. The arguments in favour of slang were about slang itself: it is vibrant, creative, and so on. These qualities might be attributed to slang-creators. The arguments against were largely about slang-users: they're unintelligent and have limited vocabularies. And that's one of the reasons why I find it hard to take sides in this argument: slang words often are witty and appealing, but not all slang-users are. On the other hand, slang-users might be perfectly charming were it not for their irritating repetition of tired slang words. The arguments are based on an entirely false dichotomy. Because new slang is creative (i.e. new), the argument implies, Standard English isn't creative. Because some slang users have limited vocabularies, people who speak Standard English know more words. This is all nonsense, as I hope you'll agree. What really sets slang apart from Standard English is the way it functions in social contexts: communicating meaning is often a secondary function for slang; it's really for communicating attitudes and cementing relationships.

Models of slang transmission

We've seen that individuals generally pick up slang terms within a social setting. If you admire a group of people you spend time with and if they all use a particular slang term, then you're likely to begin using it yourself, within that group to begin with, and perhaps more widely later on, but how and why do slang terms pass from one group to another? How did Jack, our imaginary British student, pick up *crunk* from southern American hip hop enthusiasts?

To picture the movement of a slang term from one individual to the next, let's imagine our slang term as a bacterial infection (nothing nasty, don't worry, we're talking friendly bacteria). B, C, and D pick it up from A; E and F from B; G, H, and I from C; and so on (see Figure 9). It's rarely possible to trace the elusive first user of a slang term, but that's not really important because it wasn't slang until it was adopted by a group. By collecting data about the earliest examples, we can get a good idea of when and where it arose. We may not be able to track down A, but if we have examples of the term's use by B, C, and H, we have documented its earliest use as slang. We now have six interrelated centres of infection, and it may be better to treat them as groups rather than as individuals (see Figure 10) because slang is all about social groups. In this model, the individuals will probably reinforce one another's use (reinfect one another).

At some point, the original group will probably stop using the slang term, either because they start using another term or drift apart as a social circle, but the infection lives on without them by word of mouth across interconnected social networks. Under this model, a British hip hop enthusiast would have picked up *crunk* in face-to-face conversation with an American hip hop enthusiast, enabling it to spread to Britain. The slang term may change in use or meaning

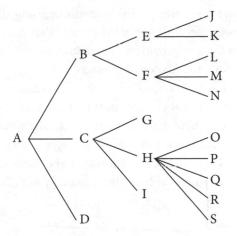

9 Slang transmission between individuals.

(mutate), and if this happens close enough to the origin of the term, the mutated form will probably coexist with or even replace the original. If the mutation occurred in circle 2, for example, it might feed back to the first circle. Alternatively, it might take place at several removes from the original users (in circle 6, for example), in which

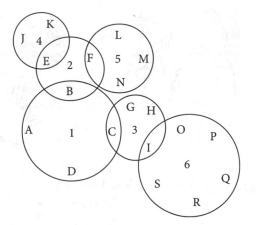

10 Slang transmission between groups.

case the original users will probably continue using the older form even though new infections are of the mutated version. On the other hand, the older form may continue spreading despite a mutation that occurs later among the first circle of users.

Before we come back to the limitations of this model, have another look at D. She's a crucial element in this transmission of slang. D is resistant to this particular strain of bacteria. She's marginal to the group and actually thinks that A is a bit of a *jerk* (1935—, originally US) or a *tosser* (1977—). She doesn't want to be like him, and doesn't think much of the others for being influenced by him. For this reason,

11 Putting the un- in cool: Betsy Streeter, 'Suzie Would Later Win a Nobel Prize'.

she doesn't pick up the slang term and doesn't pass it on. Most people will be like D some of the time, and if there were no Ds, there would be no slang because all new terms would quickly enter general use. The people who are most likely to pick up new slang terms are the ones whose self-identity isn't yet secure: the ones who worry most about what other people think of them or who are more inclined to be influenced by the people they admire. They'll be people who want to be different but need someone to show them how. Does that sound like any teenager you used to be?

Although this model might once have been a useful representation of the spread of slang, it can't possibly do justice to the current situation unless we add another dimension. Slang isn't just transmitted by face-to-face spoken contact. This infection would have to be one that could be transmitted by printed texts, by the telephone, by films, music and television programmes, but, most of all, via the Internet.

Jack wasn't mixing in hip hop circles in the southern states of the USA during the mid 1990s, when *crunk* was first used, but we can forgive him for this because he was only 3 or 4 years old at the time. Having grown up in the UK and having never been to the US, he's probably never had any personal contact with African Americans, let alone an African American who was mixing in the relevant inner hip hop circles at the right time. Jack will have picked up the term from lyrics or from discussions of hip hop online or in the media. Or, once *crunk* spread outside these inner circles, Jack might have picked it up from its use by white American hip hop enthusiasts, perhaps students like himself with whom he has communicated in person or online, figuring out its meaning much as Sam did. Or he may have acquired it at one stage further removed: from its use in British hip hop circles. Or, once its use had spread to British hip hop circles, from commentators in the British media. With all these possible routes for infection and reinfection, it's impossible (and probably futile) to try and determine the direct source of Jack's infection. The point is that he's got it and he wants Sam to know about it. He uses the term to express his emotional affiliation rather than any meaningful connection with its first users.

Slang spreads by social contact, but also via the media and the Internet. It expresses affiliations and attitudes at least as much as meaning. A small number of slang terms represent additions to the semantic range of the language: to represent a new idea, a new anxiety, or a new technology. We'll come on to the influence of the media and the Internet in the spread of slang later on, and also to the question of why so much contemporary slang comes from African American usage. The rest of this book takes a longer view of the history of English slang, which can really only be understood as part of the history of English itself.

Conclusions

Chapters 2–5 have broken the creation and development of slang into four stages: creation (spawning), early development (from fertilization), adaptation and survival (the tadpole stage), and spreading into wider use (as frogs). Each slang word or phrase will move through these processes at different rates, and some scholars use *slang* for words in all of these stages. Some scholars focus on the moment of spawning, trying to track down slang-creators. Others become interested in words only at their tadpole stage, considering the slang of tightly-knit professional and special interest groups to be more akin to jargon. There are also plenty of publications on slang that see only the frogs: discussing slang in use without reference to its origins or development. For me (and in this book), words remain only potential slang while they're restricted to a very small group of people, such as a single group of friends or a family (circle 1 in Figure 10), but once they start to spread they begin to become slang. For the early history of slang, discussed in the next few chapters, it should be assumed that a great deal of short-lived slang has come and gone without being noticed in print.

Endnotes

You can watch Goma being mistaken for a computer expert on *YouTube*. It's been posted several times, but these comments are from <http://www.youtube.com/watch?v=atfNL0_KAcs>. The student slang dialogues use terms listed in *Leicester Online Slang Glossaries* by Tom Green, Lindsey Mountford, and Alex Herring. Facebook is at <http://www.facebook.com>. Also cited is Eric Partridge, *Slang: Today and Yesterday* (London: Routledge and Kegan Paul, 1933), 6–7.

6 Prigs, Culls, and Blosses: Cant and Flash Language

We've already seen that *slang* was first used in the second half of the eighteenth century in the sense "the special vocabulary used by any set of persons of a low or disreputable character; language of a low and vulgar type". *OED* citations refer to the slang of 'the town', bailiffs, 'the lowest blackguards', thieves, 'the kennel', and 'the stable'. By about 1818, *slang* had acquired the sense with which I'm using it here: "Language of a highly colloquial type, considered as below the level of standard educated speech, and consisting either of new words or of current words employed in some special sense." The distinction between these two senses is perhaps one of social class rather than meaning: the first sense refers to the non-standard language of poor people, and the second (often) to the non-standard language of richer people. The fact remains, however, that *slang* wasn't available to label this type of language until the eighteenth century. Does this mean there was no slang as we know it until then? Or that it was called something else?

The answer is a qualified yes to both questions. There was an intermediate period when some types of slang began to develop in

English but the term wasn't yet available (there's more on this issue in Chapter 7). Various adjectives were used to describe improper language, including *knavish* (*c.*1386+*a.*1529), *lewd* (*c.*1386—), *ribaldous* (*c.*1400-1928), *bawdy* (*a.*1513—), *barbarous* (1526-1857), *base* (1549-1885), *ribaldrous* (1565—), *broad* (1580-1882), *canting* (1592—), *tavernly* (1612), *billingsgate* (1652—), *low* (1672—), *vulgar* (1716—), and *flash* (1746—). Connotations of low social status and undignified behaviour were attached to all of these terms, but conversations can be *knavish* or *lewd* without using slang. *Canting* and *flash* were different in attributing this type of language to specific social groups: beggars and thieves. *Canting* is from *cant* "to speak in the whining tone of a beggar" (1567-1750), ultimately from the Latin *cantare* "to sing". It still usually implies some type of dishonesty and is now generally used with reference to the language of beggars, criminals, estate agents, politicians, and religious hypocrites. *Flash* developed from the sense "connected to or pertaining to the class of thieves, tramps, and prostitutes" (*c.*1700—), probably derived from the noun sense "a piece of showy talk" (1605-1735) or "superficial brilliancy; ostentation" (1674—), and ultimately related to *flashes* of light. When *canting* and *flash* are used with reference to language today, they're generally used with reference to the language of specific historical periods. The non-standard language of *canting* beggars and *flash* thieves was documented earlier than slang, which was closely associated with the language of these groups. This chapter concentrates on the evidence for English canting and flash language until the nineteenth century. The next chapter will return to the subject of slang proper.

Cheating gamesters and thieving prostitutes

In his *Manifest Detection of the Most Vile and Detestable Use of Diceplay* (1555), Gilbert Walker explained that just as a carpenter uses specialized terms within his profession, so does a cheating gamester. In this extract, an experienced dice cheat teaches his craft to a young accomplice:

"Lo here", saith the cheater to this young novice "A well favoured die that seemeth good and square yet is the forehead [front part] longer on the cater and trey than any other way, and therefore holdeth the name of a langret, such be also called barred cater treys, because commonly the longer end will of its own sway draw downwards and turn up to the eye sice, sink, deuce or ace…"

Dice-players counted using terms derived from French: *ace* (*c*.1300—), *deuce* (1519—), *trey* (*c*.1386—), *cater* (1519-1730/6), *sink* (more usually <cynk> or <cynque> *c*.1386-1870), and *sice* (*c*.1386-1837). *Cater-trey*, literally "four-three", was sometimes used to refer to dice and dicing generally (*a*.1500-*a*.1700). These terms appear to have been commonly used, and many were also adopted by card-players. *Ace* and *deuce* are still used in tennis. Other specialist terms used by Walker's cheating dice-players were *langrets* (*c*.1550-1612) and *barred* (1532-1834) dice or *bars* (1545-1753), which were designed so that a certain number couldn't be thrown, in this case a three or four.

Walker emphasizes in his title that the newly leisured classes were particularly susceptible to cheating gamesters. A successful merchant could make enough money to keep his family in comfort without needing his sons' labour, and these idle young men were ideal prey for fraudsters. In this period, it would have been possible to make a living as a cheat only in the anonymity of a city like London, where there was a steady flow of new and unsuspecting victims. It wasn't a problem that was going to go away either: during the early 1590s, Robert Greene published a series of pamphlets warning of the tricks used by London *coney-catchers*[1] who tricked innocent country people by cheating at cards, committing highway robbery, robbing prostitutes' clients, cutting purses, and picking pockets. He offers a separate glossary of the terms used in each activity. Here's an extract from a conversation between a male and female coney-catcher, in

---

[1] *Coney* is recorded with the sense "a fool; a dupe" (1592-1736), from its more usual sense "rabbit" (see p. 43).

which the male begins by complimenting the female on how well and prosperous she's looking:

> **Laurence:** Faire Nan well met... have your smooth looks linked in some young novice to sweat for a favour all the bite in his bung...
>
> **Nan:** Why Laurence... fair wenches cannot want favours while the world is full of amorous fools. Where can such girls as myself be blemished with a threadbare coat as long as country farmers have full purses and wanton citizens pockets full of pence?
>
> **Laurence:** Truth if fortune so favour thy husband, that he be neither smoked nor cloyed, for I am sure all thy bravery comes by his nipping, foisting, and lifting.
>
> **Nan:** In faith sir no, did I get no more by mine own wit, than I reap by his purchase, I might both go bare and penniless the whole year. But mine eyes are stalls and my hands lime twigs (else were I not worthy the name of a she coney-catcher)...

bite "money" (*c*.1555+1592)
bung "purse" (1567-1859), probably not related to the modern slang *bung* "a bribe" (1958–)
smoke "to expose to smoke, so as to stupefy" (*c*.1154-1900), "to drive into the open by means of smoke" (1593–), or "to discover; to suspect" (1592-1913)

cloy or *cly* "to seize" (1567-1690) or "to steal; to rob" (1610-1821)
nip "to steal" (1567–)
foist probably "to cheat" (1584-1611), rather than specifically "to cheat by concealing false dice in one's hand" (1545-*a*.1618)
lift "to pick up with the intention of stealing; to steal" (1526–)

Neither smoked nor cloyed means "neither tricked/discovered/suspected nor robbed/arrested". By avoiding these fates, Nan's husband would demonstrate the quickness of his wits, but fortunately she isn't dependent on his ability to provide for her. By describing her eyes as *stalls* (*c*.1500-1592), Nan compares them with decoy birds used in hunting. A *lime twig* (*c*.1400—) is a twig smeared with a sticky substance so birds that land on it can't fly away. To *link* someone is to entrap them as if within the links of a chain (1592+1887). These last three examples are probably creative figurative uses rather than slang, and all depict the prostitute as a hunter snaring innocent men.

Pedlars and beggars

It wasn't just cheating gamesters and thieving prostitutes who were believed to be threatening the social order by developing their own vocabularies. Robert Copland's *Hyeway to the Spital-House* (1536) describes his visit to a poorhouse, guided by the door-keeper:

> **Copland:** Come none of these pedlars this way also
> With pack on back, with their bousy speech,
> Jagged and ragged, with broken hose [stockings] & breech [breeches]?
> **Porter:** Enough, enough: "with bousy cove maund nase.
> Tour the pattering cove in the darkman case
> Docked the dell for a copper make.
> His watch shall fang a prance's nabcheat.
> Cyarum by Salmon [an oath] and thou shalt peck my ire
> In thy gan. For my watch it is nase gear [clothes].
> For the bene bouse my watch hath a wyn."
> And thus they babble till their thrift is thine [until your earnings are theirs]
> I wot not what with [I don't know what in] their peddling French.

The porter doesn't understand the pedlars' French that he parrots, so it's hard for us to make sense of it. Although other uses suggest meanings for some of these words, they still don't make complete sense put together in this way:

bousy "drunken" (*a*.1529-1842), now more usually *boozy* (1592–)

cove "a man" (1536–)

maund "to beg" (1536-1864)

nase "drunken" (1536-1612)

tour "to see" (1536-1906)

pattering "that speaks rapidly or by rote" (1557/8)

darkman(s) "night" (1536-1906)

case "house; building; (later) brothel" (1536-1981)

dock "to copulate with; to deflower" (1536-1719)

dell "a girl" (1536-1834)

make "a halfpenny" (1536-1982)

watch "self" (e.g. *his watch*=himself; *my watch*=myself) (*c*.1530-1707)

fang "to steal" (*a*.1066-1922)

prance for *prancer* "a rider" (*c*.1560) or "a horse" (1567-1885)

nabcheat "a hat; a cap; ?a bridle" (1536-1890)

peck "to eat" (1536-1977, later US Black)

gan "mouth" (1536-1785)   now more usually *booze* (1674—)
bene "good" (1536-1865)   *win* "a penny" (1536-1900)
bouse "alcoholic drink" (*c.*1300-1764),

In 1561, Thomas Awdelay published a book called *The Fraternitye of Vacabondes*, which describes the various types of beggar frequenting the roads and hedges of England. For example (from the 1575 edition):

> An upright man is one that goes with the truncheon or staff, which staff they call a filchman. This man is of so much authority, that meeting with any of his profession, he may call them to account, and command a share or snap unto himself of all that they have gained by their trade in one month. And though he do them wrong, they have no remedy against him, no though he beat them, as he uses commonly to do. He may also command any of their women, which they call doxies, to serve his turn. He hath the chief place at any market, walk and other assemblies, and is not of any to be controlled.

There isn't very much canting language here. The meaning of *uprightman* (1561-1834, a compound made from two Standard English terms), *filchman* (1561-1699, which may be from *filch* "to steal" (*c.*1561—)), *snap* (1552-1897, probably slang or dialect rather than cant, and ultimately from Middle Dutch or Middle Low German), and *doxy* (*c.*1530-1861, of uncertain origin) are all explained within the passage. What's most significant about Awdelay's publication isn't his own use of cant, but the purposes to which it was put by later dictionary makers.

The first glossary of canting terms was compiled by a magistrate from Kent, called Thomas Harman. He certainly used both Copland's and Awdelay's work, and he represented some of the same types of rogue that Awdelay had listed. Harman described organized gangs of beggars roaming the land and extracting charitable donations from unsuspecting householders under false pretences of disability and misfortune. His *Caveat or Warning for Common Cursitors*[2] sets out to reveal these tricks and expose the beggars using them. They include *fraters* (*c.*1561-1749), who pretended to be collecting money for charitable causes, *freshwater mariners* or *seamen* (1567-1817), who claimed to have been shipwrecked, and *counterfeit cranks* (1567-1707), who faked epileptic fits. Named individuals to keep an eye out for included:

> Harry Smith, he drivels when he speaks
> John Stradling, with the shaking head
> Robert Brownsword he wears his hair long
> Harry Walls with the little mouth
> John Donne with one leg

Harman also provided a short glossary of terms allegedly collected from beggars under threat of a whipping. This wouldn't be considered an acceptable or reliable way to collect linguistic data nowadays. There's a pretty good chance that beggars would have told Harman whatever he wanted to hear just to avoid being whipped, so we should probably reserve judgement on the contents of his glossary even if we believe his account of how he collected it. It contains 114 entries, including *nab* "a head" (1536-1922), *famble* "a hand; a finger" (1567-1906), *skipper* "a barn" (1567-1933), and lots of words formed with *cheat* "a thing", including *fambling-cheat* "a ring" (1567-1721) and *grunting-cheat* "a pig" (1567-1684). The glossary is followed by a dialogue between an uprightman and a rogue (the second in command). After enquiring politely about one another's night's sleep, they get down to more important matters:

> **Uprightman:** ... hast thou any lour in thy bung to bouse?
> **Rogue:** But a flag, a win, and a make.
> **Uprightman:** Why where is the ken that has the bene bouse?
> **Rogue:** A bene mort hereby at the sign of the prancer.

---

[2]   *Cursitor* from Latin *currere* "to run", means "vagabond". Like a computer *cursor*, vagabonds can move about freely.

Of the canting terms in this extract, we have already seen *bung* "a purse", *make* "a halfpence", *win* "a penny", *bene* "good", and *prancer* "a horse; a rider" in earlier canting texts. Other canting terms include:

lour "money" (1567-1889)   *flag* "a groat; four pence" (1567-1851)
bouse "to drink heavily" (*c.*1300-1922),   *ken* "a house" (1567–)
now more usually *booze* (1601–)   *mort* "woman" (1567-1997)

The origins of *lour* and *ken* are unknown, but *bouse*, *mort*, and *flag* all suggest Dutch influence. Trade links with the Netherlands had been strong for centuries, and many early English books were printed there, but the 1560s saw an unprecedented influx of Dutch Protestants fleeing persecution at a time when the English were beginning to develop a stronger sense of national identity. Perhaps Harman was suggesting that the strangers roaming England's green and pleasant lands were doubly untrustworthy: not only beggars but also foreigners.

Entries from Harman's glossary were included in Thomas Dekker's *Bellman of London* (1608), in which we are told that these terms were used by London's criminals. Lists based on Harman's presented essentially the same terms, sometimes saying they belonged to criminals in general, sometimes highwaymen, and sometimes gypsies. We may have doubts about the reliability of Harman's glossary, but when later writers include the whole of Harman's list in theirs, it's impossible to believe that all of these terms were really still in use. Some of the thieves' cant used in Scorsese's *Gangs of New York* film can be traced back through various dictionaries each compiled from an earlier word list, all the way to Harman's glossary. Where there's limited evidence that English beggars really used these terms in the sixteenth century, or that anyone used them in the meantime, how likely is it that American criminals used them in the nineteenth? This 'slang' has little to do with representing linguistic reality: instead, it's being used to construct and represent groups of people as outsiders.

Canting literature

Texts like these, offering a privileged glimpse of a threatening secret language, were clearly appealing to contemporary audiences, and these early glossaries were used as source material by writers of several plays. For instance, a group of beggars sing and drink in Richard Brome's *Jovial Crew* (1641):

> **Autem Mort:** Go fiddle, patrico, and let me sing. First set me down here on both my prats. Gently, gently, for cracking of my wind, now I must use it. Hem, hem. [*she sings*]
> This is bene bouse; this is bene bouse;
> Too little is my skew.
> I bouse no lage, but a whole gage
> Of this I'll bouse to you.
> This bouse is better than rum-bouse;
> It sets the gan a-giggling.
> The autem mort finds better sport
> In bowsing than in niggling.
> This is bene bouse, &c. [*she tosses off her bowl, falls back, and is carried out*]

In addition to terms we've already seen, such as *bouse* "drink" and "to drink", *prat* "a buttock", and *gan* "a mouth", this extract includes:

patrico "a beggar priest" (*c.*1536-1993)　　*autem mort* "a married woman"
crack (wind/one off) "to fart" (1641−)　　(1567-1861)
skew "a cup; a wooden dish" (1561-1707)　*niggling* "sexual intercourse"
lage "water" (1567-1688)　　(1608-1723, but the verb *to niggle* is
gage "a quart pot" (*c.*1440-1821)　　found from 1567-1931)
rum "good" (1567-1926)

The origin of all of these terms is unknown or uncertain. Apart from *cracking wind*, they're all in Harman's glossary, and it is no accident that Brome uses so many of them in such a short extract: he was undoubtedly writing this scene with a copy of Harman's glossary (or more probably a version of Dekker's) to hand. The whole play isn't like this—that would make for terrible theatre—but this scene establishes the beggars as recognisable types. For some of these words, such as *bouse*, *niggle*, *rum*, *lift*, and *prat*, there's genuine evidence of use outside Harman's list and works closely related to it. For *autem*, *bene*, *skew*, *gage*, *lage*, *gan*, and *patrico*, there's little or no independent evidence that anyone used these terms outside canting literature or dictionaries.

It wasn't just plays that were written using Harman's glossary or related works. Songs were also constructed using cant and slang terms, and some seem to have become popular accompaniments to a night of serious drinking. Here's the beginning of 'The Canting Song' by Dekker (1612):

> Bing out bene morts, and tour, and tour,
> bing out bene morts and tour.
> for all your duds are binged awaste,
> the bene cove hath the lour.
>
> I met a dell, I viewed her well,
> she was benship to my watch:
> so she and I, did stall and cloy
> whatever we could catch.
>
> This doxy dell can cut bene whids,
> and wap well for a win:
> and prig and cloy so benshiply,
> all the deuse-avile within.

Some of this may have made sense to you. We've already seen *bene* "good", *mort* "a woman", *tour* "to look; to see", *duds* "clothes", *cove* "a man", *lour* "money", *dell* "a woman", *my watch* "myself", *cloy* "to steal", *doxy* "a woman", and *win* "a penny". Many other words can also be traced back to Harman, including:

bing (awaste) "to go (away)" (1567-1927)   *wap* "to have sexual intercourse" (1611-
benship "very good" (1567-1707)   1707+1925)
stall [see below]   *prig* "to steal" (1567–)
cut "to talk; to speak" (*c.*1500-1853)   *benshiply* "very well" (1612-1754)
whid "a word" (1567-1861)   *deuseavile* "the countryside" (1567-1859)

All of these are either found in Harman's list or derived from terms in it. *Stall* "to set in place; to establish", which appears to be a combination of Old French and Old English forms, was widely used at the time, but it's possible that it should be understood here in the sense "to screen (a pickpocket) from observation" (1592-1950, from an Anglo-French word meaning "a decoy bird"). *She and I did stall and cloy* could mean either "we became a couple and stole things together" or "we shielded one another from observation and stole things", and it's probably useful to be ambiguous when discussing these things. Both interpretations would make sense in the context: the speaker either sees that the woman is attractive or observes that she is a skilled pickpocket, either of which would be a fine basis for a relationship.

Later writers sometimes comment on the astonishing continuity of canting vocabulary across the centuries and regard this as a reliable indication that the criminal underworld is and has long been tightly knit and highly organized. Without any other evidence, we probably ought to conclude instead that people have always enjoyed scaring themselves with thoughts of a tightly knit and highly organized underworld, and that there will always be enterprising writers who will happily make money by feeding whichever fear is likely to be most profitable at the time. These writers either unthinkingly relied on their written sources as reliable representations of contemporary canting language, or didn't care about the authenticity of their dialogue at all. The important thing, in each case, is that the dialogue should sound convincing to an audience which, on the whole, knows nothing about the language of beggars and criminals other than what they've heard in other plays. Canting words came to play the same function as the striped jersey and face mask of the cartoon burglar:

they're symbols rather than realistic representations. The various versions of Harman's list tell us which groups were most frightening at different times, but they don't provide any evidence of current language use.

Other evidence of early modern cant

The Proceedings of the Old Bailey offer very few examples of these terms in their canting senses between 1674 and 1913, which suggests that criminals carefully concealed their secret language in court, that these terms had fallen from use by 1674, that although they were used in court, they were not preserved in the written record, or that they were never commonly employed. Because there's little independent evidence for many of the words they list, most of the early canting texts are of little use to us in recreating genuine usage, not least because the canting terms tend to cluster in highly stylized scenes.

Shakespeare depicts a group of thieves in *Henry IV, Part I* without resorting to the canting tradition for his vocabulary. In this scene, Hal and his friends are plotting a highway robbery (although actually Hal is planning to steal the money from his accomplices later on and return it to its original owner). The conspirators lie in wait for their victims in an isolated spot, and Falstaff complains about having to walk so far:

Falstaff: A plague upon you all! Give me my horse, you rogues; give me my horse and be hanged.

Hal: Peace, ye fat-guts. Lie down, lay thine ear close to the ground and list if thou canst hear the tread of travellers.

Falstaff: Have you any levers to lift me up again, being down? 'Sblood, I'll not bear mine own flesh so far afoot again for all the coin in thy father's exchequer. What a plague mean ye to colt me thus?

Hal: Thou liest: thou art not colted; thou art uncolted.

Falstaff: I prithee, good Prince Hal, help me to my horse, good king's son.

Hal: Out, ye rogue; shall I be your ostler?

Falstaff: Hang thyself in thine own heir-apparent garters! If I be ta'en, I'll peach for this.

Even though Hal disguises himself as a soldier before Agincourt to mingle with his troops unsuspected, he doesn't talk like this again. His language is as much an indication of his debauchery as his companions and behaviour are. We have swearing (*plague, be hanged, 'sblood*), insults (*rogue, fat-guts*), and humour, all of which indicate that this isn't a formal conversation, as does the fact that it is in prose rather than verse, but there's more to it than that. *Peach* (1570—) originated as a shortened form of the more formal *appeach* (1401-1650), meaning "to give evidence against; to impeach", but its continued use suggests that it has also been understood as an abbreviation of *impeach* (1428—). Falstaff means *colt* in the sense "to cheat; to take in" (1580-1618), but Henry pretends to understand it in the sense "to be provided with a horse" so that he can make a joke at Falstaff's expense. In each case, Shakespeare could have chosen to employ an unmarked term from Standard English: *impeach* or *cheat*, both of which he uses in other places, but here he emphasizes his characters' positions outside decent society by using terms that some members of his audience wouldn't have used, and might not even have known. Whether they represent the language of contemporary criminals is less important in the dramatic context than the fact that they sound as if they could.

Inside information from the eighteenth century

Much more information about canting language is available from the eighteenth century. An anonymous publication from 1708, called *Hell on Earth*, describes the conditions and inhabitants of London's Newgate prison. Its grammar is a little unstable, but the author seems to know what he's talking about:

> Some are very expert for the *sneak*; which is, sneaking into houses by night or day, and pike off with that which is none of their own. Some are very acute for the *running-smobble*; which is a lay two or three have together, one of 'em running into a shop, when people are in a back-room, or busy

behind a counter, snatching up something, conveys it to one of his nimble comrades, and trip it away as fast as a racehorse over Newmarket Heath. Some are very good for the *sneaking-budge*; which is, privately stealing anything off of a stall.

We can place more faith in the vocabulary presented by this writer because it's not a neat fit with the terms found in the earlier canting tradition, and because many of these terms are also recorded independently elsewhere, including *the sneak* "burglary; sneak-thievery" (1699—), *pike off* "to depart" (*c*.1529—, originally dialect and cant, later colloquial), *running-smobble* "a shop lifter; the act of shop lifting" (1703-1718), *lay* "a criminal act or scheme" (1707-1973), and *sneaking-budge* "one who robs alone" (*c*.1698-1751). *Off of* (*c*.1450—) hadn't yet become non-standard in British English.

Another individual with first-hand knowledge of London's criminal classes also published an anonymous account of their language, though we can identify him as Charles Hitchin, Under-Marshal of London. His purchased position enabled him to make a good living by charging the victims of theft for the return of their stolen property, but he was soon suspended from office and imprisoned for sodomy. Hitchin's assistant, Jonathan Wild, far exceeded his master's achievements in the field of extortion: rather than just inducing criminals to return stolen goods in return for a share of the reward, Wild arranged for them to be stolen in the first place. The speed at which he could locate stolen goods was quite remarkable. Hitchin's attempt to expose Wild suggests that housebreakers were no longer opportunistic thieves who sneaked in and snatched what they could. These thieves bring professional equipment with them and are willing to use violence if necessary:

A buzz, *alias* prig, *alias* thief. A cove, *alias* man. A dub, *alias* tilt, *alias* pick-lock-key. A glim-stick, *alias* dark-lantern. A bess, *alias* betty. Pops, *alias* pistols. To slum the ken *alias* to break into the house. All's Boman, *alias* all is safe. The Dancers, *alias* the Stairs. . . . To bundle the cull of the ken, *alias* to tie the man of the house neck and heels. . . . To lope off, *alias* to get away.

The baggage-man, *alias* that is he that carries off the booty. A Fence, *alias* or lock, *alias* a buyer of stolen goods. Ridge, *alias* gold. Wedge, *alias* silver. A boosing-ken, *alias* an ale-house. The cull is flash, *alias* that is he associates himself with thieves.

Of these terms, *cove* "a man", *betty* "a crowbar", *ken* "a house", and *flash* "associating with thieves" have already been mentioned. *Buzz*,[3] *bess*, *tilt*, *slum*, *glimstick*, and *all's boman* are only documented by later writers in the canting tradition: there's no independent evidence of their wider use. Better documented canting terms include:

prig "a thief" (*c*.1561-1980)

dub "an instrument for picking locks" (*c*.1698-1887)

pop "a pistol" (1700-1992)

dancers "stairs" (1665–)

cull "a dupe, a fool; a man" (1648-1962)

lope "to run" (*c*.1572–)

baggage-man "a pickpocket's accomplice" (1718-1768)

fence "a receiver of stolen goods" (*c*.1698–)

lock "a receiver of stolen goods" (*c*.1698-1804)

ridge "gold" (1665-1955)

wedge "silver" (1703–)

bousing-ken "an alehouse; a public house" (1567-1931)

Although many of these terms had become standard features in canting literature by this date, Hitchin appears to have learnt them from their spoken use rather than from earlier written sources.

In 1754, John Poulter gave evidence against his accomplices in a robbery, under the impression that this would help him to avoid punishment. When he realized it wouldn't, he escaped from prison, but was recaptured and hanged. This extract is from Poulter's confession, which was popular enough to be published in seventeen editions during the following quarter of a century:

---

[3] The apparently related terms, *buzz* "to steal" (1812), *buzzer* "a pickpocket" (1862), and *buzzing* "picking pockets" (1819+1884), aren't found until considerably later.

In a fair or market, where there is a throng of people, we say, "Come culls, shall us pike to the push or gaff, a rum vile for the file or lift to peter-lay or leather-lay; come let us pike, we shall nap a rum bit"; that is, "come men, shall us go to the throng or fair, a good town for the pick-pocket or shop-lifters to steal portmanteaus or leather-bags; come, let us go, we shall take a good bit." Then three or four persons go to the fair or market, and put up at the first ken (or house) they come to in the vile (or town) in order to be out of the push (or throng) as soon as we have napped (or taken) a bit; then we pike to glee if there's a cull that has a bit; if so, the files go before the cull and try his cly, and if they feel a bit, cry gammon; then two or three of us hold him up, whilst some prads or rattlers come by: if they nap the bit, they cry pike, then we go and fisk the bit and ding the empty bit, for fear it should be found...

Most of these terms are defined for us in the extract. Poulter is, after all, revealing to his readers something that they could not otherwise understand, but you'll already recognize *cull* "a fool; a man", *pike* "to go; to depart", *rum* "good", and *ken* "a house". Poulter also uses:

push "a crowd" (1718–)

gaff "a fair" (1753–), also found with the sense "a shop; a residence" (1920–)

vile or *vill(e)* "a town" (1688–)

file "a pickpocket" (1665-1848)

lift "a thief" (1591-1777)

peter-lay "the theft of a *peter*" ("a portmanteau; a large bag or trunk" (1667-1979))

leather-lay "the theft of a *leather*" ("a purse; a wallet" (1753-1955, US in later use))

nap "to steal; to take" (1665–)

bit "money" (1552-1967), used with the sense "a purse; a wallet"

glee "to squint" (c.1300-1876, particularly in Scotland and then in northern dialects), but here with the sense "to look" (1753-1799)

cly "a purse" (1699–1877)

cry/give gammon "to distract someone's attention while an accomplice robs them" (1720-1821)

hold up "to rob forcibly; to delay traffic" (1851–, although this would be a very early usage)

prad "a horse" (1703–, now chiefly Australian)

rattler "a carriage; a noisy vehicle" (1622–)

fisk [see below]

ding "to throw away", referring especially to incriminating objects (1753–)

The *OED* records *fisk* with the sense "to move briskly; to scamper" (*c*.1340-1906), but not "to search". *Fisk* is apparently related to the more familiar *frisk* "to move briskly; to scamper" (1519—), which developed the sense "to search" in about 1781. It appears that *fisk* also enjoyed short-lived use with this meaning (1724-1768).

Other evidence of eighteenth-century cant

Independent evidence of eighteenth-century canting language is provided by the publications of the Ordinaries, or chaplains, of Newgate Prison. It was their responsibility to provide spiritual comfort to condemned prisoners, and they were compensated by the profitable right to sell accounts of prisoners' lives, last words, and deaths. In these two extracts, criminals describe the circumstances of their crimes:

> We had not sat long before he fell fast asleep in the chair, having, as I observed before, drank pretty hard, and being very much tired. As soon as we found him in this condition, we began to examine the contents of his pockets, and found upwards of 15* ridges, besides a † rum fam upon his finger. We not being content with this, took his § wedges out of his || stomps, and observing before, he had a pretty rum outside and inside †† togee, we pulled them off, and made free with them likewise.
> *Guineas † Diamond ring § Buckles || Shoes †† A good coat and waistcoat

> Some short time after, they all went out again upon the old lay, and picked up another bubble in the park, whom one of them asked to take a walk, whilst the rest followed at a distance, and coming up at a time they judged convenient, they furiously catched the man by the collar, and cried, "D—n your blood! What? Are you Mollying each other?"

In addition to the terms that we have already seen, these extracts provide evidence for the use of *stomp* for *stamp* "a shoe" (recorded with the sense "a leg" (1567-1819)), *toge* "a toga; a coat" (?*a*.1400-1965), *bubble* "a dupe; someone easily fooled" (1600-1807), and *molly* "to engage in homosexual anal intercourse with" (1726-1746). Perhaps, having already been convicted, prisoners had nothing to lose by revealing their canting terms. Perhaps the Ordinary inserted them to increase sales by livening up the confessions. In either case, their inclusion suggests that some of the terms listed in the dictionaries of this period (and some that were also found in the earlier dictionaries) were widely known at this time.

Flash language

The language of London's criminals and lower orders had a guilty appeal for wealthier contemporaries. Moll King's coffee house served market traders in the morning and prostitutes later in the day, with the prostitutes' clients drawn from a broad social spectrum. In this extract from *The Life and Character of Moll King* (1747), Moll is chatting with a customer called Harry. Of the many canting terms included, we've already seen *file* "a pickpocket", *fam* "a ring", *rum* "good; excellent", *mort* "a woman", *Oliver* "the moon", *ken* "a house", and *nap* "to take":

> **Harry:** ...you must tip me your clout before I derrick, for my bloss has nailed me of mine; but I shall catch her at Maddox's gin-ken, sluicing her gob by the tinney; and if she has morrised it, knocks and socks, thumps and plumps, shall attend the frow-file buttocking b—h.
>
> **Moll:** I heard she made a fam tonight, a rum one, with dainty dasies, of a flat from t'other side; she flashed half a slat, a bull's eye, and some other rum slangs.
>
> **Harry:** I'll derrick, my blood, if I tout my mort, I'll tip her a snitch about the peeps and nasous. I shall see my jolly old codger by the tinney-side, I suppose with his daylights dim, and his trotters shivering under him.— As Oliver wheedles, I'll not touch this darkee. I'll nap the pad and see you in the morning.

tip "to give" (1610–)

clout "a handkerchief" (c.1380-1927, not originally slang)

derrick "to go" (1747+1754), from the name of a noted hangman, also referred to in the sense "a hangman; the gallows" (c.1600-1680)

bloss "a woman; a mistress or prostitute; a thief" (1699-1747)

nail "to steal; to rob" (1747–)

sluice (one's gob/mouth (etc.)) "to drink" (1747-1885)

gob "mouth" (1568–)

tinny "fire" (1747-1823)

morris "to go; to force to leave; to sell" (1726-a.1903)

frow "a woman" (1587-1953)

buttock "to have sexual intercourse" (1703+1747), from *buttock* "a prostitute" (1673-1743)

bitch "a lewd or sensual woman" (?a.1400–, never complimentary, but not always slang)

make "to steal" (1699–)

daisy "a diamond" (1747)

flat "a gullible fool" (1747-1938)

t'other side "Southwark" (1747-1897)

flash "to make a display; to show off" (1747–)

slat "a crown (five shillings); half a crown" (1703-1753), though used here with the sense "a pound"

bull's eye "five shillings" (1699-1899) slang perhaps an early use with the sense "a watch chain" (1819-1937), but it appears to mean "an object; a thing" more broadly

blood [in swearing] (1541-1950)

tout "to look for; to see" (1699-1837)

snitch "a blow" (1676-1747)

peeps "eyes" (1747-1989)

nasous "nose" (1747)

codger for *cadger* "a travelling salesman" (a.1522-1861), here presumably one who deals in stolen goods

daylights "eyes" (1747-1901)

trotter "a human foot" (c.1699–)

wheedle for *whiddle* "to turn informer" (c.1661-1834)

touch "to receive money; to steal" (1654–, cant in later use)

darkey "a night" (1747-1893)

pad "the road" (1567-1986, now dialect and Australian)

A few terms date the passage quite closely to 1732, when the dialogue is supposedly set, including *bloss, morris,* and *slat.* Recorded first in this passage are *derrick, nail, sluice (one's gob/mouth* (etc.)), *tinny, flat, t'other side, flash, peeps, daylights, Oliver,* and *darkey,* all of which are found in later texts, giving us some confidence in *nasous* "nose" and *daisy* "a diamond", even though there's no other evidence of their use. *Daylights* broadened from this sense to mean "any vital organ" (1838—), and *living daylights* are *scared* and *beaten* out of people to this day. The modern uses of *tout* "someone who resells tickets at inflated prices" (1959—), *snitch* "an informer" (1785—), oil *derricks* (1861—), *codger* "a (stingy) (old) person, usually a man" (1796—), and *flash* "to expose oneself indecently" (1846—) have all developed from these earlier slang senses. Again, this gives us confidence in their authenticity in this text.

What's most interesting about the *Moll King* dialogue is its author's comment that although the coffee house was first used by individuals associated with London's underworld, wealthy individuals began to frequent it too, presumably drawn by the prostitutes rather than the thieves. They began to use the canting terms they heard there to signal their involvement in the dubious morals of Moll's world and, simultaneously, to reject the values of more conventional society. *Moll King*'s dialogue could thus be taken as the beginning of the transition from cant to flash language.

London's fascination with its own underbelly is also evident in the success of George Parker's *Life's Painter of Variegated Characters* (1789). In this extract, a strolling ballad singer in one of London's poorest districts encourages his audience to show their appreciation:

Ballad Singer: What, no copper clinking among you, my hearties? No one to give me Hansel? What, have you got red-hot heaters in your gropers, that you're afraid to thrust your daddles in them? It won't do I say, to stand here for nicks—all hearers and no buyers—what, will none of you drop your loose kelter? Crap me but I must shove my trunk, and hop the twig—I see as how there's nothing to be got in this here place.

Female Ballad Singer: Don't mizzle yet.

Male Ballad Singer: The kelter tumbles in but queerly—however, we'll give 'em one more chaunt...

copper "a coin made of copper or bronze; (in plural) small change" (1712–)

my hearties (1789–, now chiefly pirates)

handsel [see below]

groper "a pocket" (1789-c.1830)

daddle "a hand" (1754–, historical in later use)

nix "nothing" (1781–, from German)

drop "to spend (money)" (1676–)

loose with reference to money (1760–)

kelter "money" (1789-1865)

crap (also crop) "to hang" (1772-1833)

shove my trunk [see below]

hop the twig "to depart; to die" (1785–, now often with reference to Monty Python's dead parrot)

mizzle "to depart" (1772-1976)

queerly "badly; villainously" (1699-1812)

chaunt [see below]

Parker uses *shove one's trunk*, for which there's no other evidence, quite a lot earlier than documented uses of *shove (off/out)* "to depart" (1844—). Three usages in this extract had become more slangy through the course of time. *Handsel* had been used to refer to a gift given to seal an agreement since around 1200. By 1569, it had developed the sense "a first instalment; a deposit", but by the time Parker was writing the term was specifically associated with the first successful transaction of the day (or night) made by traders or prostitutes. *This here* is first recorded in around 1460, but it doesn't appear to have been stigmatized as vulgar or dialectal until around the 1760s. *Chaunt* (now more usually <chant>) "a song" (1671-1882) was once poetic, but by this point had become associated with the language of beggars and thieves.

Not all of the attention paid to the poor in this period was motivated by idle curiosity. In 1839, W.A. Miles published a parliamentary report called *Poverty, Mendicity, and Crime*, describing the living conditions of London's poor. It included a 'Dictionary of the Flash or Cant Language' compiled by Henry Brandon, which provides 'specimens of flash' and their translations. For example:

I buzzed a bloak and a shakester of a reader and a skin. My jomer stalled. A cross-cove, who had his regulars, called out 'cop bung,' so as a pig was marking, I speeled to the crib, where I found Jim had been pulling down sawney for grub. He cracked a case last night and fenced the swag. He told me as Bill had flimped a yack and pinched a swell of a fawney, he sent the yack to church and got three finnips and a cooter for the fawney.

TRANSLATION.

I picked the pocket of a gentleman and lady of a pocket-book and a purse. My fancy girl stood near me and screened me from observation. A fellow-thief, who shared with me my plunder, called out to me to hand over the stolen property, so as somebody was observing my manœuvres, I ran away to the house, where I found James had provided something to eat, by stealing some bacon from a shop door. He committed a burglary last night and had disposed of the property plundered. He told me that Bill had hustled a person and obtained a watch; he had also robbed a well-dressed gentleman of a ring. The watch he sent to have the works taken out and put into another case, (to prevent detection,) and the ring realized him three five-pound notes and a sovereign.

Of the many flash terms in this passage, we have already seen *buzz* "to steal", *bloke* "a man", *stall* "to screen a pickpocket from observation", *cove* "a man", *pig* "a police officer", *case* "a house", and *finnip* "a five-pound note". Others include:

shakester for *shickster* "a (promiscuous) woman" (1834–, from the Yiddish *shiksa* "a gentile girl")

reader "a pocketbook" (1718-1900)

skin "a purse" (1795-1955)

jomer "a girlfriend" (1839-1882)

cross "dishonest; dishonestly acquired" (1811-1911)

regulars "a criminal's share of the profits" (1811-1937)

cop bung "look out: police!" (1839-1882)

mark [see below]

speel "to run (away)" (a.1818-1945, chiefly Australian in later use)

crib "a (small) house; a shop; a public house" (1600–)

pull down "to steal" (1839-1882), the sense "to earn" (c.1899–, originally US) appears not to be directly related to this

sawney [see below]

grub "food" (1659–)

crack "to burgle" (a.1674–)

fence "to deal in stolen property" (1610–)

swag "stolen property" (1794–)

flimp "to rob; to steal" (1824-1906)

yack "a watch" (1789-1978)

pinch "to rob; to steal" (1592–, not originally slang, now colloquial)
swell "a fashionably or stylishly dressed person" (1786–)
fawney "a ring" (1796-1906)

church "to remove the works of a stolen watch from its case" (1868-1935), though in this case it's *send to church*
counter "a sovereign" (1834–1898)

Mark had been used with the sense "to observe" since around 1400, and the *OED* cites it until 1961, commenting that it is 'now archaic or literary'. This extract suggests that it was also cant, at least for a while (1839-1882), and the sporting usage "to keep close to (and hamper) a player in the opposing team" (1887–) may have developed from this sense. *Sawney* was first used as a derisory nickname for a Scottish man (1682-1883), and is formed from *Sandy*, an abbreviation of *Alexander*, which was, at this time, characteristically Scottish. It was also used as a technical term in cloth-manufacturing and with the senses "a fool" (1699-1993) and "bacon" (1819-1906). The *OED* comments that 'the connection of the other senses [with the first] is doubtful'.

In 1857 a booklet called *The Vulgar Tongue*, published under the pen name 'Ducange Anglicus', listed some 480 terms from contemporary London English. These include:

COPPER, *n.* Policeman. *Th.*
MINCE PIES, *n.* Eyes. *Th.*
ROUND ME HOUSES, *n.* Trousers, pronounced trouses. *Th.*
ROWDY, *n.* Money. 'Got any *rowdy*, Bill?' Also *rhino*. *Gen.*

Copper "a policeman" (1838–) and *rowdy* "money" (1841-1885) were both relatively new at this date, but it's *mince pies* (1857–) and *round me* (also *the*) *houses* (1857–) that are particularly worthy of note. This glossary was the first to list any rhyming slang, labelling most of it as thieves' language. By the end of the century, rhyming slang had come to be strongly associated with London's coster-mongers through its use in cockney music hall acts and songs, and it's now useful short hand in dramatic representations of characters from London.

Conclusions

This chapter has discussed the evidence for cant, the language of thieves and beggars, from 1567 to the middle of the nineteenth century. The early part of this period provides us only with a tangled mess of interrelated glossaries and plays, but from the eighteenth century onwards there's independent evidence to suggest that some of the terms included in dictionaries of criminal language, even some of those found in the earliest glossaries, were genuinely used in contemporary canting language. We've considered some of the methods by which canting language might have spread into wider usage, and the next chapter will pick up the history of slang. As in this chapter, the evidence is largely drawn from texts written in and about London, although other large cities undoubtedly developed their own criminal language and slang. If these local cant or slang terms were recorded at all, they would probably have been treated as dialect.

Endnotes

Many of the citations in this chapter are via *Early English Books Online* <http://eebo.chadwyck.com/home>. I've modernized capitalization, spelling, and punctuation, except in the quotation from Shakespeare's *Henry the Fourth, Part I*, which was modernized by David Scott Kastan for the Arden Shakespeare edition (London: Thompson Learning, 2002), II. ii. Other quotations are from Gilbert Walker's *A Manifest Detection of the Most Vile and Detestable Use of Diceplay, and Other Practices Like the Same. A Mirror Very Necessary for all Young Gentlemen [and] Others Suddenly Enabled by Worldly Abundance, to Look in* (London: Abraham Vele, c.1555), C1r; Robert Greene, *A Disputation between a He Coney-Catcher and a She Coney-Catcher... Discovering the Secret Villainies of Alluring Strumpets* (London: T.G., 1592), A3v; Robert Copland, *Hyeway to the Spital-House* (London: Copland, c.1536), C3v; John Awdelay, *The Fraternitye of Vacabondes* (London: John Awdelay, 1575), A3v; Thomas Harman, *Caveat or Warning for Common Cursitors* (London: William Griffith, 1567), G2r and G3v; Richard Brome, *A Jovial Crew, or, The Merry Beggars* (London: E.D. and N.E., 1652), II. ii; and Thomas Dekker, *O Per Se O, or A New Crier of Lanthorn and*

Candlelight (London: John Busbie, 1612), 'The Canting Song'. Also cited in this section was Martin Scorsese's *Gangs of New York* (New York: Miramax, 2002). Information about links between England and Holland is from Ben Parsons's 'Dutch Influences on English Literary Culture in the Early Renaissance, 1470-1650', *Literary Compass* 4/6 (2007), 1577–96. *The Proceedings of the Old Bailey: London's Central Criminal Court, 1674-1913* <http://www.oldbaileyonline.org/index.jsp> provided two confessions from the *Ordinary's Account*, dating from 1741 and 1744 (OA17410731 and OA17441224). Extracts are also included from Charles Hitchin's *The Regulator or, A Discovery of the Thieves, Thief-takers and Locks* (London: T. Warner, 1718), n.p.; John Poulter's *The Discoveries of John Poulter*, 5th edn (Sherbourne: R. Goadby, 1753), 30; and George Parker, *Life's Painter of Variegated Characters* (London: R. Bassam, 1789), 126. *Hell upon Earth* (n.p., 1703), 3, and *The Life and Character of Moll King* (London: W. Price, 1747), 10–11, were both published anonymously. Also quoted are the 'Specimen of Flash' from W. A. Miles's *Poverty, Mendicity and Crime . . . to which is added a Dictionary of the Flash or Cant Language, Known to Every Thief and Beggar edited by H. Brandon, esq.* (London: Shaw and Sons, 1839), 167, along with entries from Ducange Anglicus, *The Vulgar Tongue: Comprising Two Glossaries of Slang, Cant, and Flash Words and Phrases used in London at the Present Day* (London: Bernard Quaritch, 1857).

7 Jolly Good Show: British Slang to the Twentieth Century

We've seen that there had been considerable interest in cant from the sixteenth century onwards. By that time, London was big enough to have distinct social layers, making it very different from contemporary rural parishes in which the poorest and the richest would all have been on speaking terms with one another. There were enough people in London by the end of the sixteenth century that it had become possible to socialize mainly with people of the same social class, or with shared interests, occupations, or political views, and with social isolation comes dislike and fear of other groups. The rich had more to lose than the poor, and their fear of the poor, whose nefarious designs were magnified by contemporary writers, motivated the interest in English cant that developed during the sixteenth and seventeenth centuries.

The use and documentation of slang were also influenced by socio-economic developments. As international trade grew, British merchants from humble backgrounds amassed large fortunes, blurring previously dependable class divisions. Wealth no longer provided a reliable indicator of class, so etiquette and language became more important in determining gentility. The more precisely Standard English was defined and the more fiercely its borders were policed, the more interested people became in non-standard English and in representing types of people by their use of it. This chapter provides a roughly chronological account of the early development of English slang, but it also considers the main strands of influence on the development of slang: those with new money, old money, and no money, students, soldiers, and (going full circle) criminals and their associates. Clearly there were overlaps and connections between these groups.

The medieval period

Little is or can be known about non-standard language in the medieval period. There's a tendency to refer to swear words as 'Anglo-Saxon', though most of them aren't, particularly the most forceful ones. There's no evidence that the Anglo-Saxons used swearing in the way that we do. We know that when they swore to do something they were expected to follow through ('I swear that I will not leave the battlefield alive now that my lord has fallen'), but we don't know what an Anglo-Saxon warrior shouted when he dropped his shield on his foot. Evidence that the Anglo-Saxons used slang is similarly absent. Lack of evidence doesn't necessarily mean there was no slang, but it does mean that we can't say anything definitive about it. Unless we're going to label everything that's obscene or insulting as slang by default, which I don't think we should, my feeling is that the Anglo-Saxons didn't have slang. I'm confident that no one will ever be able to prove me wrong.

This isn't to say that during the medieval period everyone spoke pure and Standard English nicely to one another in idyllic thatched cottages until the corruption of urbanization occurred. It would be nearer the truth to say that no one spoke Standard English. For most of the medieval period people didn't write Standard English either (though there was some standardization of spelling during the medieval period). This is because there was no Standard English: with no national educational system or media, everyone spoke in their own dialect, and those that could write wrote in their own dialect too: representing the sounds of their own speech. What's more, English coexisted with other languages. If Chaucer's contemporaries wanted to sound more intelligent, they didn't use better English words, they used Latin words; if they wanted to sound more cultured, they used words from French. Students might have cemented their group identity by using informal Latin rather than informal English; fashionable people would probably have commented on one another's clothes and dalliances in French. That left English to fulfil many of the other functions listed in Chapter 5 without the necessity for a special non-standard variety: English was already intrinsically undignified. But could Chaucer and his late fourteenth-century contemporaries really be rebellious, rude, offensive, vivid, and insulting without using slang? *Puh-leeze!* (1931—, originally US). This exchange comes from Chaucer's *Canterbury Tales*. A group of pilgrims travelling to Canterbury have agreed to take part in a story-telling competition. Once the Knight has told his tale, the Host invites the Monk, who is second highest in rank, to go next. The Miller isn't happy with this arrangement:

> "By arms and by blood and bones,
> I can [know] a noble tale for the nones [for the purpose],
> With which I will now quite [match] the Knight's tale."
> Our Host saw that he was drunk of ale,
> And said, "Abide [wait], Robin, my leeve [dear] brother,
> Some better man shall tell us first another,
> Abide, and let us work [proceed] thriftily [in a proper manner]."
> "By God's soul," quod [said] he, "that will not I,
> For I will speak, or else go my way."
> Our Host answered, "Tell on, a devil way [in the devil's name]!
> Thou art a fool, thy wit is overcome!"

There's lots of swearing here: by God's arms, blood, bones, and soul, and by the devil. There are also plenty of insults (*thou art a fool, thy wit is overcome*), threats (*I will...go my way*), and there are clear differences in social status. The Miller doesn't take issue with the notion that there are better men than him: only with the suggestion that he should wait until after they've spoken. Social difference is also indicated by the Host's use of *thou* to address the Miller: he had just used the politer, and originally plural, form *you* to the Knight and Monk. We've already seen *thou* used in this way in the extract from *Henry IV, Part One* in the last chapter. For Chaucer, *thou* was the appropriate way to address one's inferiors; by Shakespeare's time it was either intimate or insulting, depending on the context (in the same way that many slang terms are now). So the language here is vivid, it's expressing emotion; it's creating social groups and hierarchies. The Miller is speaking in an undignified manner. Why can't we just call this slang? The simple answer is that it's not possible to point to any of these words individually and say, 'that is slang'. The *Middle English Dictionary* (*MED*), edited by Hans Kurath, and others, doesn't use the label 'slang' at all: although we can see that words are sometimes used in ways that seem slangy, we don't have enough evidence from the early or late medieval period to allow us to say that in a particular time and place, the only people using a particular word in a particular way were young people or soldiers, or students, or any other social group.

If we can't find Middle English slang by looking at social groups, perhaps we can do it by looking at promising words. Here are some citations from the *MED*, all from John Trevisa's translation of Bartholomaeus's scientific (for the time) encyclopaedia *De Proprietatibus Rerum* ('On the Properties of Things'). The translations are my own:

> Emoroydes beþ five veynes þat strecchiþ out at þe ers [Hemorrhoids are five veins that extend out of the arse]
> Þe weies of pisse beþ I-stoppid [The passages for piss are blocked]
> Þis beest...schitiþ fleynge and nouʒt in hire hyue [This beast [the bee]... shits flying and not in her hive]

Words that became slang later appear to have been unremarkable in Middle English: arses were called *arses* because that was the word for them (and always had been). It wasn't until euphemistic substitutes became established in general use, that *arse* could be stigmatized. *Arse*, and words like it, undoubtedly featured in bawdy tavern talk, but they weren't restricted to it. There's nothing, in the medieval period, that we can safely call slang.

Slanging matches

As urban communities grew larger during the late medieval and early modern period, law-makers became increasingly involved in the task of keeping the peace by outlawing public quarrelling. Early statutes were particularly directed towards women, and several terms from this period specifically meaning "a quarrelsome or scolding woman"

12 Unfeminine language: from *The New Art and Mystery of Gossiping* (London: n.p.,?1760).

indicate that 'the gentler sex' weren't supposed to speak up for themselves: *virago* (c.1386-1891), *shrew* (c.1386-1839), *common scold* (1467-1858), *callet* (a.1528-1611), *cotquean* (1592-1633), *scold-ster* (c.1600), and *termagant* (1659-1896). We'll see later that there has been a strong sense that slang is more proper to men than to women, which means that this restriction in women's speech was essential to the early development of slang.

Slang wasn't used in the sense "to rail in abusive or vulgar language" or "to abuse or scold violently" until the nineteenth century, but it's in dramatic representations of arguments that we find some of our best evidence of what looks like early modern slang. In this extract from *The Alchemist* (1610), Ben Jonson sets the scene with a lengthy and violent argument, which begins:

Subtle: Away, you trencher-rascal!
Face: Out, you dog-leech!
   The vomit of all prisons –
Dol Common: Will you be
   Your own destructions, gentlemen?
Face: Still spewed out
   For lying too heavy o' the basket.
Subtle: Cheater!
Face: Bawd!
Subtle: Cow-herd!
Face: Conjurer!
Subtle: Cut-purse!
Face: Witch!
Dol Common: Oh me! . . .
Face: Away this brach! I'll bring thee, rogue within
   The statute of sorcery, *tricesimo tertio*
   Of Harry the Eight: ay, and perhaps thy neck
   Within a noose for laundering gold and barbing it.
Dol Common: You'll bring your head within a coxcomb, will you?
   And you, sir, with your menstrue! – Gather it up.
   'Sdeath, you abominable pair of stinkards,
   Leave off your barking, and grow one again,

Or, by the light that shines, I'll cut your throats.
I'll not be made a prey unto the marshal
For ne'er a snarling dog-bolt of you both.

Now that's what I call a row! There's lots of swearing ((*god*)'*sdeath*, *by the light that shines*) and plenty of insults (*trencher-rascal* "glutton", *bawd*, *cow-herd*, *conjurer*, *cut-purse*, *witch*, *brach* "bitch", *rogue*, *stinkard* "smelly person"). Subtle lies too heavily on the basket in which food is distributed to poor people in prison: he's so greedy that other people don't get their share. Some of these insults may have been slang when they were used figuratively, but we are on firmer ground when we can identify a clear standard alternative. For example, *spew* was once unexceptional—it's recorded in sermons and saints' lives from the Anglo-Saxon period—but by this date the more learned *vomit* (*a*.1500-1872) was also available. *Puke* (1601—, now colloquial) was also being used in medical texts alongside various politer alternatives, so *spew* may well be functioning as slang in this context. We're familiar with the idea of *laundering* money (1973—), but Jonson's use is a much more literal reference to the act of washing coins in acid to remove some of the precious metal. Another way of increasing the value derived from a coin was to *barb* it, whereby slivers of gold were clipped off to be melted down: the coin was reduced in weight but retained its face value. The existence of Standard English *clip* (*a*.1513-1855) and *wash* (1421/2-1643) suggest that *barb* and *launder* may have been slang in this context, but we can't be certain.

As we've seen in Chapter 2, slang is often figurative, and some of Jonson's figurative usages may be slang here, including *barking*, with reference to human speech (1549+1857). To continue with the canine theme, which may have been given particular force by the use of *dog* as a substitute for *God* in oaths (?1550—, now chiefly US), a *dog-bolt* is "a bolt or arrow fit to be used on a dog" (1593+1612), but it is used here to mean "a menial; a wretch" (1465-1901). Similarly, the literal meaning of *dog-leech*[1] is "a doctor for dogs" (1638-1840), but this figurative sense "an unskilled doctor; a quack" (1529-1874) appears to be slang: Jonson used both *quacksalver* (1579—, historical in later use)[2] and the more colloquial *quack* (1638—) elsewhere with the same sense, so we can be sure that more standard alternatives were available to him.

It's also worth commenting on the use of *tricesimo tertio*: the thirty-third (year) of Henry's reign and *menstrue* "a solvent used for dissolving metal". The first is Latin and characteristic of legal language at this time; the second, although related to Latin *menstruum* "menstrual blood", was restricted to the language of alchemists in this broader sense "a solvent used for dissolving metal". So Jonson's play also indicates that different professional groups were beginning to develop their own characteristic vocabularies of technical language within English.

London slang

Unfortunately for the inhabitants of London and for students of slang, no plays were performed during the period 1649–60, because the Puritans, who were no fun at all, closed the theatres. When they reopened, Restoration dramatists made up for lost time by being as risqué as possible and by depicting contemporary life, warts and all, providing much clearer examples of slang than those we've seen from Renaissance playwrights. This extract is from William Wycherley's *The Country Wife*. Mr Harcourt has been flirting with Mrs Alithia in the presence of Mr Sparkish, to whom she is betrothed.[3] Mr

---

[1] It would be satisfying if this type of *leech* was related to the name of the blood-sucking creatures still sometimes used by doctors, but the two words exist separately in Old English.

[2] This is from a Dutch word now spelt *kwakzalver*. It has nothing to do with ducks, and why would it?

[3] *Mrs* is a title of respect here, not an indication of marital status.

Pinchwife, a jealous husband, advises Sparkish to curb Mrs Alithia's inappropriate behaviour, but Sparkish refuses:

Sparkish: Why, d'ye think I'll seem to be jealous, like a country bumpkin?

Pinchwife: No, rather be a cuckold, like a credulous cit.

Harcourt: Madam, you would not have been so little generous as to have told him.

Mrs Alithia: Yes, since you could be so little generous, as to wrong him.

Harcourt: Wrong him, no man can do't, he's beneath an injury; a bubble, a coward, a senseless idiot, a wretch so contemptible to all the world but you, that—

Mrs Alithia: Hold, do not rail at him, for since he is like to be my husband, I am resolved to like him: Nay, I think I am obliged to tell him, you are not his friend.—Master Sparkish, Master Sparkish.

Sparkish: What, what; now dear rogue, has not she wit?

Harcourt: Not so much as I thought, and hoped she had.

Mrs Alithia: Mr. Sparkish, do you bring people to rail at you?

Harcourt: Madam—

Sparkish: How! no, but if he does rail at me, 'tis but in jest I warrant; what we wits do for one another, and never take any notice of it.

Wycherley uses his characters' language to emphasize the different moral standards of the town and the country. Both parties have insulting names for the other: Sparkish uses *bumpkin* "a countryman or woman" (1570 , probably from Dutch, and always informal); Pinchwife uses *cit* (1654—), a contemptuous abbreviation for *citizen* "a townsperson; a townsman" (*c*.1380—). We've already seen that a *bubble* is a person who's easily fooled. *Rogue* is a term of endearment and approval here (1593—), demonstrating the inversion of mainstream values that we've seen in other slang terms: to be accounted a *wit* one had not only to allow other men to flirt with one's fiancée, but also to take insults and abuse in good spirit. Actually, people continued to care about their reputations very much, and even fashionable wits were sometimes ready to duel to the death in response to insults. The same words might represent a facetious witticism in one setting and a deadly challenge in another. With insults, as with slang, context is all.

Thomas Shadwell's *Squire of Alsatia* (1688) depicts individuals sheltering from arrest in London's Whitefriars district, an ecclesiastical sanctuary that had become the notorious haunt of gamblers and debtors: an unfortunate combination. Belford is set to inherit his father's considerable wealth, but resents the restrictions very sensibly placed on what he can do with it. Fortunately, he can raise money in anticipation of his inheritance, and this earns him the attention of two fraudsters, called Cheatly and Shamwell:

Shamwell: This morning your clothes and liveries will come home, and thou shalt appear rich and splendid like thyself, and the mobile shall worship thee.

Belford: The mobile! That's pretty. Sweet Mr Cheatly, my best friend, let me embrace thee.

Cheatly: My sprightly son of timber and of acres; my noble heir I salute thee: the cole is coming, and shall be brought in this morning.

Belford: Cole? Why 'tis Summer, I need no firing now. Besides, I intend to burn billets [logs cut for burning].

Cheatly: My lusty rustic, learn and be instructed. Cole is in the language of the witty, money. The ready, the rhino; thou shalt be rhinocerical, my lad, thou shalt.

Belford: Admirable I swear: cole, ready, rhino, rhinocerical; Lord, how long may a man live in ignorance in the country!

Ready and *rhino*, which we've already seen, join *cole* or *coal* (1671-1870) as synonyms for "money", with *rhinocerical* meaning "wealthy" (1688-1834). *Mobile* (1676-1830) is short for *mobile vulgus* "the common (and fickle) masses" (*c*.1599—, now chiefly historical, but also medical). As in the extract from Wycherley, newcomers from the country are vulnerable until they've been corrupted by London manners and slang.

Jonathan Swift's *Polite Conversation* (published in 1738, but apparently based on notes written at least two decades earlier) depicts wealthy Londoners with nothing better to do than gossip and take part in ostentatious social events:

> **Mr Neverout:** [to Lady Smart.] Madam, have you heard, that Lady Queasy was lately at the Playhouse incog?
>
> **Lady Smart:** What! Lady Queasy of all women in the world! Do you say it upon rep?
>
> **Neverout:** Poz, I saw her with my own eyes; she sat among the mob in the gallery; her own ugly fiz: And she saw me look at her.
>
> **Colonel Atwit:** Her Ladyship was plaguily bambed; I warrant, it put her into the hips.
>
> **Neverout:** I smoked her huge nose, and egad she put me in mind of the woodcock, that strives to hide his long bill, and then thinks nobody sees him.
>
> **Colonel:** Tom, I advise you hold your tongue; for you'll never say so good a thing again.

incog "incognito" (1709–)
rep "reputation" (1677–)
poz "positive" (1710–)
mob "mobile (vulgus)" (1688–)
fiz for *phiz* "physiognomy: a face" (1687–)

plaguily "perniciously; annoyingly; very" (*a*.1586–, now archaic)
bam "to hoax; to cheat" (1738-1884)
hyps for *hypochondria* (1705-1956)
smoke "to observe" (1715–)

Swift parodies the turn-of-the-century fondness for clippings by packing six into a few lines of dialogue. He also includes a little swearing (*egad* "Ah God", but used in the sense "by God" (1673—, now archaic)) and inserts trivially used emphatic phrases, such as *with my own eyes* (1707—) and *of all the women in the world* (phrases including *of all the* . . . are found from 1738—) to emphasize the insubstantiality of the conversation. The names are carefully chosen too. Although *Atwit* isn't directly related to *twit* "a fool" (1896—), both are derived from the verb *twit* "to blame; to find fault with", ultimately derived from the Old English *atwitan*, with the same meaning. *Neverout*'s name probably implies "never out of fashion", from *out* "unfashionable" (1660—).

Smart suggests "witty" (1639—) or "stylish" (1719—). *Queasy* probably implies "sensitive; scrupulous (of the conscience)" (1545—).

Oliver Goldsmith's *She Stoops to Conquer* (1773) gives us a taste of the conversation of wealthy young men slightly later in the eighteenth century. Here Lumpkin hopes to avoid marrying his cousin by helping his friend, Hastings, to elope with her:

> **Hastings:** My honest 'Squire! I now find you a man of your word. This looks like friendship.
>
> **Lumpkin:** Ay, I'm your friend, and the best friend you have in the world, if you knew but all. This riding by night, by the bye, is cursedly tiresome. It has shook me worse than the basket of a stage-coach.
>
> **Hastings:** But how? Where did you leave your fellow travellers? Are they in safety? Are they housed?
>
> **Lumpkin:** Five and twenty miles in two and a half is no such bad driving. The poor beasts have smoked for it. Rabbit me, but I'd rather ride forty miles after a fox, than ten with such varmint.
>
> **Hastings:** Well, but where have you left the ladies? I die with impatience.

There is much about this conversation that's informal, including the swear words *cursedly* "very" (1570—) and *rabbit* "drat" (1701-1995, dialect and archaic in later use). *Varmint*, from *vermin*, is used with the sense "an objectionable or troublesome person or persons" (1773—, now chiefly US). The *OED* labels *look like* "to have the appearance of being" (*c*.1440—) as now colloquial and chiefly US, but it's also commonly used in British English. *By the bye* is related to words like *by way* and *by-law*, and literally means "by a side way", though figuratively "incidentally". This parenthetical use dates from 1708. The *basket* (1773-1840) of a stagecoach contained two external seats at the back, which offered an exhilarating but uncomfortable way to travel. *Shook* has been used for the past participle (*shaken*) since at least 1671, and although it was stigmatized as non-standard during the eighteenth century, it continued in use among those who were wealthy and fashionable enough not to care about bourgeois grammatical rules. Similarly casual is the omission of *hours* in 'five and twenty miles in two and a half', and it's possible that the use of *beast* to refer to a gentleman's horse was equivalent to describing an expensive car as a *heap* (1921—, originally US), *jalopy* (1929—, originally US), or *banger* (1962—) "an old motor car". There's also understatement in *no such bad driving* "very good driving" and exaggeration in *I die with impatience* "I am very impatient". *Smoke* "to sweat" appears to be slang here, though it could also be an entirely literal description of the evaporation of smoke from the horses' flanks.

In his *Classical Dictionary of the Vulgar Tongue* (1785), Grose observed rapid changes taking place in London slang:

> A BORE, a tedious, troublesome man or woman, one who bores the ears of his hearers with an uninteresting tale, a term much in fashion about the years 1780, and 1781.
> TWADDLE, perplexity, a confusion, or any thing else, a fashionable term that succeeded a bore.

To suffer from *the bore* "a fit of boredom" (1766-1767) was considered a French affectation, and a person who affected such ennui and the thing or person causing boredom could also be called a *bore* (1766, 1778—, and 1785—, respectively). As Grose suggests, *twaddle* replaced *bore*, but only with the narrower sense "senseless, silly, or trifling talk or writing" (1782—). Clearly *bore* didn't fall from use, but it appears that there was a short period in Regency London when using *bore* instead of *twaddle* to describe conversation was shamefully unfashionable.

Pierce Egan was a prolific sports writer who also published an edition of Grose's dictionary. His *Life in London* (1821) depicts the introduction of Jerry Hawthorn to the pleasures of London by his cousin, Corinthian Tom. It's a rambling work, produced in instalments of very variable length and quality, but it was tremendously popular at the time and gave rise to several stage plays. In this extract from W. T. Moncrieff's adaptation, Tom introduces Jerry to his student friend, Bob Logic:

Tom: I was telling him before you came in. Bob, that he must go in training for a swell, and he didn't understand what I meant.

Jerry: Oh, yes, I did, Tom.

Tom: No, no, you didn't; come, confess your ignorance.

Logic: Not know what a swell meant?

Tom: No; he wasn't up.

Jerry: Not up?

Logic: That is, you were not down.

Jerry: Not down!

Tom: No; you're green!

Jerry: Green!

Logic: Ah! not fly!

Tom: Yes, not awake!

Jerry: "Green! fly! awake!" D— me, but I'm at fault. I don't understand one word you are saying.

Logic: We know you don't, and that's what we're telling you. Poor young man very uninformed....

Green "gullible" (1605—, now old-fashioned) was long established by this time, and we have already seen *swell* used with this sense. *Fly* (1724—), *down* (1794—), *up* (1800—), and *awake* (1811—) all mean "knowing; wide awake; well informed; sharp". As we've seen, new-comers to London had to learn its fashionable ways to be accepted into the most sought-after social circles. Understanding the current slang was central to that acceptance.

In the extracts from Wycherley, Shadwell, Goldsmith, Swift, and Moncrieff, we've seen slang being used in very similar ways. It characterizes individuals as immoral, easily led, and trivial. It represents and sometimes celebrates the corruptions of modern life and London, which lure people away from the simplicity of traditional country living. Unlike Jonson's squabbling alchemists, and unlike the criminals and beggars of the last chapter, these characters are all relatively wealthy and socially elevated. Social class is central to an understanding of British slang, then as now. These writers also demonstrate what Grose explicitly observes: that fashionable speech was changing rapidly. Wealth and fashion were no longer synony-mous in this more complex network of in- and out-groups.

The lure of low London

Grose and Egan were also documenting the beginning of a new fascination among wealthy Londoners with the lives and leisure activities of the poor. While middle-class young women were begin-ning to lead increasingly restricted lives, their brothers sought out taverns, brothels, cock fights, dog-fights, and boxing bouts. There could be no better way of broadcasting one's credentials as a man of the world, perhaps even within hearing of the ladies, than casually using the latest word from the street.

The appeal of low London is also illustrated by Charles Dickens's *Pickwick Papers*, published in monthly instalments in 1836–7. It enjoyed a marked increase in popularity when Sam Weller was introduced. In his first appearance, as a shoe-cleaner in an inn, Sam described the people to be found at Doctors' Commons, a society of civil lawyers in London:

> 'Touts for licences,' replied Sam. 'Two coves in vhite aprons – touches their hats wen you walk in – "Licence, sir, licence?" Queer sort, them, and their mas'rs too, sir – Old Baily Proctors – and no mistake.'
> 'What do they do?' inquired the gentleman.
> 'Do! *You*, sir! That an't the wost on it, neither. They puts things into old gen'lm'n's heads as they never dreamed of. My father, sir, wos a coachman. A widower he wos, and fat enough for anything – uncommon fat, to be sure. His missus dies, and leaves him four hundred pound. Down he goes to the Commons, to see the lawyer and draw the blunt – wery smart – top boots on – nosegay in his button-hole – broad-brimmed tile – green shawl – quite the gen-lm-n. . . . '

Putting aside Sam's pronunciation and grammar, both of which are worthy of comment in their own right, there are a number of terms that appear to be slang. We've already seen *cove* "a man" and *tout* in the sense "to observe", but the noun *tout* was used to mean "a thief's scout or lookout" (1718-1919) and, as here, "one who solicits custom" (1853—). *Tile* "hat" (1813-1973) and *blunt* "money" (1703—) were certainly slang. *Sort* had been used to refer to a group of people since 1548, but if Sam had referred to a single tout as *a queer sort*, he would have been ahead of his time (*c.*1869-1891, colloquial). Several of Sam's idioms are marked as 'colloquial' in the *OED*, but their concentration in a single exchange may suggest a more slangy tone in this early period of their use. These are the emphatic *and no mistake* (1818—), *for anything* "excessively" (*c.*1832—), *uncommon* "uncommonly; extremely" (1784-1891), *to be sure* "undoubtedly" (1657—), *quite the*... (1752—), and the use of the singular *pound* following a number, which dates back to Old English, but is described in the *OED* as 'still common in regional and colloquial English'. People had been putting ideas into each other's heads since 1548, and an idea has been referred to as a *thing* since the Old English period, but their combination may also have seemed slangy here.

Youth and student slang

Those who disapproved of this fascination with low London tended to consider it a weakness of youth. In 1858, *The Times* published an article quoting a lecture on slang given by the Rev. A. Mursell in Carlisle:

> There are many young men who seem to consider it essential to manliness that they should be masters of slang. The sporting world, like its brother, the swell mob, has a language of its own; but this dog-English ... comes with its hordes of barbarous words, threatening the entire extinction of genuine English.

Mursell objected specifically to the use of *regular* "very; truly" (1740—), *hard up* "poor" (1800—), *up to snuff* "in the know; up to scratch" (1810—), *ugly customer* "any person or animal likely to be difficult to deal with" (1811—), *brick* "a dependable individual" (1812—), *on one's own hook* "at one's own risk" (1812—, originally American), *stump up* "to pay" (1821—), *plucky* "brave" (1835—), *make tracks* "to leave" (1835/40—, originally American), *stunner* "an excellent person or thing" (1842—), and *blow up* "to lose one's temper" (1858—). Mursell remarks that although most slang terms are harmless and expressive, their use in the presence of or in reference to family members indicates a lack of love and proper respect.

The popularity of sporting slang at this period was also commented on by *The Caledonian Mercury*:

> Our dashing young friend of today never tells
> The hotel he puts up at, or house where he dwells,
> Of his Diggins perchance we'll hear something about
> Or his Crib, or Concern, Sir, or where he Hangs out.
> Our friend has no pocket, he may have a Fob,
> Though it holds not a shilling, it may hold a Bob;
> It has not a sixpence, or any coin in,
> Though it may have a Tizzy, a Bender, or Tin.

Although their movement out of sporting circles may have been relatively recent, many of these terms had been in use for several decades already, including *crib* "a house" and *bob* "a shilling", which we have already seen. *Hang out* "to loiter; to consort" was newer, as were:

dashing "fashionably showy (of people or clothes)" (1795—)

put up "to stop or stay somewhere temporarily" (1706—), not apparently slang, but the final preposition might have made it seem so

diggings "lodgings; quarters" (1838—), abbreviated to *digs* (1893—, originally theatrical)

concern "a property; an estate" (1787 +1877)

fob "a small pocket in a trouser waistband" (1653-1839), although it appears to mean "a pocket" more generally here

tizzy "a sixpence" (1795-1946)

bender "a sixpence" (1789-1933)

tin "money" (1836-1961)

In his *Dictionary of Modern Slang, Cant, and Vulgar Words*, first published in 1859, John Camden Hotten described the slang used by

OXFORD COSTUME.

First Swell. "AWFUL SHIRT! EH?"
Second Ditto. "YA-AS, LINEN'S SO DEUCED COMMON NOW—I'M GOING
TO SPORT EMBROIDERED SILKS."
First Ditto. "HAH! CHEESY IDEA, TOO! BUT YOUR GILLS WANT
ELEVATING!"

13 Student slang II: John Lynch, 'Oxford Costume', *Punch*, 7 May 1853, 191.

various groups in his own time, including fashionable society, soldiers, and sailors, but also parliamentarians and ecclesiasts. Here he
considers the slang of students:

> The *Universities of Oxford and Cambridge*, and the great public schools, are
> the hotbeds of fashionable slang. Growing boys and high-spirited young
> fellows detest restraint of all kinds, and prefer making a dash at life in a
> slang phraseology of their own to all the set forms and syntactical rules of
> *Alma Mater*. Many of the most expressive words in a common chit-chat, or
> free-and-easy conversation, are old university vulgarisms. Cut, in the sense
> of dropping an acquaintance, was originally a Cambridge form of speech;

and HOAX, to deceive or ridicule, we are informed by Grose, was many years since an Oxford term. Among the words that fast society has borrowed from our great scholastic (I was going to say *establishments*, but I remembered the linen drapers' horrid and habitual use of the word) institutions, I find CRIB, a house or apartments; DEAD-MEN, empty wine bottles; DRAWING TEETH, wrenching off knockers;* FIZZING, first-rate, or splendid; GOVER-NOR, or RELIEVING-OFFICER, the general term for a male parent; PLUCKED, defeated or turned back; QUIZ, to scrutinise, or a prying old fellow; and ROW, a noisy disturbance. The slang words in use at Oxford and Cambridge would alone fill a volume.

*This is more especially an amusement with medical students, and is comparatively unknown out of London.

cut "to break off an acquaintance; to affect not to see or know an acquaintance" (1634–, now colloquial)

hoax "to deceive or ridicule" (1796-1869)

dead man "an empty bottle or glass" (1699–, originally military)

drawing teeth "stealing doorknockers" (1859)

fizzing "excellent; exciting" (1845–)

governor "a father" (1827-1960)

relieving officer "a father" (1858-1883)

pluck "to fail (a student)" (1713 1984)

quiz "to pry; to interrogate" (1795–)

quiz "an inquisitive person" (1781-1982)

row "a noisy disturbance; an argument" (1746–)

Hotten emphasizes the importance of youthful exuberance in the creation and adoption of slang terms, an association that's so central to our use of *slang* that it hardly needs to be made. *Governor, relieving officer, pluck,* and the use of *quiz* as a noun do appear to have originated in the slang of young men, but *hoax, row, fizzing, dead man, crib* (which we've already seen), and the verbal use of *quiz* appear to have been in wide use. There's no additional evidence for *drawing teeth.* As with the flappers and beats in Chapter 4, students were being characterized as particularly creative slang users and given credit for slang that they didn't come up with.

A complaint that was to be made increasingly during the next half century was that not only had respectable young men adopted the slang of those beneath them, but young women were adopting this slang too. In 1865, the *Glasgow Herald* published a poem bemoaning the use of slang by young women:

Oh! why should our dear English girls—
The brightest beauties in creation—
Whose words should drop like Orient pearls,
Use semi-slang in conversation?
Why should their language break the dream—
Our golden vision swift dispelling?
Like to the bright galvanic stream—
Attracting first and then repelling.

The repellent words singled out elsewhere in the verse are *jolly* "delightful; agreeable" (1549—, restricted to slang or colloquial language by the 1800s), *spoony (on)* "infatuated (with)" (1810—), *awful* "very" (1818—, dialect in later use), *slap-up* "excellent" (1823—, now usually used to describe meals, but used more broadly in the middle decades of the nineteenth century), and *stunning* "excellent" (1837/8—). Similarly emphatic terms used 'in society' were objected to by another journalist just a few years later, including *beastly* "unfit for humans; unpleasant" (1611—, slang in the weakened sense), *cropper* "a fall; a failure" (1858—, originally sporting), *awfully* "very" (1859—), *form* "(good/bad) behaviour or manners" (1868—, originally sporting),[4] *plunger* "a man of fast habits" ("a person who gambles or speculates rashly" (1868—)), and *in the swim* "up to date with current trends" (1869—). This later writer comments that *jolly* 'has become a perfect nuisance' and it was still capable of provoking wrath a decade later, when an article in the *North Wales Chronicle* argued that the leaders of society should set themselves against slang 'as resolutely as they do against other breaches of decorum and good manners'. This writer objected in particular to *ass* "a fool" (1578—, 'now disused in polite literature and speech', presumably by association with the

---

[4] This objectionable term was quickly assimilated. J. D.'s diatribe against 'Slang', published in *The Newcastle Weekly Courant* in 1892, begins 'That it is bad form to use slang, irrespective of place, no one can doubt.'

THE SLANG OF THE DAY.
(Fragment of Fashionable Conversation.)

Youth. "A—AWFUL HOT, AIN'T IT?"
Maiden. "YES, AWFUL!" *(Pause.)*
Youth. "A—AWFUL JOLLY FLOOR FOR DANCING, AIN'T IT?"
Maiden. "YES, AWFUL!" *(Pause.)*
Youth. "A—A—AWFUL JOLLY SAD ABOUT THE POOR DUCHESS, AIN'T IT?"
Maiden. "YES—QUITE TOO AWFUL——" *(And so forth.)*

14 Feminine language: George Du Maurier, 'The Slang of the Day', *Punch*, 5 Aug. 1871, 44.

unrelated *ass* "the buttocks" (1860—, US)), *briny* "the sea" (1831—), and *groom* "to make (a person or thing) tidy" (1843—). He also disliked three slang intensifiers: *dreadfully* (1602—), *immensely* (1654—, apparently in this weakened sense since around 1738), and *screamingly* (1847—).

Even those who had used slang in their own youth objected to new slang. In 1913, a writer in the *Times* wrote that:

However much slang we may use ourselves, we all dislike and despise a slang that is not our own ... We do not want new words for old discoveries that we made so long ago for ourselves; we do not want youth to be incessantly insisting upon the fact that it is young and implying that we are not ... Youth, no doubt, must be silly, but we do not see why it should get so much enjoyment out of its silliness, and it is the sense of enjoyment in slang that makes us dislike it.

This article comments on relatively few slang words: *prig* (1676-1999, now historical), *toff* (1851—, originally working class), *masher* (1875-1971, originally American), and *nut* (1904-1923, British slang), all with the sense "a fashionably dressed young man; a dandy", and each replaced in fashionable usage by the next as it lost its air of freshness and novelty. It seems unlikely that these opinions would have been expressed in the same way during or after WWI, when the balance of power between the generations was to shift irrevocably, and the idea that age equals wisdom could no longer be taken for granted.

In the interwar period, British writers continued to document the tensions between generations in wealthy families, often using slang to characterize youthful characters as modern. In this extract, John Galsworthy depicts a meeting between two cousins separated by a family feud that's never been explained to them. They're discussing the roulette game they'd met at the night before:

"I saw you last night. How did you do?"

"I didn't play."

"I won fifteen quid."

... "Rotten game, I think; I was at school with that chap. He's an awful fool."

"Oh! I don't know," said Val, as one might speak in defence of a disparaged god; "he's a pretty good sport."

They exchanged whiffs in silence.

"You met my people, didn't you?" said Jolly. "They're coming up to-morrow."

Val grew a little red.

"Really! I can give you a rare good tip for the Manchester November handicap."

"Thanks, I only take interest in the classic races."

"You can't make any money over them," said Val.

"I hate the ring," said Jolly; "there's such a row and stink. I like the paddock."

"I like to back my judgement," answered Val.

Jolly smiled; his smile was like his father's.

"I haven't got any. I always lose money if I bet."

"You have to buy experience, of course."

"Yes, but it's all messed-up with doing people in the eye."

"Of course, or they'll do you—that's the excitement."

Both of these men speak forthrightly, using emphatic language wherever possible, such as *stink* "a disgusting smell" (*a.*1300—), *rare* "splendid; excellent" (*a.*1534—), *row* "noise; clamour" (1845—), *awful* "utter" (1873—), *rotten* "horrible" (1851—), and *messed up* "spoilt; ruined" (1909—). Both use sporting terms, with Jolly apparently introducing them in a conciliatory way, to gain Val's approval. They include *the ring* "boxing" (1770—), *handicap* "a race in which horses carry weights to equalize their chances" (1812—), *the paddock* "a turf enclosure near a racecourse; horse racing" (1839—), and *classic*, used with reference to the chief annual horse races (1868—). Terms associated with betting include *do* "to cheat" (1641—), *quid* "a pound" (1661—), *back* "to bet (on)" (1697—), *tip* "a piece of insider knowledge" (1842—), and *do (someone) in the eye* "to defraud; injure; humiliate" (1891—). Other slang indicates that despite their use of terms originating in vulgar sporting circles, these men share a privileged background. *Chap* "a man" (1716—), *good sport* "a fairminded person" (*sport* had been used in this way since 1881, and was qualified with *good* from around 1916), and *people* "one's family" (1916—) identify them as upper or upper middle class. Although the differences between these modern young people and their parents are central to Galsworthy's plot, the two men are characterized more by the density of their slang than its modernity. Putting aside new terms introduced as a result of WWI, British slang was still relatively slow moving. In this period, slanginess often resided in who used a term or where it was used rather than how: it's the adoption of terms belonging to the working classes (by the middle or upper classes), to the outside world (in the drawing room), or to men (by women) that constitutes slang in this period.

Working-class slang

We've seen that, moving on from their fascination with the working classes, wealthy young people began to develop their own distinctive fashionable slang during the later part of the nineteenth century. The language of the poor had continued to move on too. Here's an extract from Arthur Morrison's short story 'The Red Cow Group', in which a gang of amateur revolutionaries plot to blow up a gas works. When one of them balks at planting the nitro-glycerine, they decide to get him drunk and use him as a human bomb so he can't betray them:

> Then his pockets were invaded by Gunno Polson, who turned out each in succession. "You won't 'ave no use for money where you're goin'," he observed, callously; "besides, it 'ud be blowed to bits an' no use to nobody. Look at the bloke at Greenwich, 'ow 'is things was blowed away. 'Ullo! 'ere's two 'arfcrowns an' some tanners. Seven an'thrippence altogether, with the browns. This is the bloke wot 'adn't got no funds. This'll be divided on free an' equal principles to 'elp pay for that beer you've wasted. 'Old up, ol' man! Think o' the glory. P'r'aps you're all right, but it's best to be on the safe side, an' dead blokes can't split to the coppers. An' you mustn't forget the glory. You 'ave to shed blood in a revolution, an' a few odd lives more or less don't matter-not a single damn. Keep your eye on the bleed'n' glory! They'll 'ave photos of you in the papers, all the broken bits in a 'eap, fac-similar as found on the spot. Wot a comfort that'll be!"

As with Sam Weller's speech, respellings represent non-standard pronunciations, and there are also non-standard grammatical constructions, such as the double negatives (*you won't have no use for money*) and past tense forms for past participles (*was blowed*).

Along with the swearing (*damn*, *bleeding*), these represent the class and place of origin of the speaker, so the use of slang is less necessary from a literary perspective. However, a few slang terms are included. We've already seen *bloke* "a man" and *copper* "a policeman", but other terms here had also been in use for some time, including *tanner* "a sixpence" (1795—, historical in later use), *split* "to turn informer" (1795—), *brown* "a coin made of copper or bronze; (in plural) small change" (1819—), and *old man* used in affectionate address to a man who isn't old (1828—). These working men's non-standard language emphasizes the difference between them and the educated reader, and makes their criminal intentions seem credible.

Similarly angry are the working-class soldiers depicted in Rudyard Kipling's *Barrack-Room Ballads* (1892):

> I went into a public-'ouse to get a pint o' beer,
> The publican 'e up an' sez, "We serve no red-coats here."
> The girls be'ind the bar they laughed an' giggled fit to die,
> I outs into the street again an' to myself sez I:
> *O it's Tommy this, an' Tommy that, an' "Tommy, go away";*
> *But it's "Thank you, Mister Atkins", when the band begins to play,*
> *The band begins to play, my boys, the band begins to play,*
> *O it's "Thank you, Mister Atkins", when the band begins to play.*

As in Morrison's work, Tommy's language is characterized as non-standard largely by respelling, though there are some non-standard grammatical features, such as *up and*, followed by a verb (1883—), the use of third-person present tense verbs in a first-person past tense narrative (e.g. *sez* (1682—)), and *out* "to go out" (for which I've found no other evidence of use). *Fit to die* isn't listed in the *OED* in its own right, but *fit* has been used in similar constructions since 1580. Many of Kipling's contemporaries would have considered all non-standard working-class speech to be slang, and so perhaps it was unnecessary to include genuine army slang, but it certainly existed:

ammunition "officially issued" (1663-1858)

dock "hospital" (1785-1963)

Johnny Raw "a new recruit" (1810-1966)

pack "a soldier's bundle of possessions" (*a*.1811—)

loaf "the, or an, act of avoiding work" (1855—, originally US)

on the peg "under arrest" (1888-1942)

quiff "a curl or lock of hair plastered down on to or brushed back from the forehead" (1890—)

get one's head down "to go to sleep" (1894—)

gong "a medal" (1894—)

tell off "to reprimand" (1894—)

gippo "gravy" (1896-1925)

As a result of the popularity of Kipling's *Barrack-Room Ballads*, *Tommy Atkins* (1883—, usually historical in later use), usually shortened to *Tommy* (1884—), came to be used as a nickname for British infantrymen, particularly those who served in WWI. It was in this context that working-class language began to be presented in a slightly more positive light. Maximilian Mügge, whose German parentage denied him a commission in the British army, joined up as an infantryman instead. His comrades were largely working class, and Mügge commented on their language in his diary:

> The "slanguage" of the boys is very forcible and stands in a peculiar contrast to the undoubtedly kind and gentle nature of their heart of hearts. [They] ... might create the impression of semi-savages to a superficial observer. But it is only their "slanguage" that does it. At heart most of them are really a good-natured lot, and with not a few I have become quite chummy.

Although Mügge was intimidated by their apparently aggressive language at first, he learns to like his comrades. His glossary includes:

- swearing, e.g. *crikey* (1832—), *blimey* (1889—)
- working-class colloquialisms, e.g. *afters* "dessert" (1909—), *cheerio* "goodbye" (1910—)
- military terms, e.g. *chit* "a letter or note; a pass" (1776—, originally Anglo-Indian), *ticket* "a pay-warrant, particularly the last pay-warrant; discharge papers; the end of a contracted period of service" (1596—)

- words and phrases picked up from French, e.g. *camouflage* "disguise; concealment" (1917—), *merci boko* "thank you" (as *mercy bucket(s)* from 1953, *mercy buckup* from 1960, and *mercy buttercups* from 1981)
- terms used by English-speaking allies, e.g. *cobber* "a companion; a mate" (1895—, Australia & NZ), *doughboy* "a US infantryman" (1847—, chiefly US).

Mügge also lists some slang that originated in or was popularized during WWI, including *scrounge* "to obtain by irregular means" (1909—, originally dialect), *pozzy* "jam; marmalade" (1915—), and *the wind-up* "a state of nervous anxiety or fear" (1917—).

Other influences on British slang

Slang interchange between the army and civilian society was a relatively straightforward process, because individuals moved between the two groups. In India, officials and soldiers picked up words from the local languages and employed them in conversations among themselves.[5] These were sometimes adopted by civilians serving in India and exported back to Britain, where they were often extended in meaning. Informal terms from Hindi and Urdu borrowed during this period include *pukka* "genuine; reliable; high class" (1776—), shading into the current slang usage "excellent" (1991—, now chiefly Jamie Oliver), *bobbery* "noisy disturbance; a row" (1795-1924), *toco* "corporal punishment" (1823-1944), *loot* "goods taken by force; booty" (1839—), *rooty* "bread; rations" (1846-1989),[6] *choky* "prison" (1866—), *baboo English* "ornate unidiomatic English spoken by an Indian" (1878—), *jildi* "haste; quick; quickly; to hurry; to enliven" (1890—), and *dekko* "a look" (1894—). Conscription during WWI helped spread some of

---

[5] Henry Yule and A. C. Burnell documented Anglo-Indian terms in a substantial dictionary called *Hobson-Jobson* (London: John Murray, 1886). Only a small fraction of Anglo-Indian terms were slang.

[6] Also occurring in the form *roti*, which refers more specifically to a type of bread originating in South Asia (1838—).

those that had remained restricted to army slang into wider civilian usage.

Other itinerant groups that introduced terms from foreign languages into English slang included criminals, gypsies, and (as we shall see in Chapter 10) entertainers. British Gypsies, speaking Anglo-Romany, have introduced *monnisher/mollisher* "a woman; a girlfriend; a prostitute" (1765—), *mang* "to beg" (1811-1979), *pani* "water; rain" (1816-1999), *posh* "money; a coin of small value" (1830-1912), *rocker* "to speak or understand (a language)" (1856-1973), *mooey* "a face; a mouth" (1859—), *chavvy* "a baby; a child" (1886—),[7] *minge* "the female genitals" (*a*.1903—), *mush* "a man", particularly used as a term of address (1936—), and *muller* "to ruin; to defeat decisively" (1990—). Although many of the earlier terms were used only in bilingual conversations or as part of criminal cant, terms borrowed from Anglo-Romani have more commonly entered general slang in the twentieth century, perhaps because the traditional separation between travelling Gypsies and the settled population became harder to maintain.

Early twentieth-century British slang

We've already seen early signs of the influence of American English on British slang. It remained a relatively minor influence until the early twentieth century, however, with the adoption of Americanisms tending to occur among those wealthy enough to move in transatlantic social networks. When he first published his *Dictionary of Slang and Unconventional English* (1937), Partridge made what must have seemed an entirely reasonable decision at the time: to include American slang terms that were used in Britain and the Commonwealth but to exclude those that were restricted to the United States. Despite this restriction, almost a fifth of entries in the first edition of Partridge's

---

[7] *Chav* "a brash and loutish working-class youth" (1998—) is probably derived from this or a closely related term. Any association with Chatham is purely circumstantial.

dictionary were labelled as American or originally American. When he undertook a major revision of the dictionary in 1949, Partridge added thousands of new terms, but labelled only around five per cent of them as originally American. During the intervening period, American troops had been stationed in Britain, British dance halls had reverberated to the sound of American dance music, and American movies had drawn crowds in British cinemas. The influence of American English on British English was growing, and Partridge realized that it was no longer possible to document all the Americanisms used in Britain, so he changed his policy to list only those that were most frequently used. He wasn't the only one troubled by this development: after WWII, newspaper complaints about the adoption of American slang terms tend to swamp earlier concerns about class and gender.

Conclusions

Socially stratified language isn't necessarily slang: working- and upper-class families can speak differently among themselves without either group using slang. Working-class terms become slang when wealthy people adopt them. When young or fashionable members of the upper classes adopt novel terms in preference to the ones used by their parents, they are using slang. However, for eighteenth- and nineteenth-century commentators, slang was a symbol of the tension between social classes, and much of what is documented during this period concerns the fashion for slumming—or, to be more accurate, a developing prohibition on social mixing. This slang was *vulgar* in the sense that it was "of or pertaining to the common people" (1597-1870) but also "coarsely commonplace; lacking in refinement or good taste" (1716-1891), and we have also seen that vulgar speech had a particular appeal to young men and (shudder to think it) young ladies. During the twentieth century, the focus shifted so that slang became associated more strongly in Britain with differences in age and with American influence, rather than with differences in class, but the association with class has never entirely gone away. As social mobility has slowed again in recent years, comedy characters such as Ali G and Vicky Pollard have given re-expression to the notion that slang is a working-class phenomenon associated with low levels of intelligence, education, and aspiration.

By the end of the nineteenth century, British slang dictionaries were almost all historical: the study of old slang appears to have been more respectable than the study of contemporary slang. Partridge's dictionary was to dominate the British slang dictionary market for almost five decades even though his coverage of contemporary slang became increasingly patchy after 1949. Because of the influence of American slang, particularly after WWII, it became harder to identify national slang in Britain. Although Partridge's dictionary documented a stratum of traditional British slang, much of which continued in use, those wanting to understand the language of young people in the 1960s could only have found the newer terms in Wentworth and Flexner's *Dictionary of American Slang*. It is to the history of American slang that we now turn.

Endnotes

The extract from Chaucer's *Canterbury Tales* is from <http://www.librarius .com/cantales.htm>, but I've modernized the spelling wherever possible. Also cited or quoted are Hans Kurath *et al.*, *Middle English Dictionary* (Ann Arbor: University of Michigan Press, 1952–2001); Ben Jonson, *The Alchemist* (London: John Stepneth, 1612), I. i; William Wycherley, *The Country Wife* (London: Thomas Dring, 1675), II. i; Thomas Shadwell, *The Squire of Alsatia* (London: James Knapton, 1688), I. i; Jonathan Swift, *Polite Conversation in Three Dialogues* (1738), ed. George Saintsbury (London: Chiswick, 1842), Dialogue I, 112–13; Oliver Goldsmith, *She Stoops to Conquer, or The Mistakes of a Night* (London: F. Newbery, 1773), V. ii; Pierce Egan, *Life in London* (London: Sherwood, Neely & Jones, 1821); W. T. Moncrieff, *Songs, Parodies, Duets, Chorusses* [sic] *&c. &c.: in an Entirely New Classic . . . in Three Acts, called Tom & Jerry, or, Life in London* (London: John Lowndes, 1821), I. iv; and Charles Dickens, *The Posthumous Papers of the Pickwick Club* (London: Chapman & Hall, 1836), Ch. 10. Newspaper articles cited in this chapter are, in order of appearance: 'Slang Words and Phrases', *The Times*, 3 Apr. 1858, 5F; 'A Chapter on Slang', *Caledonian Mercury*,

8 Jul. 1859, n.p., originally from *Punch*; 'Slang in the Salon', *Glasgow Herald*, 22 May 1865, n.p., originally from *The Owl*; 'Slang', *The Sheffield and Rotherham Independent*, 9 Nov. 1869, 7; J. D., 'Slang', *The Newcastle Weekly Courant*, 23 Jan. 1892, n.p.; Charles Mackay, 'Fashionable Slang', *North Wales Chronicle*, 18 Jan. 1879, n.p.; and 'On Slang', *The Times*, 31 Dec. 1913, 63F. John Camden Hotten's *A Dictionary of Modern Slang, Cant, and Vulgar Words* (London: Hotten, 1860), 65, is quoted from the second edition because the passage had been edited and is slightly easier to follow. Also quoted are John Galsworthy, *To Let* (London: Heinemann, 1921), Part II, Ch. 1, 'The Third Generation'; Arthur Morrison, *Tales of Mean Streets* (London: Methuen, 1865), 'The Red Cow Gang'; Rudyard Kipling, *Barrack-Room Ballads and Other Verses* (London: Methuen, 1892), 'Tommy'; and Maximilian August Mügge, *The War Diary of a Square Peg* (London: Routledge, 1920), 17, 57–8. Examples of late nineteenth-century army slang are from 'Military Slang', *Hampshire Telegraph and Sussex Chronicle*, 23 Jun. 1894, n.p., and 'Barrack-Room Slang', *Pall Mall Gazette*, 17 Dec. 1896, n.p. Also mentioned were Henry Yule and A. C. Burnell's *Hobson-Jobson* (London: John Murray, 1886); Eric Partridge's *A Dictionary of Slang and Unconventional English*, 3rd edn (London: Routledge, 1949); and Harold Wentworth and Stuart Berg Flexner's *Dictionary of American Slang* (New York: Crowell, 1960). I've written about these and other slang dictionaries in much more detail in *A History of Cant and Slang Dictionaries*, 4 vols. (Oxford: Oxford University Press, 2004–10).

8 Whangdoodles and Fixings: Early American Slang

The vocabulary of English became distinctively American in the United States as soon as the earliest settlers began to name unfamiliar animals, plants, and features of the landscape and started to interact with existing inhabitants and fellow immigrants. Terms such as *moccasin* (1612—), *wigwam* (1628—), and *tomahawk* (1634—) were borrowed from indigenous languages, and existing English words were used in new ways, as in *robin* "a migratory thrush" (1703—) and *corn* "maize; sweet corn" (1726—). New combinations were also created from within the resources of English, many of which were later introduced into international English, including *mileage* (1724—), *advisory* (1778—), and *cocktail* (1803—). Some words that had fallen from use in Britain, like *barber shop* (1579—), *sidewalk* (1739—), and *menfolk* (1749—), enjoyed continued currency in the United States, but although there are some respects in which American English is more conservative than British English:

> Many people outside the United States seem to think that American English is synonymous with slang, and that slang is a particularly American phenomenon.

The earliest settlers didn't all speak in the same way: they arrived speaking various kinds of English as well as many other languages. New settlers joined those of a similar background if they could, and regional trends in settlement sometimes explain modern dialect differences. Geographical boundaries and distance contributed towards the development of further linguistic diversity, but a tendency to describe dialect terms as *slang* in the United States, particularly those used in contemporary urban dialects, can obscure the development of American slang.

American cant

Just as in Britain, the language of criminals and beggars was documented long before there was much written about slang, and the earliest lists suggest continued use of British cant. These examples are from *The Life of Henry Tufts* (1807):

Darky: cloudy
Douse the glim: put out the light
Evening sneak: going into a house by night the doors being open
Glaze: a square of glass

Most of these terms, or ones closely related to them, appear to have been current with these senses in the language of British criminals, including *glim* (1676-1963/4), *douse* (1753—), *glaze* (1699-1889), and *sneak* (1699—). *Darky* appears to have developed from the sense "night", first recorded in *The Life and Character of Moll King* (see Chapter 6). Many early accounts of American criminal language emphasize this continuity between British and American usage, and some of the earliest lexicographers of American cant turned to British dictionaries for their word lists, including George Matsell, chief of police in New York. Although his position should have given him the knowledge necessary for writing about contemporary New York slang and cant, Matsell based his *Vocabulum, or, Rogue's Lexicon* (1859) on a selection of older British dictionaries.

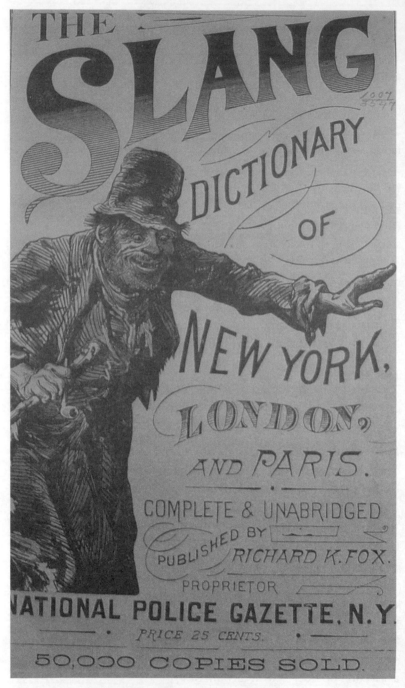

15 American cant: Alfred Trumble's *Slang Dictionary of New York, London and Paris* (New York: National Police Gazette, 1881) based on George Matsell's *Vocabulum, or, Rogue's Lexicon* (New York: Matsell, 1859).

Fortunately there were more reliable witnesses. Josiah Flynt Willard's autobiographical *Tramping with Tramps* (1899) and *World of Graft* (1901) explore connections between the language of tramps and criminals, including words that originated among British criminals like *mob* "a gang of criminals" (1791—) and *croak* "to die" (1819—), alongside newer American terms such as *graft* "a criminal technique" (1865—), *cooler* "a prison" (1872—) or "a cell used for solitary confinement" (1899—), and *beef* "to inform against a criminal" (1899—). Despite the misleading evidence of writers like Matsell, it's clear that distinctively American tramping and criminal cant was being added to the British stock during the course of the nineteenth century.

Only a few decades later, during Prohibition and after, pulp magazines, paperbacks, and films were to spread the language of American crime around the world. Henry Leverage's 'Flynn's Dictionary of the Underworld' appeared in *Flynn's* magazine in 1925, listing around 3000 words. By this stage, many more were American innovations, and some were to spread into wider usage. Terms included:

kiddy "a thief; a young thief" (1770-1863, originally UK thieves)

fin "the hand" (1785-1974, originally UK jocular)

kangaroo "an Australian" (1823-1981, originally UK)

ochre/ocher "gold; money" (1836-1894, originally UK)

cocum, used with flexible grammatical function to mean "cunning; shrewdness" (1839-c.1886, originally UK)

hush shop "an unlicensed drinking establishment" (1841-1872, originally UK)

sawbuck "ten dollars" (1850—, US)

fin "five pounds; five dollars" (1868-1992, originally UK), apparently from *finnip* "a five pound note; five dollars" rather than *fin* "hand"

lotion "alcoholic drink" (1876-1997, originally UK)

battle-ax(e) "a scolding woman" (1896—, originally US)

rustle "to steal cattle" (1902—, originally US)

tail "to follow closely" (1907—, developing from the Australian and New Zealand *tail* "to follow cattle" (1844-1890))

cherry "a virgin; virginity" (1918—, originally US)

We don't have to imagine long-tentacled criminal networks to explain the influence of British cant: repeated waves of migration would have ensured that established and new British terms were introduced during this period, and criminals probably had more reason to migrate than other people. The language of New York in particular, the main point of disembarkation, must always have been varied and fluid, with non-standard language developing differently among different ethnic groups.

Early American slang

As long as American English was being measured against British English, *slang* was a very broad category, encompassing slang terms imported from Britain as well as all American innovations. However, early commentators have relatively little to say on the subject. Noah Webster explains the need for *An American Dictionary of the English Language* (1828) by reference to differences in natural habitat and political organization, rather than with reference to colloquial speech and words of recent origin. Even dialectal differences weren't considered desirable: the United States required a unified language. Webster concedes that new words had been coined that weren't acceptable in refined circles:

> But the lexicographer is not answerable for the bad use of the privilege of coining new words. It seems to be his duty to insert and explain all words which are used by respectable writers or speakers, whether or not the words are destined to be received into general and permanent use or not... Lexicographers are sometimes censured for inserting in their vocabularies, vulgar words, and terms of art known only to particular artisans... In this work, I have not gone quite so far as Johnson and Todd have done, in admitting vulgar words. Some of them are too low to deserve notice... As to Americanisms, so called, I have not been able to find many words, in respectable use, which can be so denominated.

Webster's position was that Americans should have their own national standard with a status every bit as high as British English. This aim would have been undermined by the inclusion of slang. Aiming to be less tolerant of slang than Johnson was setting the bar pretty high, but Webster labels a number of terms as 'popular' to indicate their uncertain status, including *close* "stifling (of air)" (1591—), *bright* "clever" (1741—), *average* "arithmetical mean" (1802—), and *deed* "to convey by deed" (1816—, originally US). *Hands off* "keep away" (1563—), *piping* (1823—) or *piping hot* (1568—) "very hot", and *monstrous* "very" (1711-1968, US regional in later use), all of which originated in Britain, are labelled 'vulgar'. Webster doesn't often use the label 'low', but *fun* "pleasure; merriment" (1727—) and *slang* "low vulgar unmeaning language" are outlawed as such.

A rash of extravagant and playfully ostentatious terms from this period may have been a response to this exaggerated respect for linguistic propriety, including *sockdolager* "a powerful blow" (1824-1943), *hornswoggle* "to embarrass; to cheat; to confuse" (1829—), *catawampus* "fierce; destructive; askew" (1840-1917), *callithumpian* "discordant" (*c.*1845-1946), *whangdoodle* "an imaginary beast; an unspecified object" (1858-1979), and *skedaddle* "to retreat hastily" (1860—, originally military). Most have fallen from use, but they're all affectionately remembered.

During his first American tour, in 1842, Dickens was particularly struck by the frequent and various applications of the word *fix*:

'Will you try,' said my opposite neighbour, handing me a dish of potatoes, broken up in milk and butter, 'will you try some of these fixings?'

There are few words which perform such various duties as this word 'fix.' It is the Caleb Quotem [Jack-of-all-trades] of the American vocabulary. You call upon a gentleman in a country town, and his help informs you that he is 'fixing himself' just now, but will be down directly: by which you are to understand that he is dressing. You inquire, on board a steamboat, of a fellow-passenger, whether breakfast will be ready soon, and he tells you he should think so, for when he was last below, they were 'fixing the tables:' in other words, laying the cloth. You beg a porter to collect your luggage, and

he entreats you not to be uneasy, for he'll 'fix it presently;' and if you
complain of indisposition, you are advised to have recourse to Doctor
So-and-so, who will 'fix you' in no time.

For Dickens, *fix* meant "to fasten; to attach; to make firm or constant", in various applications, and usually carried implications of
permanence. These wider uses must have sounded comically over-
wrought to him: perhaps equivalent to a contemporary speaker using
institute or *establish* in similar contexts. *Fix* "to make ready or put in
order" has been used with various applications in the United States
since 1725, but specifically with reference to dressing since 1783, and
the preparation of food since 1830. The sense "to deal with", as used
by the porter, is recorded since 1836, and "to mend" since before
1762, though usually with reference to vehicles and other mechanical
objects rather than people. The *fixings* (1820/1—) in a meal are more
widely known as *(all the) trimmings* (1828—), with both terms
traditionally applying to everything other than the meat. What's
most significant for us, though, is that none of this is slang. Even
Webster admitted *fix* "to make ready" as proper to 'popular use'.
Dickens was struck by the colloquial American use of familiar words,
but his observations of American slang are, like Webster's, extremely
limited. We could interpret this in a variety of ways:

1. there was slang, but these writers had never heard any
2. there was slang and these writers had heard it, but chose not to
   record it
3. there was little difference between the slang used in Britain and the
   United States
4. these writers couldn't distinguish between slang and colloquial
   American English
5. there was no meaningful distinction between slang and colloquial
   American English
6. there was no slang to record.

Figure 16 attempts to answer this question using a random sample of
almost 700 entries from *HDAS*, showing the earliest examples of use

for each term. Grey indicates terms originating in the United States; black is for terms marked as 'non-North American' in origin. This suggests that in the 1820s (when Webster was compiling his dictionary), slang in the United States was broadly similar to British usage. American slang appears to have become increasingly distinctive from the 1840s (when Dickens was writing). By the 1860s, slang terms originating in the United States outnumbered those imported from Britain.

Laurence Oliphant's *Piccadilly* (1865) supports this view of American slang. In this extract, Lord Frank asks a newly arrived American traveller about his acquaintances in London:

> "Well, sir," he said, "I have only been here a few days, and I have seen considerable people; but none of them were noblemen, and they are the class I have to report upon. The Earl of Broadhem, here, is the first with whom I have conversed, and he informs me that he has just come from one of your universities, and that the sympathies of the great majority of your rising youth are entirely with the North."
>
> "You may report to your Government that the British youth of the present day, hot from the university, are very often prigs."
>
> "Most certainly I will," said Mr Wog; "the last word, however, is one with which I am not acquainted."
>
> "It is an old English term for profound thinker," I replied.
>
> Mr Wog took out a pocket-book, and made a note; while he was doing so, he said, with a sly look, "Have you an old English word for 'quite a finegurl'?"
>
> "No," I said; "they are a modern invention."
>
> "Well, sir, I can tell you the one that sat 'twixt you and me at dinner would knock the spots out of some of our 'Sent' Louis belles."

Mr Wog[1] is characterized as American by his use of *considerable* "a large quantity" (1839—, US colloquial) and *knock the spots out of*

---

[1] This name can't be derived from the racially offensive term because that wasn't recorded until 1929. It's more likely to be from *pollywog* "a tadpole" (*c.*1440—, British dialects and US), which had come to mean "a person (especially a politician) who is considered untrustworthy" (1854—, US).

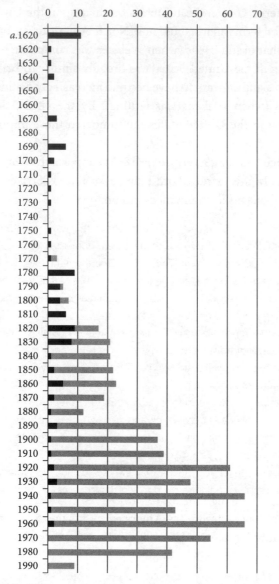

16 New American slang.

(also *off*) "to outdo; to defeat" (1856—, originally US), as well as by his pronunciation of<gurl> and <sent>, but his language is rather stilted and careful. He doesn't use anything that might be called slang until after the sly look. Perhaps because he's trying to avoid seeming vulgarly American, he comes across as pompous and out of touch. He is the one who's stumped by slang, and Frank enjoys misdefining *prig* "a conceited or self-important and didactic person" (1677—) and misrepresenting it as 'an old English term' in standard use. Oliphant may not have been aware that *prig* had been in use with this sense for long enough that it should have been familiar (Webster included it in his dictionary, for example). Because fashionable slang emanated from London at this time, Oliphant's speaker of American English is the one who has to catch up with current usage.

The late nineteenth century

Towards the end of the nineteenth century, there are signs that some British people were beginning to consider American slang to be both distinctive and useful. In 1878, an article in the London *Times* remarked that English slang lacked both wit and clarity, but 'American slang . . . is so palpable and clear that it can almost be called an art by itself'. Among the 'really admirable' American slang terms noted were *bottom dollar* "one's last dollar", used to indicate certainty of outcome (1857—), *pan out* "to conclude (successfully)" (1865—), and *die with one's boots on* "to die a violent death; to die in action or at work" (1873—). The writer particularly commended the clearness of these idioms, in which the hearer had only to understand the context to make sense of the phrase. The contexts, let it be noted, were the gold fields and gambling dens of the Wild West, far from the influence of European norms of speech and behaviour.

Figure 16 suggests a marked increase in new slang, most of it home-grown, towards the end of the nineteenth century, so Walt Whitman was ahead of the *curve* "a deflected trajectory" (1879—, originally baseball) when he wrote 'Slang in America' (1885) in celebration of what he saw as the general human and specifically American impulse to use language creatively. He commented largely on place names and nicknames, but listed a few overheard slang terms, including:

barefoot(ed) "undiluted; unmixed (of a   mystery "hash" (1882-1918)
drink)" (c.1845-1912)   sleeve-button "a codfish ball" (1883-1888)
stars and stripes "ham and beans"   nail "to work as a carpenter" (1885)
(1877/8-1952)   snatcher "a horse car conductor" (1885)

Eight years later, Stephen Crane's worldly-wise Pete impressed the heroine of *Maggie: A Girl of the Streets* with his slang fluency:

"I met a chump deh odder day way up in deh city," he said. "I was goin' teh see a frien' of mine. When I was a-crossin' deh street deh chump runned plump inteh me, an' den he turns aroun' an' says, 'Yer insolen' ruffin!' he says, like dat. 'Oh gee!' I says, 'oh gee! Git off d' eart'!' I says, like dat.... Den deh blokie he got wild... 'Gee!' I says, 'gee! Yer joshin' me,' I says... An' den I slugged 'im. See?"

Non-standard pronunciations are represented by <d> for <th> in *odder, den,* and *dat;* <eh> for unstressed vowels in *deh, teh,* and *inteh;* <'> for missing final consonants in *frien', a-crossin',* and *insolen';* and one dropped <h> in *'im.* Non-standard verb forms include *runned* and *a-crossin.* There's quite a lot of slang too, with *chump* "a fool" (1857—, originally cant), *way* plus preposition "far" (1849—), *plump* "with a sudden impact" (1594—), *turn (a)round* "to change one's stance (from friendly to hostile)" (1822—), *blokie* "a man" (1841—), and *slug* "to hit" (1862—, originally northern), all originating in Britain. *Josh* "to indulge in banter or ridicule" (1845—) and *gee* to express surprise (1851—) originated in the United States.

When James Maitland published his *American Slang Dictionary* in 1891, he took approximately two thirds of his entries from British slang dictionaries, particularly Hotten's, presumably selecting terms he was familiar with in American usage. His additions include some that originated in the United States:

highfalutin "pompous; pretentious" (1839—)

strapped "short of money" (1851—)

bach "a bachelor" (1855—)

potwalloper "a cook; a kitchen-worker (especially on board a ship)" (1859—)

hoodlum "a youthful ruffian" (1871—)

scalper "one who buys and sells (railway) tickets at a profit" (1875—)

angel "a financial backer, especially in the theatre" (1891—)

—but despite these successes, Maitland failed to list many other terms current in American slang:

toot "a drinking spree" (1790—)

brig "a military or naval prison" (1803—)

set-down "a sit-down meal" (1824-1941)

baldface [a type of whisky] (1834-1913)

jism "energy; strength" (1842-1978), developing the sense "semen" (1854—)

dinero "money; cash" (1856—)

pine-top [a type of illicit whisky] *(1858-1985)*

canoodle "to indulge in caresses and fondling endearments" (1864—)

dope "any mixture or drug; heroin; marijuana" (1872—)

God-awful "terrible" (1877—)

keister "a suitcase or bag" (1881-1962)

belly ache "to complain" (1881—)

A body of distinctively American slang had undoubtedly developed during the nineteenth century, but it wasn't possible to record it all because slang wasn't a national phenomenon in this period. Each of these terms must have been used first in a distinct locality or among a restricted group of people: Maitland notes, for example, that *hoodlum* originated in San Francisco. It would have been impossible for him, or anyone else, to travel widely enough or mingle in sufficiently varied social circles to collect them all.

In 1894, a British newspaper discussed American slang in an article in the *Detroit Free Press*, including *stake* "to lend" (1853—), *cop* "a policeman" (1859—), *on one's uppers* "poor" (1886—), *play horse with* "to treat roughly" (1892-1923, from *horseplay* "rough or inappropriate play" (1590—)), *Easy Street* "a comfortable situation" (1894—), and *well-heeled* "having plenty of money" (1894—), which all originated in the United States. Neither the American author of the article nor its British commentator appeared aware that *come down (with)* "to pay" (1700-1877), *mug* "a fool" (1838—), and *lush* "a drunkard" (1851—) had originated in Britain. Similarly, a British reviewer of the *New Century Dictionary* described the following American slang terms and phrases (ironically) as 'charming', 'tasteful', 'polite', and 'elegant': *face the music* "to accept the inevitable blame; to face up to reality" (1824—), *drummer* "a commercial traveller" (1827—), *keep one's eyes skinned* "to remain alert" (1828—, now more usually *keep one's eyes peeled* (1844—)), *splurge* "to make an ostentatious display" (*a*.1848+1888, now more usually "to spend money extravagantly" (1934—)), and *bone-pit* "a cemetery" (1872+1894). Because these terms were selected from a dictionary, they were all fairly well established, but the article also includes *idea-pot* "head" (1751—). This may have been misidentified as American because it's vivid and metaphorical: qualities that were felt to be characteristic of American slang. British reviewers wouldn't necessarily have been authorities on British slang, and it's similarly unlikely that a well-informed chronicler of American slang in this period would have known which terms were also used in Britain. Because speakers of both British and American English were starting to feel that American English was slangy, slang terms were beginning to be attributed to American English regardless of their actual origin, in the same way that we've seen flappers, beats, and other groups being given the credit (or blame) for slang that originated elsewhere.

Even those American writers who conceded that slang enlivens speech and allows for vivid expression generally tended to come down against it. Sherman Malcolm wrote that slang terms:

> are drifting us away into a carelessness of speech or a want of gracefulness in our deportment, which, in the case of many is to be much lamented... others, not quite so fortunate, will be vitiated, debauched, and finally by reading slang novels, slinging slangs and associating with the companions

who use them and love the low dens in which they are nurtured, will be landed into irretrievable ruin.

British commentators from this period were worrying that slang-users lowered themselves socially; American commentators, working within a more flexible social structure, tended to focus more squarely on morality and self-respect:

Still another reason why slang can never gain a permanent foothold in the language is its utter lack of dignity. No subject can be seriously treated in slanguage. Its sole function is to tickle by its patness or its grotesqueness. It reflects a fugitive iridescence upon current wit and humor, but, like the bubble, it vanishes even while you behold it.

Words and phrases objected to by this writer included *sand* "boldness; courage" (1864—),[2] *I should smile*, used to ridicule an idea (1874-1957), *off one's trolley* "crazy" (1896—),[3] and *not on your tintype* "certainly not" (1900—, referring to a photograph taken as a positive on a tin plate). The writer concludes by remarking that although some slang is useful, 'concerning its misuse there can hardly be two opinions among people whose opinions are worth anything'. The people who habitually use slang, he reasons, are the most forceful arguments against it: slang not only causes but also reveals its users' vulgarity.

Specialized and localized slangs

George Ade's *Fables in Slang* were written at the end of the nineteenth century, in the first wave of the 'Chicago Renaissance', which

---

[2] This occurs earlier in the phrase *knock the sand from under (someone)* (1847 +c.1858), but later uses suggest that *sand* is inside, rather than underneath, the courageous individual. It may be related to *grit* "determination; courage" (1825—), also originally US.

[3] This originally referred to trolley-cars (trams), but British users may understand it with reference to *trolleys* that transport patients in hospitals or shopping in supermarkets.

celebrated representations of real life and real language. This extract is from 'The Fable of the Baseball Fan who Took the Only Known Cure':

> Once upon a Time a Base Ball Fan lay on his Death-Bed. He had been a Rooter from the days of Underhand Pitching... More than once he had let drive with a Pop Bottle at the Umpire and then yelled "Robber" until his Pipes gave out. For many Summers he would come Home, one Evening after Another, with his Collar melted, and tell his Wife that the Giants made the Colts look like a lot of Colonial Dames playing Bean Bag in a Weedy Lot back of an Orphan Asylum, and they ought to put a Trained Nurse on Third, and the Dummy at Right needed an Automobile, and the New Man couldn't jump out of a Boat and hit the Water, and the Short-Stop wouldn't be able to pick up a Ball if it was handed to him on a Platter with Water Cress around it, and the Easy One to Third that ought to have been Sponge Cake was fielded like a One-Legged Man with St. Vitus dance trying to do the Nashville Salute.
>
> Of course she never knew what he was Talking about...

Obviously this is exaggerated for comic effect. It's unlikely that anyone would use slang this densely, particularly in conversation with a spouse who's showing neither understanding nor interest. To avoid tedium, sportswriters have to find new ways of saying that someone hit, missed, threw, or caught a ball, and the vivid language of sporting commentaries often finds its way into the conversations of sports fans and then into more general use. *Rooter* "a supporter" (1889—) and *shortstop* "an infielder standing between second and third base" (*c.*1837—) originated in baseball slang, as did *third* (1891—, from *third base* (1845—)) and *right* (1867—, from *right field* (1857—)). However, much of the colourful language used here was general American slang, including many terms that weren't restricted to the United States, such as *let drive* "to aim a blow or missile" (*c.*1380—), *pipes* "the voice; the vocal cords" (1567—), *dummy* "a fool" (1796—), and *pop* "a carbonated drink" (1812—). *Dame* "a woman" (1744—, British dialect and US slang) developed from the sense "the mistress of a household" (*c.*1330-1855). *Sponge* *cake* "something easily accomplished" (1899+1947) wasn't transported to Britain, but a similar image emerged there in the use of *piece of cake* (1936—) with the same meaning. *The Dial* magazine, which had long railed against the danger posed to correct speech by immigrants and the uneducated, reviewed Ade's *Fables* in positive terms, 'conceding that certain kinds of slang were actually of Anglo-Saxon derivation'. Slang may be vulgar, but at least it can be pure.

Sportswriters and enthusiasts weren't the only groups developing their own slang terms. In 1908, a British article on 'Restaurant Slang' described a couple's visit to 'a cheap restaurant' in New York. The man orders his food:

> "Give me two eggs fried on one side and three slices of crisp, broiled breakfast bacon," ordered the man.
>
> "Two cackles slapped in the face and three squeals crisp," howled the waiter while the woman looked aghast...
>
> "What would you like to drink?" he asked.
>
> The woman ordered a cup of coffee with cream, two lumps of sugar, and, of course, a spoon. The man wanted a cup of coffee without cream.
>
> Here is what the waiter ordered –
>
> "Cup of mud, two chunks of ballast, milk the Jersey, and throw in a piece of scrap-iron; draw another in the dark."

Mud "coffee" (1855—), *cackle* "an egg" (1908-1946), *squeal* "bacon; ham" (1908-1949), and *draw one (in the dark)* "pour a (black) coffee" (1886—) all occur in later lists of American restaurant slang. The other terms may have been ad hoc coinages or enjoyed only a limited period of use, but several informal terms originating in restaurant slang are now widely found, including *BLT* "a bacon, lettuce, and tomato sandwich" ([1941]+1952—), *OJ* "orange juice" (1934—), and *sub* "a large sandwich" (1949—, also *submarine* (1955—)).

Other groups were also originating new terms that were spreading into wider use and, sometimes, developing extended meanings. Cowboys were using words like *red eye* "whisky" (1819—), *round up* "the driving of cattle into an enclosure" (1873—), and *wrangler* "one who herds horses or cattle" (1888—) that hovered between slang, dialect, and jargon. Circus and carnival workers were responsible for *plant* "a salesman's confederate who masquerades as a member of the public" (1926—) and *wow* "to impress; to excite" (1924—). It's probable that many other occupational groups were also using words distinctively in this period, particularly newer occupations without a traditional jargon. It should come as no surprise that the groups whose words were documented and disseminated were, on the whole, the glamorous and appealing ones.[4] During the twentieth century, America's film-makers, journalists, and musicians were to bring their own slang, and those of these other groups, to wider public knowledge not only around the world, but also throughout the United States. In a country this vast and varied, syndication and national media outlets were essential to the development of a national slang alongside the specialized and local slang terms developing in America's professions and growing cities (see Chapter 10).

The twentieth century

Until the end of the nineteenth century, American slang received relatively little attention, and relatively little of that was positive. It was only under the influence of broader modernist trends in the early decades of the twentieth century that slang was celebrated for its newness. Sportswriters and journalists weren't the only ones turning away from linguistic conservatism. For example, in 1913 the *University Missourian* published an article citing the opinions of various professors, many of whom argued that slang could be a valuable resource for those who knew how to use it properly:

> There are two kinds of slang—the kind that is a natural expression of a
> vulgar mind, and the kind that is used occasionally by persons of culture as

---

[4] Hoboes might not strike you as particularly appealing, but think factory/office job or family farm in the Depression: hoboes were still living the pioneer life, going where the work was and working only when they needed money.

a form of relief... Even men of classical training occasionally indulge in slang for the sake of humor or local color.

For others, slang was becoming an emblem of equality in contrast with the elitism of written English (still largely conforming to eighteenth-century rules). Another professor commented:

> That particular brand [of slang] that appeals to me most is the kind you get from the working classes... We go in for slang more in this country because it makes its point so quickly and because we usually have a dislike of anything that sounds academic.

The conservative voice remained dominant in American educational circles, however:

> I have always abhorred slang, abhor it now, and shall abhor it as long as I live. I do not like emotions put into language, and a person who uses slang seems to show that he has no rational argument, and that he has to substitute emotion for reason.

Oh dear. Someone was bullied by the cool kids. Although this article is largely theoretical, it does list a few slang phrases, including *get someone's goat* "to irritate (someone)" (1904—) and *I should worry* (1913—, originally Yiddish).

In 1919, when he published the first edition of *The American Language*, Henry Mencken devoted only 8 of his 380 pages to slang. This should come as no surprise. Mencken's purpose, like Webster's, was to enhance the status of American English. His eight pages are largely taken up with theoretical discussions of earlier and current approaches to slang, and although Mencken remarks that American slang deserved greater attention, his own attitudes were hardly more egalitarian than those of his British contemporaries:

> In its origin it is nearly always respectable; it is devised not by the stupid populace, but by individuals of wit and ingenuity... But when its inventions happen to strike the popular fancy and are adopted by the mob, they are soon worn threadbare and so lose all piquancy and significance.

Mencken cites a number of terms that had once seemed slangy but were, by his account, acceptable in Standard American English, including *nice* "agreeable, pleasant; attractive" (1747—), *slacker* "a person who avoids work or exertion" (1898—), *muck-raker* "a scandal monger" (1906—), and *steam roller* "to overwhelm (political opposition)" (1912—). He contrasts these with *shoo-fly* [an expression of annoyance] (1867-1919), *fall for* "to be deceived by" (1903—), *let George do it* "leave it to someone else" (1910—), and *have a heart* "show some pity" (1917—). These, Mencken claims, were perfectly good words and phrases that might have been granted entry to the standard language if they hadn't been so enthusiastically adopted by the vulgar masses.

Slang and gender

Attempts to standardize American English led to high levels of conservative prescriptivism. For example, Jo is berated for using slang in the early pages of Louisa May Alcott's *Little Women* (1868):

> " . . . though we do have to work, we make fun for ourselves, and are a pretty jolly set, as Jo would say."
> "Jo does use such slang words!" observed Amy . . . Jo immediately sat up, put her hands in her pockets, and began to whistle.
> "Don't Jo; it's so boyish!"
> "That's why I do it."
> "I detest rude, unladylike girls!"
> "I hate affected, niminy-pimimy chits!"

A group of relatively well-to-do young women living in a small town aren't obvious candidates as slang innovators, so it should come as no surprise that Jo's slang is made up of well-established terms that she could have encountered in general conversation or in printed sources: *pretty* "fairly" (1565—), *jolly*, which we've already seen, *chit* "a young woman" (*a*.1657-1879), *set* "a select social group" (1780—), and *niminy-piminy* "mincing; affected" (1786—). Perhaps, given Webster's view, *fun* is also being identified as slang here. In the absence of their father, the appearance of propriety is paramount in the March household. As in Britain, the same terms wouldn't have been considered so slangy used by a man.

The careful and occasional use of slang in appropriate contexts was gradually becoming acceptable among educated men by the early twentieth century, but the use of slang by women indicated an unmistakeable lack of refinement. An article in a British newspaper reported that the pupils of a San Francisco ladies' school were campaigning to suppress slang. When asked if this was likely to succeed, their spokeswoman said *You bet!* "absolutely" (1857—). A similar article from the *Rambler*, reprinted in *The Hampshire Telegraph and Sussex Chronicle* in 1885, included an interview in which a Chicago woman responded to the suggestion that women in Chicago used more slang than those in Boston:

> "Come off" she ejaculated playfully. "Take me, for example. I can paw the ivory with the best of 'em. I can warble a few warbs, and I can elocute too. No, sir, I can tell you, Boston girls have got to hustle to keep even with us, and it's very seldom I hear say of the girls use slang. Well, I must go and get ready for the matinée, so, over the river.

The joke, of course, is that the poor vulgar girl doesn't realize how much slang she's using, and this is a criticism still frequently made, on both sides of the Atlantic, of any American who professes to dislike slang. In this case, the offences against propriety include the use of American colloquialisms like *come off* "to desist" (1711-1958, now more usually *come off it* (1920—)), *no sir* "certainly not" (1863—), and *elocute* "to practise elocution" (1884—). The Chicago girl also uses informal language that originated in Britain, such as *with the best of them* "as well as anyone" (1748—), *hustle* "to move quickly" (1821—), and *ivory* "the keys of a piano" (1818—). *Warb* is a slangy clipping of *warble* "to modulate the voice in singing" (1530—), which had been jocular since the mid nineteenth century with the sense "to sing". *Keep even with* "to keep up with" is neither distinctively American nor slang, but perhaps it should be understood with reference to *get even with* "to take revenge on" (1846—, originally US). Also, although they aren't slang, her use of *paw* "to touch", *I can tell you*, *hear say of*, *go and*, and *get ready* were all too informal to be properly ladylike, as was *over the river*, a jocular representation of *au revoir*. Similarly regrettable is the final revelation that the young woman works in the theatre, presumably as a chorus girl. A personification of vulgar pretension, her dubious moral status is revealed by the way she speaks.

Although British readers could bolster their self-esteem by sneering at American slang in this period, some Americans did value it, up to a point:

> There is no especial harm in boys using boys' slang and girls using girls' slang because it is American. But when the girl uses the boys' slang it becomes coarse, and when a boy says a thing is "perfectly lovely" or "simply sweet" you at once set him down as effeminate. As for boys, you may as well let them have it out, for it is a kind of fever; but slang is not so essential to a girl, and fortunately she sooner outgrows it.

Following WWI and the Depression, the United States became increasingly isolationist, and patriotic approval of American styles of speech grew. Qualities that would once have been used to discredit slang terms began to count in their favour: they were American, they were novel, they were witty and irreverent, and they didn't originate with social elites.

African American slang

It's necessary to stop here and take a step backwards in time. I've omitted to mention the one group that has influenced contemporary American (and international English) slang more than any other: African Americans. It would be impossible to discuss the development of American slang without reference to race, in the same way that the history of British slang is infused with issues of class. Educated middle-class youths wanting to sound knowing and cool, have long imitated

17   African American slang: Mark Parisi, 'House Cat Who Thinks He Has Alley Cred'.

the language of those living on the margins: in Britain, the urban working classes; in the US, urban African Americans.

It's impossible to generalize about African American Vernacular English (AAVE) at any single point in history, let alone across the centuries, but there's a long tradition of representing African Americans with a distinctive speech style. Here, for example, Huckleberry Finn and Jim, an escaping slave, discuss King Solomon's approach to mediation:

"I doan k'yer what de widder say, he *warn't* no wise man, nuther. He had some er de dad-fetchedes' ways I ever see. Does you know 'bout dat chile dat he 'uz gwyne to chop in two?"

"Yes, the widow told me all about it."

"*Well*, den! Warn' dat de beatenes' notion in de worl'? You jes' take en look at it a minute. Dah's de stump, dah—dat's one er de women; heah's you—dat's de yuther one; I's Sollermun; en dish-yer dollar bill's de chile. Bofe un you claims it. What does I do? Does I shin aroun' mongs' de neighbours en fine out which un you de bill *do* b'long to, en han' it over to de right one, all safe en soun', de way dat anybody dat had any gumption would? No—I take en whack de bill in *two*, en give half un it to you, en de yuther half to de yuther woman."

There are no prizes for guessing which one's Jim. This representation of AAVE was written by a white man who chose to characterize Jim with numerous non-standard linguistic features: pronunciation (*doan k'yer, de, dat*), double negatives (*he warn't no wise man*), non-standard verb forms and tenses (*I ever see, does you know*), and euphemistic swearing (*dad-fetchedes'*). There's no way of knowing how accurate Twain's representation was because we don't have any objective evidence about how slaves spoke, and even if we did, we couldn't treat it as representative of all slaves. What reliable evidence there is, in recordings of ex-slaves, comes from long after abolition, and it suggests that slaves and their descendants spoke with local dialects not unlike those of their white neighbours. Many linguists no longer subscribe to the idea that AAVE is an African creole created by necessity among speakers of different languages, arguing instead that contemporary AAVE grew out of the concentration of southern dialect forms in black zones in northern cities. Wolfram and Torbert remark that it 'has become a transregional variety that is more ethnically distinct today than it was a century ago'.

Many features of AAVE tended to be categorized as slang until the growth of black radicalism in the 1970s and the Ebonics debates of the late 1990s, but in our terms Jim isn't using much slang. *Shin* "to move quickly" (1838—) and *gumption* "common sense" (1719—) were both colloquial, and *beatenest* "most excellent" (1860—) was dialect. Only *whack* "to share" (1812—), apparently adopted from the language of criminals, may have been slang here. Twain's representation of AAVE fifty years before his own time is driven more by pronunciation and grammar than by a distinctive choice of words.

Although white writers often represented African Americans as illiterate, African Americans generally wrote in formal Standard English, even when they were representing speech. When they did represent AAVE, it was often to emphasize the difference between educated and/or emancipated African Americans and their illiterate and/or enslaved counterparts, rather than to group them together by skin colour. Here Booker T. Washington presents a conversation in which an elderly slave asks a favour of his young master:

> the young man, not having much faith in the ability of the slave to master the guitar at his age, sought to discourage him by telling him: "Uncle Jake, I will give you guitar lessons; but, Jake, I will have to charge you three dollars for the first lesson, two dollars for the second lesson, and one dollar for the third lesson. But I will charge you only twenty-five cents for the last lesson."
>
> Uncle Jake answered: "All right, boss, I hires you on dem terms. But, boss! I wants yer to be sure an' give me dat las' lesson first."

Jake's language isn't signalling that he's black: it's signalling that he's a slave who's been denied the opportunity of an education. If he were educated, like Washington, he would speak and write in Standard American English. The stereotype was used for comic effect by black-faced white (and black) stage-performers and, later on, by Hollywood.

After the abolition of slavery, many African Americans moved from the south to the north in search of a better life. There they were corralled into poor quality housing and low-paid work, generally coming into contact with white America only in subservient roles. If you look back to the favourable conditions for slang development listed in Chapter 3, you'll see that the situation of emancipated African Americans in northern cities fulfilled them almost perfectly. In the 1920s and 1930s, scholars began publishing articles about 'negro language', with a particular interest in recent developments in the north. One commentator, Van Patten, remarked that:

> For seventy-five years, we have been gaining a false impression as to the
> speech of the Negro in America. Hundreds of novels and countless short
> stories have been written by authors with no first-hand knowledge of how
> a Negro speaks…

He sought to rectify this situation by drawing upon recent publications by African American writers, concentrating particularly on works emanating from the 'Harlem Renaissance', listing a number of contemporary slang terms, such as *ofay* "a white person" (1899—), *bull dyke(r)* "a (masculine) lesbian" (1906—), *snow* "cocaine" (1913—), *copacetic* "excellent" (1919—), *happy dust* "heroin; cocaine" (1919—), *hoof* "to dance" (1922—), *faggoty* "homosexual; effeminate" (1927—), and *sweetman* "a pimp" (1928—). Although Van Patten was modern enough to be interested in urban language, he was still relying on literary representations, apparently believing that the language of a small group of writers could be taken as typical.

By the 1930s, it was felt that African American students were using a style of speech that was not only distinct from the language of white American students, but also distinct from the language of other African Americans. Their slang included *hellacious* "outstanding" (1847—), *man* "a policeman; anyone in authority" (1918—), *psyche* "to probe someone's motivations; to outwit" (1929—), *satchel mouth* "someone with a large mouth" (1934—, now generally referring to Louis Armstrong), and *biff(er)* "an unattractive woman" (1934-1980).

Musicians were another group of African Americans who were also using distinctive slang, and some early studies noted their use of the following terms:

number "a recorded track" (used with reference to items in a musical programme 1865—)
cut it "to succeed; to do something well" (1900—)
canary "a female vocalist" (1901—)

jive "misleading or dishonest speech" (1926—)
corny "outdated; unsophisticated; sentimental" (1932—)
jitterbug "a jazz or swing enthusiast" (1934—, now usually historical)
jam "to improvise" (1935—)

These terms, along with others discussed in Chapter 4, could easily have solidified into musicians' jargon, and remained unknown to all but the most enthusiastic fans if it hadn't been for the development of commercial radio, which brought jazz and its language to those white Americans who weren't brave or independent enough to experience it in the flesh.

From black slang to youth slang

In the middle years of the twentieth century, a number of factors came together to create the beginnings of a more or less national youth slang in the United States. Jazz music, and then swing (and later blues, rhythm and blues, rock and roll, soul, disco, and hip hop) brought the slang used by African American musicians to the attention of white youths, sometimes through the mediating influence of white musicians and DJs. This offered a potent form of rebellion, particularly under segregation, causing parents to worry that their pure white daughters would be seduced into a drug-induced frenzy while dancing to hypnotic beats. As long as segregation was still in place, some white music stations refused to play records by black artists, and many southern states imposed racial restrictions on live performances. In the face of these obstacles, a white youth using the latest African American slang acquired an enviable worldly-wise glamour. From the 1940s, we begin to see terms originating in African American slang, particularly in the slang of musicians, being depicted as general youth slang. But this isn't the whole story. This could have been a passing fad if it hadn't been for WWII.

WWI military slang was used by a large number of Americans for a short period; WWII military slang was used much more influentially, by a much larger number of Americans, and for longer. The greater mobilization of the population, women as well as men, clearly played a role in the greater influence of WWII military slang during and after the war, but it was also popularized in films and in morale-boosting journalism. Depictions and descriptions of the young men who were risking their lives for their country brought a mixture of general American and African American slang to wider attention. Entertaining and educational films emphasized the camaraderie that developed among (unrealistically) ethnically mixed servicemen from a wide range of geographical, social, and educational backgrounds. Special Services, the entertainment branch, wasn't segregated, and entertainments organized for military personnel brought live jazz and swing to young men and women who might never have experienced it if they had stayed in their parents' homes. Even if the young people who served during WWII had stopped using these slang terms when they got home, and settled down into proper jobs, it's likely that their younger brothers and sisters would have picked them up from films and records.

But many veterans didn't settle down into proper jobs straight after the war. The G.I. Bill funded college education for many of these slightly older men whose dangerous and exotic experiences gave them a well-founded disrespect for authority, particularly for toothless civilian officials. They must have been irresistibly attractive to female students and to younger males looking for role models. Tertiary education expanded dramatically in the post-war years, and ex-servicemen contributed to a significant change in the nature of university experience in the United States. Veterans of the Korean and Vietnam wars also found their way on to university campuses, and because young men were still subject to the draft, there was a constant interchange of people and slang between these two groups. Moral supervision of students' social lives became a thing of the past, and students' energies became more involved with the social trends and political issues of the world off campus. During the 1960s, an informal journal called *Current Slang* documented their use of terms such as:

dude "a man" (1883–, used earlier with more specific senses)

roach "the butt of a cigarette or joint" (1938–)

prang "a crash" (1944–)

honky "a Caucasian" (1946–)

bash "an attempt" (1948–)

ride shotgun "to sit in the seat next to the driver of a vehicle" (1963–)

all-nighter "an activity that lasts all night" (1964–)

moon "to bare one's buttocks" (1965–)

mega "extremely" (1966–)

As we've seen before, the people given credit for creating new slang don't always deserve it. Among these examples, *bash* appears to have originated in military slang, *prang* in the RAF, *honky* among African Americans, *all-nighter* in the entertainment business, and *roach* among drug-users. *Ride shotgun* and *dude* seem to have been in reasonably wide use by the late 1960s, but it isn't possible to identify their earliest users with any certainty. *Mega* and *moon* may be student coinages from around this period.

There's one final reason why American black/youth slang became so influential and innovative during and after WWII, and that's the growth in consumerism. In constantly striving for the latest new thing, the music and film industries, along with commercial radio and television, advertisers and promoters, did much to promulgate the slang that was already in use, and also sometimes created their own slang in an attempt to appeal to the youth market. Slang can make products seem modern, novel, amusing, intriguing, aspirational, and rebellious, all at once, but it's necessary to renew this appeal to the youth market with great regularity, and this has contributed to a rapid turnover of slang terms in the postwar period. Since WWII, advertisers and the media have used black slang to imbue their products with coolness, and the commercialization of existing slang necessitates the creation of new terms to reestablish the rejection of white values, with these new terms and trends often being commercialized in their turn. Just as fashion-designers have adapted street wear and the music industry has promoted African American musical forms, advertisers have co-opted contemporary African American slang, sometimes operating differently for black and white consumers, to give their products an aura of coolness, modernity, rebellion, and humour. There's more on the influence of the media on slang in Chapter 10.

Other influences on American slang

American English has adopted terms from the many languages spoken by immigrants, including French (e.g. *chowder, prairie*), Dutch (e.g. *boss, coleslaw*), German (e.g. *pretzel, sauerkraut*), and Italian (e.g. *barista, macchiato*). Many of these terms became standard in American English and have been exported to other parts of the English-speaking world. Some American slang has also been borrowed from languages other than English, particularly the languages of later and poorer immigrants. Yiddish provided, among other terms, *nebbish* "a nobody; a loser" (1890—) and "innocuous; ineffectual" (1941—), *potch* "to slap; to smack" (1892—), *boychick* "a boy; a young man" (1921—), *schlump* "a slob; a fool" (1941—), *tsatske* "a trinket; a pretty girl" (1964—), and *schlong* "the penis; a despised person" (1967/8—). It tends to be names from Irish that turn up in American slang, including *mulligan (stew)* "a stew made from whatever is available" (1895—), *Kelly* for a type of hat (1908-1972), *paddy wagon* "a police van or car" (1909—), *the life of Riley* "a luxurious or carefree existence" (1911—), and *Murphy*, referring to a confidence trick (1954-1990).[5] Slang from Spanish, largely Mexican Spanish, includes *bunco* "a swindle" (1872—), *loco* "insane" (1887—), *Tico* "Costa Rican" (1905—), *hoosegow* "prison" (1908—), and *mootah* "marijuana" (1926—).

[5] Daniel Cassidy's *How the Irish Invented Slang* (Oakland, CA: CounterPunch, 2007) suggests Irish etymologies for lots of slang terms whose origins remain obscure (and some that don't). More detailed research is necessary to verify them.

Conclusions

Early commentators who sought to raise the status of American English tended to ignore or disown slang terms. Towards the end of the nineteenth century, and especially in the early twentieth century, writers began to argue in favour of American slang, and a greater openness to linguistic innovation developed, with slang sometimes becoming a symbol of national identity. The driving forces in the development of American slang in the twentieth century were urbanization, segregation and continued inequality after the civil rights era, the expansion of higher education, the G.I. bill, and the development of mass media and advertising. American slang has undoubtedly been nurtured by inequality and consumerism, but it has also functioned as a voice of protest against establishment values. Although linguistic prescriptivism remains a powerful force in the United States, American slang is often held up as an emblem of the creativity and vigour of its users. As we shall see in the remaining chapters, American influence was to be central to the development of English slang around the world in the post-war period.

Endnotes

Figure 16 was constructed by taking the earliest citation for the first full entry on each odd-numbered page in *HDAS*, producing a sample size of 699, with the decrease in the 1990s reflecting the dictionary's publication dates. First citations marked with an asterisk are represented in black. The graph doesn't tell us anything about frequency of use and it may reveal more about the documentation than the use of slang.

The first quotation is from Gunnel Tottie, *An Introduction to American English* (Oxford: Blackwell, 2002), 103, who describes slang as 'an important phenomenon', but devotes only two pages to it. The development of American dialects is discussed in Walt Wolfram and Ben Ward (eds.), *American Voices: How Dialects Differ from Coast to Coast* (Oxford: Blackwell, 2006). Walt Wolfram and Benjamin Torbert are quoted from their chapter in this book, 'When Linguistic Worlds Collide (African American English)', 225–32 (231). The origins of AAVE remains a contentious subject, but both sides of the argument are represented in Sonja L. Lanehart (ed.), *Sociocultural and Historical Contexts of African American English* (Amsterdam: John Benjamins, 2001).

The lists of criminal and tramps' language mentioned were *A Narrative of the Life, Adventures, Travels and Sufferings of Henry Tufts* (Dover, NH: Samuel Bragg, 1807), Glossary, Matsell's *Vocabulum*, Josiah Flynt Willard's *Tramping with Tramps* (London: T. Fisher Unwin, 1899) and *The World of Graft* (London/ New York: McClure, Phillips & Co., 1901), and Henry Leverage's 'Flynn's Dictionary of the Underworld', *Flynn's* 3–6 (3 Jan.–2 May 1925), Vol. 3: 690–3, 874–7, 1056–7; Vol. 4: 118–19, 488–9, 664–5, 868–9, 1150–1; Vol. 5: 191–2, 280–1, 511–12, 660–1, 818–19, 968–9; Vol. 6: 116–17, 211–12, 426–7.

Extracts in this chapter are from Noah Webster, *An American Dictionary of the English Language*, 2 vols. (New York: S. Converse, 1828), 'Introduction'; Charles Dickens, *American Notes* (London: Chapman & Hall, 1842), Ch. 10; and Laurence Oliphant, *Piccadilly* (Edinburgh: W. Blackwood and Sons, 1870), Part I, 'Love', first published in *Blackwood's Magazine* in 1865. Whitman's 'Slang in America' is from his *Complete Prose Works* (Whitefish, MT: Kessinger, 2004), 445–9. Also quoted is Stephen Crane's *Maggie: A Girl of the Streets* (New York: Appleton, 1896), 46–7, first published in 1893. James Maitland's *American Slang Dictionary* was privately printed in Chicago (1891). The review of the *New Century Dictionary* is from 'American Slang', *The Weekly Standard and Express*, 19 Aug. 1899, 3, and the comparison between British and American slang from 'Slang', *The Star*, 3 Apr. 1875, n.p. The same article appeared in *The Morning Post* (3 Apr.), *Trewman's Exeter Flying Post* (14 Apr.), *The Dundee Courier and Argus* (26 Apr.), and *The Times* (30 May), demonstrating the appeal of slang to journalists under pressure to fill a column. Sherman Malcolm bemoans the use of slang in *The American Slangist* (Blenheim, Ont.: n.p., 1888), 5–6, and its lack of dignity is remarked upon in 'A Study in Current Slanguage', *The San Francisco Call*, 31 Oct. 1897, 23. Also quoted are George Ade's *Fables in Slang* (Chicago & New York: Stone, 1899), 27–30, and its evaluation by *The Dial* from Lisa Woolley, *American Voices of the Chicago Renaissance* (Dekalb: Northern Illinois University Press, 2000), 30.

Other sources were 'Restaurant Slang', *Penny Illustrated Paper and Illustrated Times*, 10 Oct. 1908, 234; 'What They Say about Slang', *University Missourian* 80, 17 Dec. 1913, 2 (three quotations); 'A Society for the Suppression of Slang', *The Penny Illustrated Paper and Illustrated Times*, 22 Feb. 1873, 115; 'A Chicago Girl's Slang', *Hampshire Telegraph and Sussex Chronicle*, 7 Nov. 1885, 1; and 'Slang in Women's Colleges', *New York Tribune*, 19 Jan. 1901, 7. Other extracts are from H. L. Mencken's *The American Language* (New York: Knopf, 1919), 308; Louisa May Alcott's *Little Women* (Boston: Roberts, 1868), Ch. 1 (quoted first in Adams, *Slang*, 78–9); Mark Twain's *Adventures of Huckleberry Finn* (New York: Century, 1884), Ch. 14; and Booker T. Washington's *Up From Slavery* (Garden City, New York: Doubleday, 1901), Ch. 6. Recordings of ex-slaves are available at the Library of Congress: *Voices from the Days of Slavery* <http:// memory.loc.gov/ammem/collections/voices>. This chapter also quotes from

Nathan Van Patten's 'The Vocabulary of the American Negro as Set Forth in Contemporary Literature', *American Speech* 7 (1931), 24–31 (24), and cites terms from Hugh Sebastian's 'Negro Slang in Lincoln University', *American Speech* 9 (1934), 287–90 (290); Russel B. Nye's 'A Musician's Word-List', *American Speech* 12 (1937), 45–8; and H. Brook Webb's 'The Slang of Jazz', *American Speech* 12 (1937), 179–84. Adams, *Slang*, 55–78, offers an interesting account of the current use of African American slang. Student slang is from Stephen H. Dill and Clyde Burkholder's *Current Slang: A Biennial Cumulation* (Vermillion: University of South Dakota, Department of English, 1969), with a second biennial collection edited by Dill and Donald Bebeau in 1970.

9 Bludgers, Sooks, and Moffies: English Slang around the World

As we've seen in the last chapter, before there was a clear sense of what Standard American English was, it was difficult to determine the status of informal American terms. This distinction can be harder still with reference to other national forms of English, particularly where there's still no codified national variety to act as a standard of correctness. The competing authority of British and American English complicate the picture still further.

Australian cant and slang

Speakers of various dialects of British English were transported to Australia between 1788 and 1868. Others went voluntarily to control the prisoners, and governors were appointed to oversee the development of these new colonies. Along with these varied roles, the values and social structure of Britain were transported to the other side of the world, complicated by the fact that people's new roles didn't always correspond with their relative status back home. Some free migrants considered themselves better than convicts and the descendants of convicts. Some of those who were Australian-born considered themselves better than migrants who'd just arrived. Words such as *walkabout* "a journey on foot in the bush" (1897—) and *currawong* [a type of bird] (1911—) were adopted by necessity from pidgin English and aboriginal languages, and some existing words were redefined, such as *run* "to graze (cattle, sheep, etc.)" (1795—), *sterling* "an individual born in Britain" (1825—, historical in later use), and *currency* "a native-born white Australian" (1824—, historical in later use). As in the United States, new and unfamiliar terms were often considered to be slang merely because they weren't part of standard British English, but new arrivals were expected to adapt to established patterns of behaviour, and the acquisition of Australianisms was to become a conspicuous symbol of the acceptance of Australian values of egalitarianism, irreverence, and informality.

Early commentators remarked on the purity of Australian English, as the varied dialects and accents of the first generation were levelled out in the second. A distinctive Australian accent was first remarked upon in the early nineteenth century, but it wasn't until the end of the century that vigorous attempts were made to promote Received Pronunciation in Australia, with a corresponding decline in the status of Australian accents. In 1892, a newspaper commented that 'it will come to many Australians as a surprise to find that they have a distinct accent of their own', which 'like all peculiarities of pronunciation, has little to recommend it'. Linguists now divide Australian accents into cultivated, general, and broad, representing a continuum from Received Pronunciation to the strongest Australian accents. The second half of the twentieth century saw a significant shift away from the cultivated to the general accent, but it took several more decades before distinctively Australian accents and words again became a source of pride rather than an embarrassing indication of low social status and lack of education.

Some of the earliest dictionaries of non-standard language in Australia concentrated on the language of criminals in a pattern we've seen before, in both Britain and America, but we might expect the language of criminals to be particularly prominent in a penal colony. James Hardy Vaux's *Memoirs* (written in 1812, published in

1819) suggest that, in the early years, British-born convicts continued to use the cant they had learnt before transportation. Vaux lists:

> AWAKE, an expression used on many occasions; as a thief will say to his accomplice, on perceiving the person they are about to rob is aware of their intention, and upon his guard, stow it, the cove's awake. To be awake to any scheme, deception, or design, means, generally, to see through or comprehend it.
>
> NAIL, to nail a person, is to over-reach, or take advantage of him in the course of trade or traffic; also, to rob, or steal; as, I nail'd him for (or of) his reader, I robbed him of his pocket-book; I nail'd the swell's montra in the push, I picked the gentleman's pocket of his watch in the crowd, &c. A person of an over-reaching, imposing disposition, is called a nail, a dead nail, a nailing rascal, a rank needle, or a needle pointer.

Much of this language is familiar from the British publications cited in earlier chapters. *Awake* "alert", *cove* "a man", *nail* "to steal", *swell* "a fashionably or stylishly dressed person", *reader* "a pocket book", and *push* "a crowd" were all derived from British slang or cant of the period. *Needle* (1790+1821) and *nail* (1819-1823), both meaning "a cheat; a cheating gamester", are also recorded in British cant. We could hardly expect that British criminals would stop using terms they were familiar with just because a judge had seen fit to send them to the other side of the world, particularly when the trip was likely to bring them into close contact with other users of the same terms. Vaux's *Memoirs* describe his return to England and transportation twice more, indicating that transported felons weren't as isolated from current British speech as the geographical distance might suggest. Vaux's glossary tells us as much about the speech of criminals in London as Australia, but some of his terms hadn't been recorded before in the way he defines them, and these may indicate changes that had taken place in or on the way to Australia. For example, *stow* "to stop talking" (1567—) is recorded in Harman's *Caveat*, but Vaux provides the first citation for the broader sense "to stop". *Montra* "a watch" is recorded only by Vaux and later dictionaries.

The play *Life in Sydney* (1843) was written in response to the success of Egan's *Life in London*. Newly arrived Jerry, who is 'up to the knowing ones at home, but sadly out of order here', has only just learnt that *twig* means "to understand" (*a.*1790—) when he hears another unfamiliar term:

Jerry: I say Tom what does he mean by office?

Tom: Why you see Jerry, this is Dan's private friend's room, and as the big-wigs are so devilish moral here, a game of cards is almost equal to high treason. In short, Bill's station is to give us the wink if any of the traps should walk in.

Jerry: I twig, a wink's as good as a nod to a blind horse....

Twig, office "a warning; a signal" (1759—, from sporting slang), *big-wig* "a person of high standing" (1703—), *devilish* "excessively" (1612—), *the wink* "a surreptitious (glance or movement of the eye as a) signal" (1757—), and *trap* "a thief-taker; a policeman" (1705 , historical in later use) were all well established in the language of British criminals. Their wider use in Australian English was an inevitable product of the penal settlements, but they wouldn't have been amusing in this play if they were acceptable in all Australian contexts.

The gold rushes of the 1850s brought new waves of settlers, particularly from the United States. Many miners who'd given up on the Californian goldfields decided to try their luck, and by the time Cornelius Crowe documented Australian criminals' language in 1895, they appear to have been using several terms that originated in the United States:

LYNCH LAW, the American manner of quickly getting rid of evil-doers (1811—)

ABSQUATULATE, to disappear; to decamp (1830—)

BUNKUM, talking nonsense ("tall talk; humbug", 1847—)

However, Crowe also included a flash letter, which could easily have been written by a contemporary British thief:

Church Bill,
Meet me at net to darkman in blooming slum near the old padding ken to dispose of the swag. I know a lavender-cove and a swag chovey bloke that will take some of the white yacks. We must get a thimble faker to christen and church the redge yacks. I gave a shickster's red thimble and slang and a cat to my mollishe[r] for stalling while we cracked the faker's chovey ...

We've already seen *darkman(s)* "night", *swag* "stolen property", *bloke* "a man", *yack* "a watch", *shickster* "a promiscuous woman", *slang* "a watch chain", and *mollisher* "a woman; a girlfriend; a prostitute". We've observed criminals *cracking* houses, *churching* watches, and *stalling* for their associates. Other terms also found in British sources include:

blooming [in swearing] (*c*.1850–)	*thimble* "a watch" (1795-1901)
slum "a narrow alley surrounded by squalid housing" (1845–)	*faker* "one who creates fakes or forgeries" (*c*.1845–)
padding-ken "a lodging house" (1839–, now historical)	*christen* "to re-engrave a stolen watch" (1753-1901)
chovey "a shop" (1791-1882)	*cat* "a muff" (1839)

Redge "silver" appears to have arisen by confusion between *wedge* "silver" and *ridge* "gold", both of which we've seen in eighteenth-century English cant. *Ridge* developed the sense "genuine" in Australia (1938–), and was later expanded to *ridgy-didge* (1953–), with the same meaning. *Red* had referred to gold and *white* to silver since the Old English period, but they both appear to have been restricted to cant by this date. There's no independent evidence for *church* "dear", *net* "ten" (from back slang), or *lavender-cove* "a pawnbroker". Whether or not we believe Crowe's letter is a genuine example of Australian criminals' language, there's little evidence of distinctively Australian cant from this period.

Thomas Browne (1826-1915), who wrote under the pseudonym 'Rolf Boldrewood', was born in London and moved to Sydney as a child. His *Robbery Under Arms* makes careful use of non-standard language to characterize an individual living a less than respectable life. It begins:

> My name's Dick Marston, Sydney-side native. I'm twenty-nine years old, six feet in my stocking soles, and thirteen stone weight. Pretty strong and active with it, so they say. I don't want to blow — not here, any road — but it takes a good man to put me on my back, or stand up to me with the gloves, or the naked mauleys. I can ride anything — anything that ever was lapped in horsehide — swim like a musk-duck, and track like a Myall black-fellow. Most things that a man can do I'm up to, and that's all about it. As I lift myself now I can feel the muscle swell on my arm like a cricket ball, in spite of the — well, in spite of everything.

Colloquial phrases like *with it*, *so they say*, *up to* "capable of" (1785—), and *any road* "anyway" (1896—) suggest that Marston hasn't been taught to write in a formal style, creating a sense of unvarnished revelation and intimacy. Boldrewood doesn't represent non-standard features of grammar or pronunciation, but he characterizes Marston as Australian by what he says as well as by how he says it. *Blow* "to boast" (*c*.1420—), *blackfellow* "an Australian aboriginal" (1738—), *native* "a white person born in Australia" (1806—), and *Sydney-side* "the Sydney area" (1888—) were all restricted to Australia and New Zealand at this time, though *blow* and *blackfellow* had once been more widely used.

Although it was necessary for English to develop to express new conditions in Australia, many Australians were starting to be embarrassed by deviations from Standard British English. A letter published in *The Sydney Morning Herald* in 1894 distinguished between linguistic developments that were 'lawful and reasonable' responses to differences in climate and geography, and those developments that arose from an unreasoning fondness for innovation:

> Democracy . . . like childhood, is eager for novelty. There is great joy to a child in repeating an oath which he has heard by chance; the more so that in his desperately wicked little soul he feels it to be naughty. Fresh terminology, that of the music-hall and the market, is full of charm for those

who, feeling no responsibility in their precious inheritance of speech, delight to flout the old and reverend.

Objectionable terms included:

township "a prospective town; a village" (1790—)

bush "uncultivated open countryside" (1803—)

new chum "a newly arrived convict; a recent immigrant" (1819—)

down "a grudge" (1828—)

spell "a rest period" (1831—)

bail up "to rob (on the highway)" (1838—)

stick up "to rob (on the highway)" (1843—)

rouseabout "an (unskilled) employee on a sheep station" (1861—)

(old) identity "a person who is a long resident or well known in a place" (1862—)

push "a gang of hooligans or criminals" (1866—, originally American)

larrikin "a hooligan" (1868—)

jackaroo "an inexperienced colonist working on a sheep station to gain experience" (1870—)

give (someone) best "to concede defeat" (1888—)

The objections are largely on the grounds of etymology, sense, and utility, though the consistency with which the writer picks out Australian terms suggests that it's really national innovations that offend him. Length of use didn't qualify these terms for approval: although most had been in use for many decades, this writer still considered them illegitimate.

Following an exchange in *The Argus* (Melbourne), in which parents and teachers objected to children being asked to correct examples of idiomatic Australian English lest they be contaminated by it, *The Western Australian* (Perth) published an exchange on the subject of grown men using slang:

To listen to these up-to-date men one would suppose that they had graduated in Whitechapel, London, or the High-street of Edinburgh, instead of having spent their lives in a great many instances in the Australian bush. True, in years gone by, the boy had a language of his own mostly confined to the playground, but which he gave up as he did the playing of marbles and top-spinning, as something too childish for one coming to years of discretion. Such, however, is not the case now, as you may daily hear middle-aged men speaking about "chucking" their job, or being "out of collar". It is pitiful and almost painful to hear expressions such as these used by hard-working well-meaning men, and the only wonder is that a habit so silly should not be more frequently and vigorously protested against.

This writer objects to vulgarisms newly imported from Britain, including *jude* (1887—) for *judy* (1819—) "a woman", *peg out* "to die" (1852—), *screw* "salary; wages" (1858—), *collar* "regular employment" (1862—), *chuck (out/up/over)* "to dismiss; to discharge; to resign" (1869—), and *trot (out)* "to escort (a woman)" (1888—). As in the last extract, the writer has an accurate sense of which terms are Australian.

A greater pride in informal Australianisms developed with the growth of nationalistic feelings during and after WWI. In 1915, C. J. Dennis published a book of verses that had previously appeared in the *Sydney Bulletin*, called *Songs of a Sentimental Bloke*. Dennis wrote of the trials and tribulations of a young working man who falls in love, marries, and, in a later volume, serves in the war. Written in colloquial Australian English, *Sentimental Bloke* was a huge success. In this extract, Dennis's narrator bemoans the uncertainty of love:

THE world 'as got me snouted jist a treat;
Crool Forchin's dirty left 'as smote me soul;
An' all them joys o' life I 'eld so sweet
Is up the pole.
Fer, as the poit sez, me 'eart 'as got
The pip wie yearnin' fer—I dunno wot.

I'm crook; me name is Mud; I've done me dash;
Me flamin' spirit's got the flamin' 'ump!
I'm longin' to let loose on somethin' rash . . .
Aw, I'm a chump!
I know it; but this blimed ole Springtime craze
Fair outs me, on these dilly, silly days.

Unlike Boldrewood, Dennis used non-standard spellings to represent non-standard pronunciation. The sentimental bloke speaks broad Australian: he drops 'h's (*'as, 'eld, 'eart*), simplifies final consonant clusters (*an', yearnin', flamin'*), and pronounces *blamed* "blasted" (1838—) as <blimed>. Dennis could have indicated broad pronunciations for more words, but only at the cost of making his verses harder to read.

There are also a few non-standard grammatical features: *me* (for *my*), *smote* (for *smitten*), *them* (for *those*), and the use of *is* following a plural subject. The *OED* labels *a treat* "extremely well" (1898—) as colloquial. *Left* (1898—) abbreviates the boxing term *left hook* "a punch with the left arm bent" (1898—), and *out* "to knock out" (1896-1951) was also boxing slang. *Up the/a pole* has been used with various senses since its first appearance in military slang: "in favour" (1890), "in confusion; in trouble" (1896—), "teetotal" (1899/ 1900-1944), "drunk" (1897-1922), "crazy" (1904—), and "pregnant" (1918—). Here it appears to mean "destroyed" or "lost". *Get the pip* "to become depressed, unwell, or irritated" (1837/8—) comes from the name of a poultry ailment, now more commonly found in *give the pip* "to annoy or irritate" (1896—). Terms also used in Britain include *the hump* "a fit of ill humour" (1727—), *his/her* (etc.) *name is mud* (1823—), and others already discussed. None of this is specifically or even characteristically Australian, though these terms all contribute to the creation of a character who's down to earth and unspoilt by education.

Specifically or usually Australian terms in this verse include *dilly* "silly" (1873—), *flaming* [in swearing] (1885—), *crook* "out of sorts; unwell; angry" (1906—), *snout* "to treat with disfavour" (1913-1981), and *do one's dash* "to fall in love" (1915-1919), related to the more frequent *have a dash* "to make an attempt" (1843—). *Fair* had been used adverbially with the sense "completely" since *c.*1330, but had been non-standard in Britain since the mid nineteenth century. The Director of Education in Victoria asked Dennis where he learnt all this slang:

'Four-fifths of the people of Victoria talk it and seven-eighths of the children in your schools.' He was surprised. I think he did not like what I said. You see he had moved amongst people who talked correctly. But...some months afterwards he came to me and said, 'I believe you are nearly right.'

Newspaper coverage of slang in Australia changed during WWI. No longer was slang merely a sign of vulgarity: it came to represent vitality, virility, and defiantly high morale in the face of unimaginable danger. As Australia's sons died for the Empire, particularly in the disastrous Gallipoli campaign, loyalties began to shift and a more positive sense of national identity developed. This article quotes a report from London's *Pall Mall Gazette*:

The Australians are not very rich in slang...but the following conversation I caught the other day might prove mystifying to the uninitiated.
"Hullo, —chum! I've just heard some bonza news."
"What! Another furfie?" "No, dinkum oil this time; the boys have imshied the Turks on the right, and got fifty prisoners, who say they have had mafeesh tucker for two days."...

Hullo and *chum* might both have been used in this way by a speaker of British English, and a British soldier might have learnt both *imshi* "to hurry (someone) along" (1915-1918, more usually "to hurry; to go away" (1815—)) and *mafeesh* "finished; none; good for nothing" (1855-1931, usually as a free-standing interjection) from Arabic. However, *tucker* "food" (1858—), *bonzer* "good" (1904—), *dinkum oil* "true information" (1915—), and *furphy* "a (false) rumour" (1915—, from Furphy water carts) were all distinctively Australian slang. Far from being a source of shame, this slang provided a bond between Australian troops and became emblematic of their stoicism and sacrifice.

There are several glossaries of the slang used by Australian soldiers in WWI, including one compiled after the war at the Australian War Museum (now Memorial). Distinctively Australasian terms in this list include:

shivoo "a celebration; a disturbance" (1844–)

cow "an objectionable person, thing, or situation" ([1864]+1891–)

dag "a tough, eccentric, or amusing individual" (1875–)

(fair) dinkum "good; genuine; honest" (1894–)

cliner "a girl; a sweetheart" (1895–)

inked "drunk" (1898-1969)

fair go "fair treatment; a fair chance" (1899–)

banjo "a shovel" (1900/10–)

put the acid on "to exert pressure on" (1906–)

give it a burl "to have a go" (1917–)

gutzer "a heavy fall" (1918–)

put the hard word on "to ask for an unlikely favour" (1918–)

chop "a share" (1919–)

Although Australian cities, and particularly Sydney, were clearly seeing the beginnings of Australian slang, WWI played a major role in its spread, development, and documentation, as well as in the developing belief that Australian English was, and ought to be, distinctive.

In the interwar period, Australian newspapers focused on the undesirable influence of American slang on Australian speech. Professor Stable, chair of English literature at the University of Queensland, argued that the use of Americanisms was a 'passing phase':

> He had no objection to the use of "native" slang with discrimination and moderation. In distinction from foreign words that entered into the common speech, without a local or apt application, it might express the thoughts and feelings of the people within their own conditions and environment. In the development of the language, words might be incorporated which expressed an accepted meaning, and in time ceased to be slang.

Stable felt that parents who spoke incorrectly were the main obstacle that teachers faced in improving the speech of their pupils. Standard British English was still the ideal being taught, despite an incipient grass-roots consensus that Australian English was actually better: more down to earth, more practical, and more masculine.

18 Australian and New Zealand slang: Park Kendall, *Dictionary of Service Slang*
(New York: Mill, 1944), n.p.

The tendency to consider national forms as slang persisted later in
Australia than in the US. Sidney J. Baker presented a broad and
contradictory definition of *slang* to justify the contents of his *Popular
Dictionary*:

> Slang is too small a word to describe the evolution of a new way of
> speaking, of a national idiom. But it is a flexible term, and for the purpose
> of this brief dictionary it must be taken to include many Australian expres-
> sions that have long since ceased to be slang in the strict sense of that word
> and have become "standard." It even includes a few of those many indige-
> nous terms which probably never were slang, but which became part of
> our speech without any probationary period. And it includes also some
> still-born expressions which flourished ephemerally. They are included to
> show that Australia has something to say for herself that extends a good
> deal past the limitations of a few sickly colloquialisms of the bonzer-
> dinkum-strike-me-up-a-gum-tree brand.

In order to compile even a small dictionary of Australian slang at this
period, then, it was necessary to include obsolete words and words
that, although Australian, were no longer slang or never had been. In

fact, Baker cut out various terms in later editions when he realized they weren't distinctively Australian. Why, if there was so little genuine Australian slang to document, did Baker bother compiling a dictionary of it? And why did it sell well enough to go through several editions? Part of the answer must lie in Churchill's failure to defend Australia against a feared Japanese invasion: although Australian troops were fighting for the Empire, once again, in Europe, the defence of Australia wasn't considered a strategic priority. Just as Australia was breaking its emotional ties with Britain, American troops flooded in. As in Britain, the Americans were greeted with a mixture of gratitude and resentment: some Australians enthusiastically adopting American slang, others standing firm against it. Britain's entry into the European Economic Community gave a further boost to Australian nationalism. These shifting and conflicting affinities changed the balance between different forms of English in Australia and, as speakers with cultured accents were gradually outnumbered by those with general accents, distinctive Australian terms and American slang also came to be more widely used.

This has led to a curious dichotomy in discussions of Australian English. Scholars often avoid using *slang* altogether, arguing that Australian English is, by its nature, so informal that it's impossible to distinguish meaningfully between slang and colloquialisms, while popular writers often label all distinctively Australian words (and sometimes also pronunciations and grammatical features) as slang:

> Australians don't seem to evolve their own language. For example, from the highly scientific standpoint of observing my wife, I've noticed the Australian slang and idioms (from the Latin "idiom", meaning "drinking beer and talking a lot") she uses are identical to those her parents used. Nothing new developed over a generation.

It's certainly true that Australian English tends towards greater informality than British English, and probably also American English, but no matter how informal a term is, if everyone knows and uses it, it's colloquial rather than slang. Nevertheless, traditional Australian terms are endowed with the values normally associated with slang:

> Young city people rarely greet each other in the time-honoured Australian way: "G'day mate." These days it is likely to be: "Hi guys" or "Hey dude", grating imports from the United States.... How often, these days, do we hear words like ... bludger, drongo, ... sheila, ... jiffy, strewth, ... arvo and Buckley's? Most people in the older generations know what they mean, but already they are lost among the young. How sad.

This writer blames the dominance of American film and television and the underfunding of the Australian media for the decline in traditional Australianisms, but he also identifies multiculturalism as a cause of this decline. Terms like *jiffy* "a moment" (1785—, originally UK), *sheila* "a girl; a young woman" (1839—, originally Irish), *strewth* "God's truth" (1883—, originally UK), *Buckley's (hope/chance)* "a forlorn hope" (1895—), *bludger* "a hanger-on; a sponger" (1900—), *arvo* (1927—), and *drongo* "a fool" (1941—) have come to be symbolic of a particular version of Australian national identity, and Australian teenagers who want to seem modern or to rebel against their parents can do so most effectively by using other slang terms.

Since neither British nor American slang is pure of external influence, there's no reason to think that Australian slang should (or could) be. A recently updated glossary of 'Australian slang' on a website called *Koala Net* is designed to help the tourist 'feel at home on your first day Down Under'. Of its almost 500 words, many are derived from British dialects, including:

whinge "to complain" (*a.*1150—)
wag (off) "to play truant" (1848—)
fossick "to hunt about (for)" (1853—)
spiffy "smart; excellent" (1853—)

chook (also *chookie, chucky*) "a chicken" (1855—)
lolly "any piece of confectionary; a sweet; a candy" (1864—)
boozer "a pub" (1895—)

Plenty of others originated in the United States, including:

knock "to criticize" (1860–)	*moolah* "money" (1939–)
cream "to kill; to defeat decisively" (1929–)	*veg (out)* "to relax or do nothing" (1967/8–)
dog "an unattractive woman" (1937–)	*boogie board* "a small surfboard" (1976–)

The American terms are generally later than the British ones, and most have also spread to Britain. It may well be that the compilers of the list weren't aware that these terms originated outside Australia, but they may have taken the view that if a term is slang and it's used in Australia then it's Australian slang no matter where it was coined. Omitting terms that originated outside Australia from this list would be doing a disservice to tourists who were unfamiliar with British or American slang.

Conversely, many of the Australian terms in the list have been exported to other parts of the English-speaking world. I've heard all of these Australian slang terms used unselfconsciously by speakers of British English:

knockback "a disappointment; a refusal" (1898–)	*earbash* "to talk too much (to)" (1944–)
uni "university" (1898–)	*no-hoper* "a born failure" (1944–)
Aussie "an Australian" (1917–)	*perv* "a pervert" (1948–)
too right "certainly; definitely" (1918–)	*in the nuddy* "in the nude" (1953–)
plonk "cheap wine" (1933–)	*rubbish* "to criticize or denigrate" (1953–)
perv "to look (at) lecherously" (1941–)	*dob on/in* "to inform against" (1954–)
	no worries "no problem" (1967–)

The *Koala Net* list also reveals the difficulty of distinguishing between levels of use in Australia. Colloquial and standard terms in the list include *brumby* "a wild horse" (1880—), *wowser* "a strait-laced person; a spoilsport; a teetotaller" (1899—), and *outback* "the interior of Australia" (1904—). Several are now restricted to historical and self-consciously Australianized use. These include *jumbuck* "a sheep" (1824—), *Matilda* "a sleeping roll carried by an itinerant worker" (1892—), and *come the raw prawn* "to attempt to deceive" (1940—). *Dinky-di* "genuine" (1916—) is now more often used with the sense "unconvincingly or self-seekingly Australian".

A striking feature in this list is the number of abbreviations ending with *-ie* or *-y*, which is often identified as a distinctive feature of Australian slang (or colloquialism). These include:

bushie "a dweller in the outback" (1885—)
possie "a position" (1915—)
blowey "a blowfly" (1916—)
coldie "a cold beer" (1953—)
esky (generic use of a brand name) "a cool box" (1953—)
truckie "a truck-driver" (1958—)

kindy "kindergarten" (1959—)
surfie "a surfer" (1962—)
pokie "a poker machine; a slot machine" (1965—)
Chrissy "Christmas" (1966—)
greenie "an environmentalist" (1973—)
sunnies "sunglasses" (1981—)

Some have spread to British English, including:

footy "(Australian rules) football" (1906—)
mozzie "a mosquito" (1917—)
chewie "chewing gum" (1924—)
cozzie "a swimming costume" (1926—)
hottie "a hot water bottle" (1947—)

sickie "a sick day taken dishonestly" (1953—)
lippy "lipstick" (1955—)
u-ey "a u-turn" (1967/8—)

The *Koala Net* list also includes a few *-ie* abbreviations that originated in Britain, including:

brekkie "breakfast" (1904—)
choccy "chocolate" (1918—)
rellie "a relative" (1921—)
bikkie "biscuit" (1930—)

prezzie "a present" (1933—)
veggy "a vegetable" (1955—)
trackie(s) "a tracksuit" (1986—)

In British usage these are usually childish forms, though occupational names with the same ending belong in general colloquial language rather than in the nursery, including *postie* "a postman" (1871—) and *brickie* "a bricklayer" (1873—). In this list, only *polly* "a politician"

(1932—) appears to have originated in the United States, presumably by clipping. These British and American terms may have merged with the Australian stream in Australia or been reinvented there.

A smaller group of abbreviated terms in the *Koala Net* list end in *-o*, another distinctively Australian form:

smoko "a (smoke) break" (1865—)

Salvo "(a member of) the Salvation Army" (1891—)

bottle-o "a collector of empty bottles" (1898—), now more usually "a shop selling alcohol" (1997—)

milko "a milkman" (1905—)

kero "kerosene" (1930—)

metho "methylated spirits" (1933—)

compo "compensation" (1938—)

reffo "refugee" (1941—)

garbo "a garbage-collector" (1953—)

nasho "national service; a person doing national service" (1962—)

derro "a derelict: a tramp" (1963—)

rego "registration (of a vehicle)" (1967—)

bizzo "business" (1969—)

rello "a relative" (1982—)

servo "a service station" (1985—)

Only *troppo* "mentally ill (through spending too long in the tropics)" (1941—) and *journo* "journalist" (1967—), from this list, have spread to British usage. That this is still an active combining form is indicated by examples in *The Australian* newspaper of *ambo* "ambulance; ambulance driver", *doco* "documentary", *fisho* "a fishmonger; a fisherman", and *vego* "vegetarian", none of which is listed in the *OED* or *AND*. Having decided, understandably, that all nouns ending in *-o* are Australian, the *Koala Net* glossary also lists *yobbo* "an uncouth person" (1922—, originally UK). Related words from the rest of the English-speaking world include *alive* (*alive*) *oh* [a cry used by fish-sellers] (c.1709—, now chiefly Molly Malone), *beano* "a bean feast; a festivity" (1888—), *righto* "ok" (1893—), *cheerio*, and *daddy-o*, both mentioned earlier. In the rest of the world, *-o* is usually added to a complete word, while in Australia it's used with clipped forms, but the distinction isn't foolproof.

Another feature of Australian slang in this list and others like it is the profusion of colourful idioms. Some of these are also attested in

The Australian newspaper and elsewhere online, including *busy as a cat burying shit, cross as a frog in a sock, cunning as a dunny rat, dry as a dead dingo's donger* (or *a nun's nasty* or *a pommy's towel*), *fit as a Mallee bull, mad as a cut snake,* and *mean as cat's piss.* It doesn't matter whether you know what a *nun's nasty* and a *Mallee bull* are: it's entirely possible to understand these phrases from the adjective. The remaining words convey attitude and affiliation rather than meaning. Based on Internet evidence, many of these phrases are talked about and included in glossaries more than they're actually used: like the traditional slang, some of these phrases have become emblems rather than examples of Australian English.

The history of Australian English sees a gradual narrowing in the groups of words for which 'Australian slang' seems an appropriate label. For some commentators, it has narrowed so far that only traditional Australianisms are worthy of the label, but in truth Australian slang remains both creative in its own right and receptive to slang from other English-speaking nations.

New Zealand slang

Although speakers of English arrived in New Zealand from 1792 onwards, large-scale settlement didn't begin until after the Treaty of Waitangi in 1840. Many of the early settlers spoke Australian English, which was already a mixture of various British and American dialects, but they also picked up some distinctive New Zealand terms from the Maori language, such as *Pakeha* "a European" (1817—), *haka* "a ceremonial dance" (1832—), and *goorie* "a (mongrel) dog" (1937-1970). By about 1900, the development of a New Zealand accent had been identified as a cause for concern and a threat to the maintenance of Standard British English in New Zealand, but a century later commentators were troubled that American English was influencing New Zealand pronunciation and vocabulary. Sidney Baker published a book called *New Zealand Slang* in 1940, but we've already seen that he understood *slang* to include everything non-standard and/or national, and many of the terms and phrases he lists were normal features of colloquial New Zealand English. General dictionaries had sometimes included New Zealand supplements since as early as 1914, but it wasn't until 1979 that a comprehensive dictionary of New Zealand English was published. Its author later co-edited a *New Zealand Slang Dictionary*, including a great deal of colloquial language as well as slang.

A website aimed at new and potential immigrants to New Zealand provides a list of about 180 slang terms to 'give you a better understanding of what your Kiwi mates are really trying to tell ya!' A great many of the terms listed are also found in Australian English, including *ropeable* "very angry" (1874—), *sook* "a softy; a wimp" (1933—), *scroggin* "a high energy snack eaten by walkers" (1949—), and *pav* "a pavlova (a type of dessert)" (1966—). Of the terms that are also used in Britain, several are colloquial, like *dole* "unemployment benefit" (1362—) and *cardy* "cardigan" (1968—), or even standard, like *petrol* "gasoline" (1895—). This suggests that the compilers of the list are taking American rather than British usage as the standard against which to identify slang terms. Terms in the list that did originate in New Zealand include *bach* or *batch* "a makeshift house; a holiday home" (1927—), *jandal* "a flip-flop; a sandal", from a proprietary name (1950—), and *fizzboat* "a motorboat" (1977—). *Greasies* "fish and chips", *scarfie* "a student", and *wop-wops* "a far away and insignificant place" aren't listed in the *OED*, but other evidence of their use in New Zealand supports their inclusion in this list.

New Zealand English shares the informality of Australian English, creating the same difficulty in distinguishing between slang and colloquialisms. It can also be difficult to determine whether individual terms originated in Australia or New Zealand. The competing currents of slang from Britain and the United States add to the challenge of distinguishing a body of 'New Zealand slang', but if we focus on usage rather than origins, it will be clear that there are slang terms available to play the same social functions in New Zealand as they do in the rest of the English-speaking world. Like Australian English,

New Zealand English can be both slangy and distinctively national, but the two don't necessarily coincide.

Canadian slang

Canada was settled by European speakers of English and French from the seventeenth century. Canadian English developed from the dialect of the north-eastern United States, but political loyalties and later immigration superimposed a British influence on its pan-American forms. In the first half of the twentieth century, however, Canadian newspapers were focusing on the influence of American slang on Canadian English, apparently believing that Canadian English would be 'pure' without this contamination. For example, in 1906, an unnamed politician was criticized for using American terms such as *slick* "excellent" (1833—), *dough* "money" (1848—), *get out and dust* "to leave" (*dust* had been used with the same sense since 1860—), and *deliver the goods* "to fulfil a promise; to bring a task to successful completion" (1879—). Despite this resistance to American slang, it was regularly introduced into Canadian newspaper articles in the early twentieth century to make points more forcefully, though writers often took care to indicate that they both recognized and regretted their own use of slang.

In 1932, an article in a student newspaper criticized Canadian students for adopting slang terms:

> Why shouldn't these young Canadians, here in the University, take a genuine pride, not in aping cheap American slang, but in keeping themselves free from it? Why can't they get the silly notion out of their heads that a student who speaks good English is any the less a 'good sport'?

Various slang terms used by Canadian students are listed in the article, including *cut* "to skip; to miss" (1791—, originally UK), the interjection *say* (used on its own since 1830, but *I say* had been used with the same function since 1611), *low-down* "inside information" (1908—), and *uh-huh* "yes" (1924—), all of which either originated or were current in the United States. However, at least one of the objectionable terms mentioned appears to be derived from British school and college slang: *tuck*, apparently meaning "a café" or "a dining hall". *Wet* "unappealing (of a course)" could be related to the American *all wet* "mistaken; completely wrong" (1923—), or British *wet* "spineless; ineffectual" (1916—). In objecting to American slang, this writer assumes that all slang is American.

By 1939, a female Canadian student might have dismissed an unappealing admirer as a *droopy drawers* "an untidy, sloppy person; a slow-witted person" (1932—, originally UK), *dimwit* "a stupid, slow-witted person" (1922—, originally US), or *screwball* "an eccentric; a fool" (1933—, chiefly US). Female students apparently also employed the interjection *fluff!* to express disgust without trespassing against decency, which may be related to *fluff* "to make a mistake" (1884—, originally UK theatrical).

In 1973, a Canadian MA student called Donald Wesley Preston set out 'to determine if there is such an entity as Canadian English slang'. He worked on material collected for, but not included in, Avis's *Dictionary of Canadianisms*, comparing it with dictionaries of slang from Britain and America (but not Australia or New Zealand). Preston concluded that over half of the slang terms used in Canada were of Canadian origin, but his reference works weren't very up to date and some of the terms he considered to be Canadian slang weren't in the slang dictionaries he used because they were colloquial or dialectal elsewhere. The proportion of slang terms used in Canada that originated in Canada is certainly lower than Preston's figure.

Modern Internet sources for Canadian slang tend to repeat a hoary list of national and colloquial terms that are equivalent to totemic Australian 'slang', such as *Canuck* "a Canadian, specifically a French Canadian" (1825—, originally US), *tuque* "a knitted winter hat" (1871—), *chesterfield* "a sofa" (1900—), *Newfie* "a Newfoundlander" (1942—), *poutine* "a dish of chips topped with cheese curds and gravy" (1982—), and *loonie* "a Canadian dollar" (1987—). Slang terms that appear to have originated in Canada, some of which are now used more widely, include:

dogan "an Irish Roman Catholic" (1854 +1933)

muffin "a man's female companion at social engagements" (1854-1965)

jawbone "credit" (1862-1971)

bindle "a bundle" (1897–)

stakey "flush; having plenty of money" (1919-1973)

zombie "a man conscripted for home defence" (1943–, historical in later use)

stubble-jumper "a prairie farmer" (1946–)

mud-pup "an English student of agriculture" (1955-1994)

suckhole "to curry favour" (1961–)

suck "a worthless person" (1965–)

Many Canadian slang terms are specific to Canada in meaning if not use, including:

pea-soup "a French Canadian" (1866-1912)

herring-choker "an inhabitant of the Maritime Provinces" (1899–)

pea-souper "a French Canadian" (1930–)

spud-islander "an inhabitant of Prince Edward Island" (1957–)

Joe "a French Canadian" (1963+1966)

pepsi "a French Canadian" (1978-1996)

hoser "a loutish Canadian" (1981–)

It's possible that terms promoting a regional sense of what it means to be Canadian are less likely to be embraced as national colloquialisms, and thus more likely to remain stigmatized as slang.

Caribbean slang

Distinctive slang terms are also found in the Caribbean, where the development of English has been influenced by pidgins and creoles used among slaves who didn't share a common language. Although the local patois is a source of pride for some speakers, it co exists with a higher-status local standard form. Terms used in the patois are not slang in that context, but they may function as slang when they're introduced into what is otherwise standard or colloquial English. Slang terms originating in Jamaican patios include:

rass (also *raas*) "arse: nonsense; a
despicable individual" (1790–)
politricks "politics" (1908–)
facety "impudent; arrogant" (1927–)
facey "bold; impertinent" (1929–)
rass "to make a fool of; to insult" (1952–)
criss "attractive; smart; fashionable"
(1954–)

rassclaat "a despicable person" (1969–)
mash it up "to liven up (a musical
performance)" (1979–)
selector "a DJ's assistant; a DJ"
(1980–)
posse "a criminal gang" (1986–)
rassclaat [used as an intensifier]
(1993–)

The *OED* labels *niggergram* "a scandalous rumour" (1957—) as chiefly Trinidadian and *conch* "a black West Indian" (1833-1875) as 'Bahamas slang'. Terms used more widely in the Caribbean include:

batty "the bottom; buttocks" (1935–)
pick up a nail "to catch venereal disease"
(1938-1994)
battyman "a male homosexual" (1967–)
pum-pum "the female genitals; women"
(1983–)
punani "the female genitals; women"
(1987–)

massive "a group or gang of young
people defined by their shared
interests or place of origin" (1989–)
batty-riders "a pair of tight (women's)
shorts" (1992–)
big up "to praise" (1992–)

Many of these have been carried into American and particularly British usage by immigration and the influence of reggae and ska. In British hip hop, they're used alongside African American terms.

Indian slang

British influence in India began with traders in the sixteenth century. In 1858, the British government took over direct control from the East India Company, but native English-speakers were always in a small minority. The earliest Anglo-Indian terms were used by British officers and officials in India, and some reached wider use, particularly through military slang (see Chapter 7). These include *poggle* "a crazy person" (1783-1989), *griffin* "a newcomer to India" (1793-1883), *tiffin* "a light midday meal" (1800-1906), *oont* "a camel" (1815—), *soor* "a pig", used as a term of abuse for a person (1848-1936), *puckerow* "to seize; to lay hold of" (1864-1943),[1] *sub-cheese* "the lot; everything" ([1864]+1874-1992), *ek dum* "at once; immediately" (1895-1977), and *poggle* "mad" (1925-1989).

English remains an official language in India, and the model for educated Indians is British English, but many informal usages have developed in speech and writing. The *OED* lists:

telephone "a telephone call" (1935+1979)

phut-phut "a motorized vehicle" (1951–)

tribal "a member of a tribal community" (1958–)

airdash "to make a quick journey by air" (1968–)

military hotel "a restaurant serving meat" (1979+1990)

cabin "an office; a cubicle" (1979–)

masala "pep; vigour" (1986–)

history-sheeter "a person with a criminal record" (1988–)

matrimonial "a classified advertisement for a potential spouse" (1989–)

kitty party "a lunch at which the guests contribute money towards the cost of hosting the next gathering" (1991–)

skin show "exposure of the skin" (1999–)

Whether these qualify as slang would depend on which standard they're being compared to: if the standard is British English, they're all slang; but if the standard is Indian English, we first have to determine what Standard Indian English is, and that task has yet to be undertaken. Speakers in multilingual contexts regularly switch from one language to another within a single sentence, so it can be hard to decide whether an informal term should be considered to be part of English. Newspaper articles have identified the following examples as Indian slang from the past decade: *champu* "a loser", *chewing gum* "an irritating person", and *dadda-baaji* "basketball"

---

[1] This isn't related to the New Zealand slang *puckeroo* "to break; to destroy" (1840—).

(from 2002); *Bunty* "a rich Punjabi kid from Delhi", *fatta* "bullshit", and *jhakkas* "perfect" (from 2004); *bombat* "excellent", *chope* "to snub", and *gubbal* "idiot" (from 2005). Because there are no authoritative dictionaries of Standard Indian English or of Indian slang, only a native speaker could hope to determine how frequently or widely these terms are used.

South African slang

South African English has been influenced by indigenous languages as well as by Afrikaans, as spoken by the Dutch settlers who began to arrive in the seventeenth century. Britain's political interest in the Cape dates from the end of the eighteenth century, and British settlers began to arrive during the early decades of the nineteenth. Originally or chiefly South African slang terms include some derived from English, such as *blerry* "bloody" (1920—), *mailer* "a supplier of illegal alcohol" (1950-1986), *rugger bugger* "a boorish (young) man who is fanatical about rugby or other sports" (1959—), *rock spider* "an Afrikaner" (1973—), and *motherless* "drunk" (1988—). Slang terms from Afrikaans include *stompie* "a cigarette butt; a partially smoked cigarette" (1947—), *moffie* "effeminate; homosexual" (1954—) or "a male homosexual" (1959—), and *min dae* "the last few weeks of one's (compulsory) military service" (1971—). *Majita* "a (young black) man" (1963-1990) and *okapi* "a single-bladed knife" (1974—, from a trade name) are from African languages. Military and civilian movement between different parts of the British Empire may account for terms ultimately from Arabic, which include *kaffir* "bad; unreliable" (1934-1961, from the sense "African" 1854—, derogatory) and *majat* "poor quality marijuana" (1956-1990).

In South Africa, English is an ethnic heritage as well as an international language. The use of national forms of English expresses local affiliations. For this reason, not only is South African English better documented than Indian English, by Rhodes University's Dictionary Unit for South African English, but its non-standard forms have also received more attention. Ken Cage's *Gayle: The Language of Kinks and Queens* (2003) is 'a history and dictionary of gay language in South Africa', which places particular emphasis on the freedoms offered to white gay men by life as an air steward. Among the terms Cage lists are *baby-batter* "semen", *harry* "a hangover", *ina* "to iron", *nongolozi* "a (Zulu) gay man", *optert* "to dress up; to make oneself presentable" (from *tart up* (1947—, originally UK), with the same sense), *reeva* "revolting", and *skesana* "a (Zulu) passive partner in anal sex". A number of terms found in early British gay slang and Polari (see Chapter 10) are also found in Cage's dictionary, including *bona* "good; pleasant" (1846—), *varda* "to look at" (1859—), *lally* "a leg" (1962—), and *zhoosh (up)* "to make more exciting or stylish" (1977—).

British slang?

Some regions that formed part of the British Empire are still entirely or partially governed by it. There never has been a body of language that could meaningfully be described as 'British slang'. There are different non-standard forms of English in Wales, Scotland, Northern Ireland, England, and in their various regions. Books and films, such as *Trainspotting*, *The Commitments*, and *The Full Monty*, have brought greater exposure to some of these local terms which sometimes function as slang when they're more widely adopted, even if they originated in dialect or colloquialisms.

The last few years have seen the production of several dictionaries of Irish and Scottish slang, which tend to include colloquialisms alongside words, phrases, pronunciations, and grammatical constructions characteristic of local or national dialect, in the same way that early dictionaries of Australian slang did. Most focus on the slang terms of a single city rather than attempting to present a national slang, and with that caution in mind, slang terms originating or chiefly used in Ireland include:

mazard "the head (of a coin)" (1802)

oil "alcohol" (1833-1998)

cod "to kid; to fool" (1859—)

gas "fun; a joke" (1914—)

stocious "drunk" (1937—)

banjax "to destroy; to wreck" (1939—)

culchie "a rustic; a yokel" (1958—)

snapper "an (unborn) infant" (1959—)

gobdaw "a foolish or pretentious person" (*a.*1966—)

act the maggot "to play the fool; to behave stupidly" (1972—)

nut "to kill" (1974-1992)

Slang originating or chiefly used in Scotland includes:

(Glasgow) magistrate "a herring" (1833-1950)

raw "neat whisky" (1844-1967)

scuffer "a policeman" (1860—)

ned "a layabout; a hooligan" (1910—)

chib "a knife used as a weapon" (1929—)

buroo "the Labour Exchange" (1933—, also Ulster)

sucky "sore (of a wound)" (1934—)

lumber "to pick up; to have sex with" (1938-1991)

Tim "a Roman Catholic; a supporter of Glasgow Celtic football club" (1958—)

chib "to stab" (1962—)

lumber "sexual caressing; a casual sexual partner" (1966-1987)

minging "stinking; very drunk" (1970—)

malky "a bladed weapon; a razor used as a weapon" (1973—), "to wound (with a razor)" (1973—)

numpty "an idiot" (1988—)

jakey "a homeless drunkard; a wino" (1988—)

Slang terms originating or chiefly used in Wales include *tidy* as an expression of approval (1805—), *cutch* "a cuddle" (1992—), *butt* "mate" (2001, abbreviation of northern English *butty*, with the same sense (1837—)), *baddy* "a minor wound", *badgered* "drunk", and *chopsy* "talkative".

Conclusions

For many English-speaking nations, the standard form remained (and in some cases remains) Standard British English, though the influence of American English has grown since WWII. Commentators on developing national forms often dismiss anything distinctively national as slang, and in reaction against this, lexicographers of international Englishes are now sometimes reluctant to stigmatize any distinctively national forms as slang. Other writers, particularly in Australia, embrace the concept of slang as an act of rebellion against the standard, and continue to celebrate everything national as slang as well as to claim everything non-standard as national, even where it's more widely used. The picture is further complicated by the tendency to distinguish between the pure national form (good) and terms imported from American English (slang). Greater informality, particularly in Australian English, can make it difficult to draw a line between slang and colloquial language.

There are important differences between national forms of English throughout the world, but these don't necessarily reside primarily in their slang. The spread of English throughout the world has been a story of recurring and interrelated influences. We've seen that terms originating in each of these countries have spread to others, but the idea of national slang remains powerful in people's minds. If you're willing to identify only words that originated in and are restricted to New Zealand (for example) as 'New Zealand slang', you'll be left with a relatively small selection of examples. If you applied the same criteria to British or American slang, you'd be left with similarly diminished lists. A dictionary of 'New Zealand slang' that included words imported from other parts of the world would be considerably larger, and more useful for anyone attempting to keep up with conversational English in New Zealand. The origins and distribution of slang terms are a secondary consideration for most users of slang dictionaries.

The influences of national forms upon one another were felt even when they were dependent upon the movement of people and printed books, but many of the slang terms found in international usage are more modern. The remaining chapters will explore the effect of the media and the Internet on the development and movement of English slang around the world in the twentieth and twenty-first centuries.

Endnotes

This chapter had to present rather sweeping accounts of the linguistic situation in each country, largely based on Robert Burchfield (ed.), *The Cambridge History of the English Language, Vol. 5: English in Britain and Overseas* (Cambridge: Cambridge University Press, 1994), though this book offers little information about slang. The account of Australian English is based on George W. Turner's chapter and on Bruce Moore's *Speaking Our Language: The Story of Australian English* (Oxford: Oxford University Press, 2006). K. S. D. commented on the distinctiveness of Australian accents in 'Slang and Accent', *The West Australian*, 12 Sept. 1892, 3. Other newspaper articles cited are, in order of appearance: E. E. D., 'Of Some Australian Slang', *The Sydney Morning Herald*, 6 Oct. 1894, 5; 'Slang Teaching in State Schools', *The Argus* (Melbourne), by 'Indignant' (20 Mar. 1896, 3), 'A Parent' (23 Mar. 1896, 6), and 'Teacher' (27 Mar. 1896, 6); 'Bushman', 'The Prevalence of Slang', *The West Australian*, 21 Aug. 1897, 6; 'The Sentimental Bloke', *The Advertiser* (Adelaide), 10 Apr. 1918, 7; 'Anzac Slang', *The Argus* (Melbourne), 25 Dec. 1915, 4; 'May Use Native Slang But Professor Bans Americanisms', *The Courier-Mail* (Brisbane), 13 Dec. 1933, 12; P. Ruehl, 'Dinkum Slang gets the Gong', *Sunday Herald Sun*, 9 Apr. 1995, News, 6; and Rex Jory, 'Aussie Slang is on the Endangered List Like Animals and Plants Facing Extinction', *The Advertiser*, 10 Aug. 2009, Opinion, 18 (from which I omitted terms I'd already discussed). The online *Australian Slang Dictionary* is at *Koala Net* <http://www.koalanet.com.au/australian-slang.html>. Also quoted are James Hardy Vaux, *Memoirs of James Hardy Vaux* (London: W. Clowes, 1819) and H. C. O'Flaherty, *Life in Sydney*, ed. Richard Fotheringham, *Australian Plays for the Colonial Stage 1834-1899* (Queensland: University of Queensland Press, 2006), I. iii (located through Moore's book and modernized here). Cornelius Crowe, *Australian Slang Dictionary: Containing the Words and Phrases of the Thieving Fraternity, Together with the Unauthorised, though Popular Expressions Now in Vogue with All Classes in Australia* (Fitzroy: Barr, 1895), 99; Rolf Bolderwood [*sic*], *Robbery Under Arms* (Leipzig: Tauchnitz, 1889), Ch. 1; C. J. Dennis, *The Songs of a Sentimental Bloke*, reprinted edn (Sydney: Angus & Robertson, 1915), 'A Spring Song'; and Sidney J. Baker, *A Popular Dictionary of Australian Slang* (Melbourne: Robertson & Mullens, 1941), 'Foreword', were also cited. A. G. Pretty's *Glossary of A.I.F. Slang* (typescript, Australian War Memorial) is available online as Amanda Laugesen (ed.), *Glossary of Slang and Peculiar Terms in Use in the A.I.F. 1921-1924* <http://andc.anu.edu.au/australian-words/aif-slang>.

The section on the development of New Zealand English summarizes information from Laurie Bauer's chapter in Burchfield's *Cambridge History* and Donn Bayard's 'New Zealand English: Origins, Relationships, and Prospects', *Moderna Språk* 94/1 (2000), 8–14. New Zealand dictionaries mentioned here are Sidney J. Baker's *New Zealand Slang: A Dictionary of Colloquialisms* (Christchurch:

Whitcombe & Tombs, 1941), H. W. Orsman's *Heinemann New Zealand Dictionary* (Auckland: Heinemann, 1979), and H. W. Orsman and Des Hurley's *New Zealand Slang Dictionary* (Auckland: Reed, 1992). The website for potential New Zealanders is Danny De Hek, *New Zealand's Information Pack* <http://www.nz-immigration.co.nz/lifestyle/slang-words.html>, and most of the examples quoted in this section are from that site, with additional information from my main dictionary sources.

Newspaper articles on Canadian slang are, in order of appearance, 'Editorial Notes', *Red Deer News*, 3 Apr. 1906, 4; E. K. Broadus, 'Campus English', *The Gateway*, 12 Feb. 1932, 5; and 'College Colloquialisms are a Mystery', *The Gateway*, 7 Nov. 1939, 2. Also cited in the section on Canadian English are Donald Wesley Preston, *A Survey of Canadian English Slang* (University of Victoria: MA thesis, 1973), i, and Walter S. Avis, *A Dictionary of Canadianisms on Historical Principles* (Toronto: Gage, 1967), which is currently being revised.

The sections on other international Englishes are reliant on chapters by Braj B. Kachru, William Branford, John A. Holm, J. Derrick McClure, Alan R. Thomas, and Jeffrey L. Kallen in Burchfield's *Cambridge History*. Indian slang terms were located using the *Times of India* website <http://timesofindia .indiatimes.com>. The South African Dictionary Unit website is at <http://www.ru.ac.za/dsae>. Also mentioned are Ken Cage's *Gayle: The Language of Kinks and Queens* (Houghton, SA: Jacana Media, 2003), Roddy Doyle's *The Commitments* (London: King Farouk, 1987), and Irving Welsh's *Trainspotting* (London: Secker & Warburg, 1993). Regional slang was given greater exposure in films such as Alan Parker's *The Commitments* (Los Angeles: 20th Century Fox, 1991), Danny Boyle's *Trainspotting* (London: PolyGram, 1996), and Peter Cattaneo's *The Full Monty* (Los Angeles: 20th Century Fox, 1997). Welsh slang terms are from the *Leicester Online Slang Glossary* by Lindy Bannon. She found that many of her terms had their origins in Lancashire dialect, and it is probable that some of these are also used elsewhere.

10 Top Bananas and Bunny-boilers: The Media and Entertainment Age

Slang developed in relative isolation in different parts of the English-speaking world until the end of the nineteenth century, but we've already seen that the isolation was never total. A trickle (and sometimes a flood) of migrants carried new developments from one English-speaking country or continent to another, with the tide largely flowing from the British Isles outwards, at least to begin with. Sailors and some wealthy travellers went back and forth often, but for most people exposure to new slang from other parts of the world could only ever be sporadic. No matter how determined they were to return, for example, few convicts on board the First Fleet to Botany Bay could have hoped to raise the money for the eight-month return trip once they'd completed their sentence. Because travel was time-consuming, expensive, and dangerous, the interchange of national linguistic developments was limited. By the end of the nineteenth century, ocean-going steamships had shortened long sea journeys, making them safer and cheaper, and by 1880 the crossing between New York and Liverpool took only 6 days and cost considerably less than it had fifty years before.

For those who looked to Europe for their cultural standards, the latest British slang term may have seemed smart and fashionable. However, where new national forms of English began to be valued in their own right, British slang terms lost this status. In Britain, on the other hand, colonial terms were quaint curiosities necessitated by extraordinary conditions or lack of education, seeming ridiculous or vulgar in a British context. Only among those who valued novelty over tradition could other nations' slang make any inroads into British usage, but these potential slang-adopters would still need to have been exposed to it in some way.

It's possible for new words to be transmitted in print, but this works better for technical or educated language. Slang learnt from printed sources is likely to remain in an individual's passive vocabulary (that is, they'll understand it when they see it, but not use it themselves) unless a group of people begin to employ it as an allusion to their shared reading experience. This happens a lot with fancy literary allusions, which prove how well read and clever we are, but much less often with non-standard language. Only a very small number of informal terms derived from popular books entered conversational usage during this period, even within the United Kingdom, including *gamp* "an (untidily tied) umbrella" (1864—), from *Mrs Gamp* in Dickens's *Martin Chuzzlewit* (1843/4) and *Kim's game* "a memory-testing game" (1908—), from Kipling's *Kim* (1901). If informal terms from such well-read British authors are in short supply, we shouldn't expect to see slang terms from other parts of the English-speaking world being disseminated via the printed word. It would have been hard work to introduce an American slang term into everyday speech in nineteenth-century London when other people didn't recognize, understand, or feel the need for it. The adoption of slang terms is promoted by repeated exposure, and this can only be delivered in everyday conversation or by the mass media.

The press

Newspapers were available long before the twentieth century, and cheaply too, but they remained relatively formal, with slang generally used only in the sporting pages and occasionally in court reports. However, we've seen in the last three chapters that anecdotal accounts of slang usage began to make occasional appearances in newspapers and magazines in the 1850s, becoming considerably more frequent by the end of the century. We've also seen that prominent individuals' pronouncements on linguistic progress or decay were reported to drum up controversy, even when they weren't actually saying anything particularly original: it would be far more newsworthy if a day went by during which no one complained about the way young people talk (though harder to write about).

Articles listing current slang are both controversial and new, and although this type of exposure to slang might sometimes have played a part in its wider spread, it's unlikely that many newspaper readers adopted new slang from second-hand commentary. We've already seen that the flappers of the 1920s received considerable media attention, but the successful transmission of flapper slang in print could only have taken place within tightly knit groups with shared aspirations: it's possible that would-be flappers tentatively tried out the slang they read in newspapers, and just about possible that these terms found a receptive audience among like-minded friends who'd read the same article, but the slang of such impressionable conformists could only ever be transient. It's more usual for writers to mine articles like these for a convenient shorthand in depicting a stereotype. Real flappers would have learnt their slang socially, and it is unlikely that the slang listed in the papers was used nationally. Articles like these really just demonstrate that journalists were interested in language variation, particularly in novelty, and that they thought their readers would be too. Publishers still cash in on this

19 Slang in comic strips: Richard Felton Outcault, 'The Yellow Kid Takes a Hand at Golf', *New York Journal*, 24 Oct. 1897, 8.

interest by filling press releases with new words to be found in the latest edition of their dictionary.[1]

Newspapers did include some more promising vehicles for slang, however. With their colourful depictions of exaggeratedly everyday characters, comic strips included slang terms from their earliest inception in the last decade of the nineteenth century. These terms had a much greater chance of entering daily use than those discussed in articles: not only were they more immediate, but they were often used repeatedly. This meant that they could function as in-jokes: as ways of signalling and testing a shared sense of humour. Some comic strips were syndicated in newspapers throughout the United States and further afield, ensuring wide recognition of the terms they included. For example, *Mutt and Jeff* "a comically mismatched pair" (1917—),

---

[1] While I was putting the finishing touches to this book, the *OED* issued a press release about new additions, including *FYI* "for your information" (1941—, originally US), *muffin top* "a roll of flesh above a waistband" (2003—), *LOL*, and *OMG*. The discussion that trended on Twitter expressed the following attitudes: a) about time too, b) now students can't be criticized for using them in their essays, and c) this is the end of the world. The list of words falsely alleged to have been added is growing before my eyes.

"a good cop/bad cop team" (1940—), or "deaf" (*a*.1945—, rhyming slang) first featured in a comic strip of the same name by Harry Conway ('Bud') Fisher in 1907. Ham Fisher's *Joe Palooka* strip, appearing in newspapers from 1930, depicted an inept prizefighter of that name. *Palooka* was already established with the meaning "a clumsy or stupid person" (1920—), but the term's reach was undoubtedly extended by its daily exposure, and it came to refer specifically to a clumsy fighter. Popeye appeared first in E. C. Segar's *Thimble Theatre* in 1929, and terms associated with him were reinforced by their use in cartoons for cinema and television, and by later incarnations in film and computer games. These included *arf arf* as a representation of laughter (1931—) and *jeep* "a small four-wheeled vehicle, as used in the army" (1941—). Although Segar didn't originate *wimp* "a weakling; an indecisive person" (1911—), Wellington Wimpey contributed to its spread, also inspiring *Wimpy* "(a proprietary name for) a hamburger" (1935—) and "a Wellington bomber plane" (1942—, historical in later use). Al Capp (Alfred Caplin)'s *Li'l Abner* strip was syndicated in hundreds of American and Canadian newspapers from the 1930s, introducing terms such as *Sadie Hawkins Day* "a day on which gender roles are reversed" (1938—), *Dogpatch* "an unsophisticated rural community" (1951—), and *skunk works* "(the location of) a group working on a secret project" (1962—). Capp was also responsible for introducing *(double) whammy* "an evil influence or hex; an intense look; something effective, upsetting, etc." (1939—).[2] Other comic strips introduced *malarkey* "humbug, nonsense; a racket; a palaver" (1924—), *milquetoast* "a timid or ineffectual person" (1932—), *sad sack* "an inept or foolish person; a social misfit" (1943—), *dragon lady* "a domineering or powerful woman" (1949—), and *security blanket* "a blanket or other object

---

[2] This is a current favourite among British politicians and journalists, with the sense "a misfortune; a setback; a disadvantage". The *triple whammy* is now commonplace, and newspaper searches also threw up a few examples of the *quadruple* or *quintuple whammy*. Further inflation may be countered by the attention span required to encompass lumbering *multiple whammies* (this non-specific plural also occurs in British newspapers).

providing comfort through familiarity" (1971—). For some users, these terms may still function as in-jokes, but many others will be entirely unaware of their origins. These terms became living slang by frequent reuse, and some have passed into general usage.

From newspaper comic strips grew comic books, dominated by action heroes, and from these it was often the names of characters that reached wider allusive use. For example, *brainiac* meaning "very intelligent" (1976—) or "a very intelligent person" (1982—) originated in the name of Superman's extraterrestrial enemy, though it was also (and earlier) the name of a self-assembly computer kit. Not yet listed in the *OED* are *wonder woman* "a successful woman, especially one who multitasks effectively" (since at least 1951—) and *kryptonite* "an Achilles' heel; a thing or person causing aversion" (since at least 1968—). With endearing hyperbole, my sons call any child with whom they have a minor disagreement at school their *arch-enemy* "a rival; a threat" (since at least 1975—).[3]

Parodies of the speech of ethnic groups were found in newspapers on both sides of the Atlantic. For example, Finley Peter Dunne's Mr Dooley, an Irish-American bartender, commented on current affairs in the Chicago *Evening Post* from 1893 to 1926. In this extract, he compares the Prime Minister of Spain to a card sharp:

> "I'll explain it to ye," said Mr. Dooley. "'Tis this way. Ye see, this here Sagasta is a boonco steerer like Canada Bill, an' th' likes iv him. A smart man is this Sagasta, an' wan that can put a crimp in th' ca-ards that ye cudden't take out with a washerwoman's wringer. He's been through many a ha-ard game. Talk about th' County Dimocracy picnic, where a three ca-ard man goes in debt ivry time he hurls th' broads, 'tis nawthin' to what this here Spanish onion has been against an' beat."

Representations of non-standard pronunciation and grammar aside, we do see some informal terms in this brief extract: *bunco-steerer* "a

---

[3] These dates are from Nexis newspaper searches. There are probably earlier examples elsewhere.

confidence man" (1875—, US slang), *put a crimp in* "to interfere with" (1889—, US colloq), *three card man* "a card sharp" (1854—, originally US), and *broads* "playing cards" (1753-1962, originally UK). *Hurl* "to play cards" may be related to *throw* "to discard a card" (1879—).

Newspapers gradually began to use more informal language during the course of the twentieth century, particularly in short stories and in sports, lifestyle, and opinion columns. O. Henry, Damon Runyon, and Ring Lardner were some of the earliest American journalists to develop their own distinctively slangy idioms in the early decades of the twentieth century. In the meantime, newspaper workers were developing their own professional slang, some of which they transmitted to their readers. For example, American newspapers gave rise to *dogwatch* "(the staff on) the night shift" (1901—), *POTUS* "the President of the United States" (1903—), *Fortean* "relating to paranormal phenomena" (1932—, from Charles Fort, journalist of the paranormal), *Dorothy Dix* "a question designed to elicit a prepared answer" (1941—, Australian, from an American question-and-answer columnist), *funnies* "comic strips" (1852—), *sob sister* "a female sentimental journalist" (1912—), and *deadline* "the time by which something (originally text for publication) has to be ready" (1920—). British journalists are responsible for *hatches, matches, and dispatches* "births, marriages, and deaths" (1878—), *abominable snowman* "yeti" (1921—), *lonely heart* "a single person seeking love" (1931—), and *bonk-buster* "a best-selling sexually explicit book" (1988—). *Maffick* "to celebrate uproariously" (1900—) is a humorous journalistic back-formation from Mafeking (now Mafikeng), a British garrison relieved from besiegement during the Boer War.

Amateur newspapers also documented slang usage in the late nineteenth and early twentieth century, usually for the benefit of slang-users. During WWI, with looser censorship than in WWII, British soldiers ran off numerous issues of what are now known as trench journals. They commented on many aspects of their daily lives, and sometimes provided glossaries of current slang terms, which included:

gubbins "an explosive shell" (*OED*: "fish parings; anything of little value; a gadget; cables" (1553–))

joyride "a pleasure trip (in a stolen car)" (1908–)

joystick "the control lever of an aeroplane or computer game" (1910–)

gasper "a cigarette" (1914–)

spikebozzle "to destroy completely" (1915-1962)

buckshee "free" (1916–)

swing the lead "to malinger; to fake illness" (1917–)

zoom "to fly fast" (1917–)

wangle "to acquire by dubious means" (1918–)

salvage "to acquire by dubious means" (1918–)

Student newspapers also began to comment on current slang usage at about this time. Articles published in the *Columbia Jester* largely gave comic definitions, such as *naughty* "but nice", *nightgown* "hey! hey!", *loan* "a gift", and *neckerchief* "what the boys cried when they found the chief of police in Lonesome Lill's cell", but a few slang terms are defined, and others are implied, including:

juice "alcohol" (1387–, slang in later use)

kick-off "a beginning" (1875–, in sport since 1857)

keen "good" (1914–, now dated)

frosh "a college freshman; a first-year student" (1915–)

heavy "intense (of a date or relationship)" (1928–)

In these publications by soldiers and students, the writers and intended readers belonged to the same group. The slang they listed would have been reinforced in daily conversation, but the printed explanations might well have contributed to their spread.

The music hall, vaudeville, and the theatre

At the end of the nineteenth century, London's masses were being entertained in grandly decorated music halls, where they saw variety performances that reflected their way of life and commented on current affairs. The music-hall experience was infused with rebellious frisson: men dressed as women, women wore revealing clothes or dressed as men, and performers satirized the behaviour of the government, the upper classes, and the police. Audiences participated by shouting out catchphrases and singing along with choruses. Music-hall circuits throughout the country ensured that acts were known nationally, and informal terms derived from music-hall songs include *cure* "an eccentric person" (1856–1971, popularized by a music-hall song with the chorus 'The cure, the cure, the perfect cure'), *jingoism* "unthinking and belligerent patriotism" (1878—, from a patriotic chorus including the words *by jingo* "by Jove" (1694—)), and possibly *hooligan* "a street rough" (1898—, from a music-hall song depicting a rowdy Irish family of that name). *Tich* (now often <titch>) "a small person" (1934—) is derived from a stage name of the diminutive performer Harry Relph.[4] *Harry Tate* "characterized by disorganization; late (by rhyming slang)" (1925-1935) is from R. M. Hutchison's comedic persona. *Fred Karno's Army* was the name of a troupe of British slapstick comedians (including Charlie Chaplain and Stan Laurel), used with the sense "a group of disorganized or incompetent people" (1933—).

Music-hall workers largely adopted existing theatrical slang in their own usage, and they undoubtedly helped some of these terms to enter into wider currency. Terms that originated as theatrical or music-hall slang include *star* "a popular performer" (1824—), *prop* "an article used on stage" (1841—), *make-up* "a disguise; costume and cosmetics adopted for a performance" (1852—), *pro* "a professional (performer)" (1856—), *wheeze* "an impromptu joke" (1864—), *barnstorm* "to tour

---

[4] The name implied that he was another ludicrous claimant of the Tichborne title and fortune. Roger Tichborne, son of the 9th Baronet, was lost at sea in 1854. His heart-broken mother refused to accept that he was dead, and in response to her repeated requests for further information, a London-born Australian butcher named Arthur Orton presented himself as the missing man. Lady Tichborne accepted the imposter as her son but Roger's nephew, who had inherited the title, was less willing to be convinced. After a civil and then a criminal case, Orton was sentenced to fourteen years hard labour in 1874.

rural districts with performances designed to appeal to unsophisticated audiences" (1883—), and *wing (it)* "to undertake a performance, or any other activity, without the necessary preparation" (1885—).

At about the same period, vaudeville shows were fulfilling similar functions in the United States. In what was still a more rural economy, vaudevillians would have reached a smaller proportion of the population than British music-hall stars, but their appeal was broader, in that comedians, singers, acrobats, dancers, and actors combined to present shows that were intended to be suitable for reasonably respectable families. Circuits across various cities increased the stars' exposure and kept audiences entertained with ever-changing novelty. General theatrical slang was also used by these performers, but new vaudevillian terms included *flop* "a failure; a person or enterprise that is a failure" (1893—), *headliner* "the first and most popular act listed in a bill" (1896—), *jazzbo* "slapstick" (1914—), *mammy song* "a sentimental song" (1923—), *straight man* "a comedian's stooge" (1923—), and *single act* "a solo performance or performer" (1952—). Some vaudevillian slang leaked into more general usage, often in figurative meanings, including:

hamfatter "a bad actor" (1880-1966)

ham "a bad actor" (1882—)

song and dance "a rigmarole; a fuss" (1895—), with literal reference to an act since 1872

can "to put a stop to" (1906—)

grand "a thousand dollars (or pounds)" (1909—)

hokum "nonsense" (1926—), with reference to onstage nonsense since 1908

small-timer "an insignificant person" (1931—), with reference to a second-rate vaudeville theatre or act since 1910

stooge "a subordinate; a lackey" (1934—), with reference to an on-stage subordinate since 1913

top banana "the leader in any field" (1974—), with reference to the highest-ranking comedian in an act or troupe since 1953

246 The Life of Slang

Many music-hall and vaudeville acts used local speech to create vivid and amusing characters, exposing national audiences to restricted or local slang. By 1910 it seems that rhyming slang owed as much to music halls as to working-class usage, and the *Penny Illustrated Paper* depicted an actor travelling between engagements:

> He may then partake of two hard-boiled "borrows" ("borrow and beg" –
> egg), explaining to his fellow-travellers that he had no breakfast, as the
> "New York Nippers" were burnt up to a "Bertha Winder", and that the
> "treacle" ("treacle toffee" – coffee) was stone "Harry" ("Harry Gold" – cold).
> The limit is perhaps reached when he orders a cup of tea during the
> journey. "Cup of Harrigan", he says. "Harrigan?" asks the barmaid; "what's
> Harrigan?" "Why, Harrigan—that's *me*."

Although several of these unusual rhyming slang terms are found in dictionaries, I haven't been able to find any examples of genuine use. The identities of the original *Bertha Winder* and *Harry Gold* remain unclear, if any such originals existed.[5] Like *Harrigan* (me) as a rhyme for *tea*, these terms were probably rarely (if ever) used. Their purpose in this context, as in many stage renditions of slang, is to amuse by exaggerating a stereotype.

Audiences in the United States were also enjoying performances involving parodies of local or ethnic speech styles. Bert Little (d.1933), for example, enjoyed great success as Hogan, a bartender from New York's disreputable Bowery area. A newspaper interview includes a boxed section entitled 'Bert Translates Himself', in which he describes his first encounter with the Hyde theatre 'speciality company'. The Standard English version is headed *straight* "straightforward; honest" (1894–, colloquial) or "the truth" (1866–, US); Bert's own language is headed *dope* "(inside) information" (1899–):

> Straight: That was something which, of course, I must see. They opened at a
> matinee and the place was the Olympic theatre. I didn't dare to tell the family of my

---

[5] The jazz saxophonist and the Soviet spy called Harry Gold were both born too late to have inspired this term.

plans, but on the morning of the eventful day I took my lunch as usual in my little basket and started ostensibly for the shop, but in reality for the water front, where I idled the forenoon away in anticipation of the afternoon treat that was coming.

Dope: Then the bug fever stole softly to me brain patch and de merry ticker of de grand old heart worked overtime and when I stole softly from me pillows in de morning de Mountebanks arrived I began to oil up me thinking cogs and saying boldly to de party of de first part "I will not go forth on de long path that leads to de print shop. Nay! nay! bold foreman. I must hike to de Hyde Speciality company where me favrites will hold visiting day that we must pay for catching them at their stunts." I started for work at 6 o'clock in de top end of de day with my lunch pinned securely under me arm.

As in the representations of non-standard speech we've already seen, the indications of pronunciation (*de* for *the*; *favrites* for *favourites*) and non-standard grammatical features (*me* for *my*) outnumber the slang terms. Nevertheless, the *dope* does employ terms that were slang at the time, including *stunt* "a dangerous feat; a gimmick" (1878—) and *catch* "to watch; to listen to" (1906—). *Bug fever*, which isn't in the *OED*, can be understood as a combination of *bug* "an enthusiast; an enthusiasm" (1841—, originally US) and *fever* "a state of nervous excitement" (1586—). *Hike* "to go for a long walk (in the country-side)" (1809—, colloquial, originally dialect and US) may have seemed slangy in this context. The interviewer remarked, with some surprise, that Little was well dressed and well educated in real life:

He says his gift of slang is due to imagination. He thinks it out carefully and then "springs" it as though it were spontaneous.

The extract uses a number of vivid metaphors that aren't documented in dictionaries. Little may, therefore, have invented *brain patch* "brain" (not found elsewhere with this sense), *(thinking) cogs* "(the workings of) the brain" (1910—), and *top end of the day* "first thing in the morning" (1910—), or it may be that he was reflecting spoken usage. Perhaps he should also be given credit for coining *ticker* "the heartbeat; a heart", because this example antedates the *OED*'s (1930—) first citation by twenty years.

Formal theatre also played a role in the dissemination of slang in this period, particularly among wealthier people, and it's likely that playwrights reworked one another's slang in depicting similar types. Improvements in transatlantic travel meant that audiences began to be exposed to modern plays by travelling companies from the opposite side of *the pond* "the Atlantic; any ocean" (1612—). In these countries divided by a common language, minor differences have long occupied a borderland between fascination and irritation. In 1900, Lillie Langtry starred in an American tour of a British play called *The Degenerates*. Her talent had 'never been a matter of much moment', but audiences flocked to see the erstwhile mistress of the Prince of Wales in the flesh. The *Chicago Daily Tribune* promoted the play by publishing a glossary of fashionable London slang lifted from a British newspaper, including *nightie* "a nightgown" (1871—, now colloquial), *deevy* "divine; charming" (1900-1942), *frillikies* "frills" (*frillies* has been used with reference to women's clothing, and particularly underwear, 1900—), *mackie* "mackintosh: a waterproof coat" (*mac* has been used with the same sense, 1901—), *twee* "sweet; dainty" (1905—), and *pyjies* "pyjamas" (this spelling is still sometimes used, but *PJs* (1930—) is now more common). In 1909, two plays in New York gave a theatre critic an opportunity to compare the slang of London and New York, with satisfying patriotically results:

> American wins in this case as she did at Bunker Hill...American slang is metaphor. London slang is artificially contrived and based on rhyme... 'American slang is much more picturesque, I think, and is developed out of the imagination of the unlettered. They are hidden poets, these fellows who invent slang.' [quoting Dallas Welford, a Scottish actor]

Commentators comparing British and American slang in this period, whatever their origins, often observed that while American slang enabled clear and vivid expression, British slang (particularly rhyming slang) obscured meaning.

Newspapers reported in 1928 that British audiences of the American comedy *Is Zat So?* were given glossaries of slang to help them understand it. Terms listed included:

ride "to tease; to criticize" (1891—)   *wisecrack* "a witty remark; a joke" (1911—)
hooch "poor quality whisky" (1897—)   *broad* "a woman" (1913—)
aces "perfect" (1901—)   *stall* "to loiter; to kill time" (1916—)
goof "a fool" (1902—)   *apple sauce* "nonsense" (1925—, now
wise up "to learn; to inform" (1905—)   dated)

Other terms in the glossary were also in use in Britain, but perhaps not in the circles frequented by London's theatre-goers, including *mill* "a prize fight" (1812-1996, boxing slang) and *shut-eye* "sleep" (1899—, originally army slang).

The cinema

The cinema was also to have a dramatic effect on the development and dissemination of slang. Film-makers adopted and adapted terms to describe aspects of their new industry, and many of these acquired extended meanings in slang and colloquial usage, including *fade out* "departure; death" (1933—), from the sense "the gradual disappearance of a picture" (1918—), *pan* "to scan with the eyes" (1968—), from the sense "to take a panoramic shot (of)" (1913—), and *big picture* "a broad overview" (1935—), from the sense "the main film in a programme; a major film" (1913—). A few informal terms originated in specific films, such as *the usual suspects* "people habitually suspected of having committed a crime" (1942—) from *Casablanca* (1942), and *gaslight* "to manipulate someone into believing they are insane" (1969—) from the 1944 film of the same name. In more general slang, the cinema is responsible for *valentino* "a gigolo" (1927-1974, with reference to the screen idol Rudolph Valentino), *It girl* "a glamorous female celebrity" (1927—, originally referring to Clara Bow, star of the 1927 film *It*, revived in Britain in the 1990s), and *bogart* "to take more than one's share of a joint" (1967—, with reference to Humphrey Bogart's deep drags upon more conventional cigarettes). Film characters featuring in slang include *Keystone (cops)* "slapstick; comically incompetent" (1913—, from the bumbling policemen featuring in Keystone productions since only the previous year) and *Mickey Mouse* "ineffectual; insignificant; second-rate; easy" (1931—, relatively soon after his 1928 debut). *The Wizard of Oz* (1939) acquired recognition in *friend of Dorothy* "a homosexual man" (1972—) and *munchkin* "a small and endearing person, especially a child" (1976—). The Watergate informant, Deep Throat, took his code name from the title of a pornographic film of 1972, and *deep throat* has come to mean "a provider of inside information" more generally (1974—). *Rambo* "a tough and aggressive man" (1985—) is from the Vietnam vet played by Sylvester Stallone in *First Blood* (1982), and three sequels so far. Glenn Close was the original *bunny-boiler* "a woman obsessed with a lover who has spurned her" (1990—, British slang), in *Fatal Attraction* (1987). The Austen Powers films originated *shagadelic* "sexy; excellent" (1997—) and popularized *mini-me* "a smaller version of oneself, specifically one's child" (1996—) as well as revitalizing some genuine 1960s slang.

Slang terms with cinematic origins are relatively few in number, but cinema has played a central role in disseminating slang already in use. Slang used in films received considerable journalistic attention even when it was restricted to the written captions of silent movies (see p. 5). In 1913, the *Boston Daily Globe* reported that a British newspaper had provided a list of American slang to aid cinema-goers. These included *mutt* "a fool" (1900—), *boob* "a fool" (1909—, derived from British dialect and colloquial *booby*, used with the same sense since 1599), and *junk* "worthless goods or possessions" (1842—, from a nautical term meaning "an old or inferior cable", first recorded in 1485). In the same year, *The Daily Mail* complained that American slang heard in the cinema was encouraging British youths towards 'mental indiscipline' in their choice of vocabulary. A journalist in the Melbourne *Argus* (1918) identified *two-fisted* "ambidextrous; aggressive (of a fighter)" (1878—), *tenderloin* "a red-light district" (1887—), and *highball* "a drink of whisky and soda" (1898—) as examples of American slang encountered by uncomprehending Australian audiences. In 1932, an article in *The Sydney Morning Herald* remarked that:

> Perhaps, the most distressing feature of this invasion of Australia by American slang is the deleterious effect it is producing upon not only the speech, but also upon the morals of the younger generation. The mind of a child is a singularly receptive organ, and constant repetition is not needed for it to assimilate quickly these American vulgarisms

This writer objected to Australians using *ok* to express agreement (1839—), *oh yeah* to express incredulity (1927—), *I'll be seeing you* (1937—), and the terms of address *baby* (1898—), *kid* (1917—), and *big boy* (1918—).

Because films usually represent unusual situations (real life being rather dull in comparison), and because characterization often relies on stereotype, cinema contributed towards a sense that there were clear differences between national slangs. In 1929, *Film Daily* provided a glossary of terms used in an early talkie called *Fast Life*, starring Douglas Fairbanks Junior. The glossary was compiled from an earlier American dictionary, and included many terms originating in the United States:

jug "a bank" (1845–, from the earlier sense "a jail", first recorded in 1815)
heeled "armed" (1852–, now historical)
con "one who talks fluently and dishonestly; dishonest talk" (1889–)
con "a convict" (1893–)
gat "a gun" (1904–)
hijacker "one who commandeers a vehicle (carrying bootleg liquor)" (1923–)

It also included several terms from British criminal slang: *uncle* "a pawnbroker" (1756—), *benjamin* "an overcoat" (1781–1909), *turnip* "a gold watch" (1823-1970), and *grease* "money given as a bribe; protection money" (1823—). British audiences who'd never had to *grease* an *uncle* must have assumed that these were all American innovations.

The dominance of American cinema soon meant that reviewers and audiences around the world became familiar enough with American slang that it no longer seemed worthy of comment, while slang from other parts of the English-speaking world remained unacceptable to American audiences. For example, the American distributors of *Crocodile Dundee* (1986) cut out Australian terms such as the collo-quial *stickybeak* "an inquisitive person" (1920—) and standard *billa-bong* "a backwater or stagnant pool" (1865—), after negative feedback from test screenings in the United States. As we've already seen, the 1990s saw an interesting turnaround, when films such as *The Full Monty* and *Trainspotting* employed contemporary slang in their reve-lations of a grittier side of British life. One journalist commented:

> Trouble is, don't you know, Brits are just so good with words. Even their slang sounds so bloody refined. See! See how insidious it is!

British slang terms noted in this article include *knock up* "to wake up (by knocking)" (1603—),[6] *shag* "to have sex (with)" (1786—), and *telly* "television" (1942—, now colloquial). I haven't found many examples of *bell (up)* "to telephone" (2005—), though *give someone a bell* "to telephone" (1933—) is common. At a loss for other exam-ples of British slang, this writer falls back on rhyming slang terms like *skyrocket* "pocket" (1879—) and *whistle and flute* "suit" (1930—), along with nicknames like *Chalky* White and *Dusty* Miller in use in the armed forces during (and perhaps also before) WWI.

Slang and realism

Popular magazines offered the promise of easy money for writers of fiction in the early twentieth century, and enterprising publishers put

---

[6] The sense "to make a woman pregnant; to have sex with a woman" (1813—) originated in the United States, but is also current in Britain.

together lists of slang terms used in particular settings and professions, promising that these would help aspiring writers to create a sense of authority and authenticity not provided by their own life experiences. National differences in slang created particular problems for writers trying to represent the speech of other nationalities. In 1929, *Variety* published a glossary of British slang, including *tar* "a sailor" (1676—, now historical), *rag* "to tease" (1749—), *clear out* "to go away" (1823—), *bad egg* "a person or plan destined to disappoint" (1855—), *bad hat* "a scoundrel" (1876—), and *tec* "a detective" (1879—). Like similar articles published today, this one assumes that a term used by one British speaker is used by all, and conflates various types of slang that are unlikely to have been used by the same individual. *Variety*'s glossary of 'English Underworld Slang' (1931) was probably intended as an aid to scriptwriters attempting to represent British villainy. It included many long-established terms, including *spark* "a diamond" (1599–1924), *poof* "an effeminate man; a homosexual" (1833—), and *drum* "a house; a residence; a drinking den; a brothel" (1846—). Names for various sums of money were also explained, including *pony* "£25" (1797—), *monkey* "£500" (1827—), *tenner* "£10; a ten-pound note" (1845—), and *nicker* "a pound (note)" (1871—). Screenplays based on this list might have convinced American audiences or upper- and middle-class British audiences, but they would be unlikely to have represented realistic speech.

Aspiring writers were also offered help with specialized American slang. In 1916, *The Editor* magazine offered writers a list of 'Tramp Jargon', including:

scoff "to eat" (1798–, originally British)

moniker "a (false) name" (1851–, originally British or Australian)

kettle "a watch" (1865-1981, originally British)

punk "bread" (1891-1991)

bull "a uniformed policeman" (1893–)

soup "nitroglycerine" (1902–1970)

flop "to sleep" (1907–)

flop "sleep" (1916–1925), now more usually "a place to sleep" (1910–)

Presumably this glossary was a hit with *The Editor*'s readers, because in 1917 a further list of terms used by America's homeless was published, by Patrick Casey. It too lists terms originating in Britain, including *office* "a warning; a signal", which we've already seen, and *screw* "a turnkey; a prison officer" (1812—). Terms originating in the United States include:

slope "to leave; to run away" (1830—)
squeal "to inform" (1846—)
stool "an informer" (1859—)
crook "a professional criminal" (1879—)
yap "a fool; an unsophisticated person" (1890–1977)
jocker "an older tramp who travels with a boy; a predatory homosexual" (1893—)

prushun "a boy travelling with a tramp" (1893–, now historical)
bughouse "crazy" (1895—)
mug "to photograph for the purpose of identification" (1899–1990)
dick "a detective" (1908—)

Randolph Jordan offered a similar service to aspiring writers in an article in *Writer's Monthly* magazine in 1925. He suggested that depictions of hobo life should be sprinkled with terms like *oiled* "drunk" (1701—), *fall guy* "a scapegoat" (1983—), *jack* "money" (1890—), *ice* "diamonds" (1896—), *Mary Ann* "marijuana" (1916-1971), *frame* "to implicate in a crime" (1919—), and *needle artist* "an injecting drug-user" (1925+1990).

In 1932, aspiring writers who read *The Editor* were offered an opportunity to add 'underworld lingo' to their repertoire. This glossary included plenty of terms that were well established in use, such as:

on the make "seeking personal gain" (1863—)
hood "hoodlum: a petty gangster" (1880—)
lam "to flee" (1886—)
lug "a big stupid man; a hanger-on" (1887—)
rock "a diamond" (1888—)
glom "to steal" (1897—)

apple-knocker "a baseball player; a yokel; a fool" (1902—)
rap "an accusation; a criminal charge" (1903—)
cluck "a fool" (1904—)
cannon "a pickpocket" (1910—)
chisel(l)er "a petty thief" (1918—)

Newer terms in the list include *bug* "a burglar alarm" (1925–1955), *pay-off* "protection money; a bribe" (1928—), *scram* "to depart quickly" (1928—), *finger* "to accuse; to inform against" (1930—), and *in the doghouse* "in trouble; out of favour" (1931—). Some of these lists may have been compiled from crime stories and films, further perpetuating stereotypes.

In part through their prominence in films, American gangsters also received a great deal of attention in newspapers. In 1930, the *American Mercury* published a glossary of the slang used by racketeers, including *plant* "a hiding place for stolen or illegal goods" (1785—, originally British), *roscoe* "a handgun" (1914—, later, and less frequently, *John Roscoe*), and *heat* "pressure; police attention" (1925—). *Tommy* "a machine gun" (1931—) is short for *Tommy gun* (1929—), derived from the name of the general after whom it was originally named a *Thompson* (1920—). *McCoy* "genuine" (1928-1996) is also listed, from the more common phrase *the real McCoy* "the genuine article" (1856—), whose etymology is still much debated. In 1931, the *Saturday Review of Literature* included a glossary of 'New Words' used by racketeers, including *college* "jail" (1620-1990, originally British), *yen* "a desire for anything" (1906—, from the earlier sense "a craving for opium" (1876-1974), probably from Cantonese), and *creep joint* "a gambling joint that moves nightly; any disreputable establishment" (1921—). The Associated Press issued a 'Dispatch from Chicago' in 1932, listing the latest terms used by gunmen in the city, which included *troops* "a criminal gang" (1932—), *gunsel* "a stupid or untrustworthy person" (1932—, derived from the sense "a naive youth; a homosexual" (1912—)), and *(big) wheel* "a big shot; the leader of a criminal gang" (1932—). Cross-fertilization between the various accounts and representations of criminal language from the media and entertainment industries probably also influenced the development of criminal language itself, in that many of those who aspired to a life of crime would, initially at least, have copied the language used by their fictional heroes.

The radio

When radio broadcasting began in earnest after WWI, it need hardly be said that the BBC used Standard English, but within a few decades light entertainment was beginning to expose listeners to various types of non-standard language, and entertainers' catchphrases began to be repeated in the same way that music-hall performers' catchphrases had been: to signal a shared sense of humour and create group identity. Tommy Handley's show *It's That Man Again* (later *ITMA*) began broadcasting topical entertainment shortly before the outbreak of WWII, alluding in its title both to the German Chancellor, who seemed to be constantly in the news, and to the burgeoning use of acronyms and initialisms. Catchphrases like *I don't mind if I do, ta-ta for now*, and *Can I do you now, sir?* enabled listeners to bond with one another by signalling their enjoyment of the programme's irreverent humour. Variety shows, such as *Workers' Playtime* and *Variety Bandbox*, brought numerous other music-hall catchphrases to the public's attention, such as *how's your father* and *Can you hear me mother?*, to a considerably wider audience. *The Goon Show* introduced (or popularized) the fictitious diseases the dreaded *lurgy* (1947—) and the *nadger plague* or *nadgers* (1956—), from which the sense "a testicle" (1967—) developed.

British radio also preserved one form of slang that might otherwise have fallen from use altogether. Polari, a semi-secret language used by travelling entertainers and actors, borrowed words from Romany, Italian, Spanish, and back slang. While homosexuality was illegal in Britain, and particularly during the post-war period when laws were enforced with particular rigour, Polari was used among gay men as a way of signalling and cementing their gay self-image. In the 1960s, a radio programme called *Round the Horne* combined Polari with innuendo and a camp style of delivery to deliver deliberately ambiguous comedy. In 'Body Bona', a sketch based in a gym, Julian (Hugh Paddick) describes his physical transformation to Kenneth Horne (who plays himself), prompted by Sandy (Kenneth Williams), using *varda* "to look" and *lally* "leg", which we've already seen:

> J: I used to be a puny little omi. I had lallies like a flamingo – and narrow shoulders.
> S: Yes. He had to cross his braces to keep his trousers up.
> J: And a little pale eek, and lifeless riah.
> S: He was like a wallflower Mr Horne.
> KH: That wasn't the flower that came to mind.
> S: A wallflower he was. Now he's a hardy annual aren't you Jule?
> J: Thanks to Sand and his method. He showed me his dynamic tension and overnight I became the great butch omi you vada now.

omee "a man; a landlord" (1859–, Polari)	*pansy* "a homosexual or effeminate man" (1926–) [implied]
eek or *ecaf* "a face" (1962–, back slang)	*butch* "overtly masculine" (1941–)
riah "hair" (1962 , back slang)	

Listeners' understanding of these sketches would have varied dramatically depending on their ability to pick up on the subtext. Julian and Sandy are described as out-of-work actors, and their extravagant speech and camp intonation might have sound merely theatrical to less alert members of the audience. Others, perhaps in the same room, would have understood and relished the coded humour. *Round the Horne* also offers the earliest *OED* citation for *naff* "unfashionable; vulgar; lacking in style" (1966–). The origins of *rumpo* "sexual intercourse" (1986–) may lie in *Round the Horne*'s Rambling Syd Rumpo, a singer of nonsensical innuendo.

With less regulation of the airwaves in the United States, commercial stations were freer to make use of non-standard language where it helped listener figures. By the 1950s, individual DJs were developing distinctive speech styles to attract specific target audiences. In 1956, Hy Lit's *Rock 'en Roll Kingdom* show would begin something like this:

Calling all my beats, beards, Buddhist cats, big time spenders, money
lenders, tea totallers [sic], elbow benders, hog callers, home run hitters,
finger poppin' daddy's [sic], and cool baby sitters. For all my carrot tops,
lollipops, and extremely delicate gum drops. It's Hyski 'O Roonie McVouti
'O Zoot calling, up town, down town, cross town. Here there, everywhere.
Your man with the plan, on the scene with the record machine.

The immediacy, informality, and intimacy of radio, and its appeal to
tightly defined groups made it an extremely effective medium for the
transmission of slang. Its role was largely one of dissemination rather
than creation, however. Lit shows himself to be up to date and in the
know (for a white man), by using Vout,[7] playful rhyme, and slang,
including some terms discussed above:

beat "a beatnik" (1955–)

beard "a person with a beard" (1928–) or
possibly "a betting go-between" (1953–)

big time "notable; famous" (1913–)

elbow-bender "a heavy drinker" (1942–)

hog-caller "a person who shouts or
complains loudly" (1889–)

finger-popping "finger-snapping (in time
with music)" (1955–)

daddy "a man" (1926–)

babysitter "a childminder" (1937–)

carrot top "a red-haired person"
(1889–)

lollipop ?"an attractive woman" (1860-
1985)

gumdrop ?"a sweetheart" (1896+1901),
but its real purpose is the rhyme
-ski [as a suffix] (1902–)

Although Lit's listeners were at many removes from the origins of
these terms, they could also acquire coolness by copying his slang.
British pirate radio stations and (from 1967) Radio One played a
similar role in disseminating youth slang within and around the
records they played. Radio continued to have a disproportionate
influence on the language of young people as long as televisions
were restricted to living rooms and viewing remained a family activity. With the advent of cheap and portable transistor radios in the

---

[7] Vout is a form of wordplay invented by Slim Gaillard, a jazz musician and singer.
Lit adopts its characteristic addition of -oroonee (though Gaillard seems to have
preferred -oreenee) and -vouti.

1960s, young people could listen to programmes targeting their own age group wherever they were. Crucially, listening to the radio could be a social activity, overlapping with and feeding into everyday conversation. These circumstances were particularly favourable to the adoption of new slang.

Television

The 1930s saw the establishment of television broadcasting on a limited basis, with domestic sets becoming more affordable in the decades after WWII. By the end of the 1960s, homes without a television set were in a minority in both Britain and the United States. Words introduced by American television shows include *cowabunga* "yippee" (1954—, from the *Howdy Doody* show, but further popularized by *The Simpsons*), *bippy* "buttocks" (1968—, from *Rowan & Martin's Laugh-In*), *gomer* "a difficult elderly patient" (1972—, from *The Andy Griffith Show*), *muppet* "an idiot" (1989—), *dibble* "a policeman; the police" (1989—, from *Top Cat*), and *scooby (-doo)* "a clue" (1993—, by rhyming slang). The last three, although originating in American programmes, are originally and chiefly British. American programmes also popularized *not!* to highlight the sarcasm of a previous statement (1888—, *Saturday Night Live* and *Wayne's World*), *doh* in recognition of one's own stupidity (1945—, *The Simpsons*), and *noogie(s)* "a poke or grind with the knuckles" (1968—, *Saturday Night Live*).

Informal terms from British television shows include *nudge nudge (wink wink)* used to imply sexual innuendo (1969—, from *Monty Python's Flying Circus*), *plonker* "an idiot" (1966—, popularized by *Only Fools and Horses*), *tardis* "anything apparently bigger on the inside than the outside" (1985—, from *Doctor Who*), *lovely jubbly* "excellent" (1989—, from *Only Fools and Horses*), *wibble* "to talk nonsense" (1994—, from *Blackadder*), and *spam* "unsolicited mass emails" (1994—, inspired by a *Monty Python* sketch). The last two both appear to have arisen among computer users, who we'll return to

20 Slang on television: Robertson Royston, 'EastEnders Canteen'.

in the next chapter. Terms like these often function as in-jokes to begin with, but if they last for long enough and pass into wider use, they can become slang.

Television provided an unprecedented opportunity for the spread of slang, and this has increased as production companies have become more alert to the profits offered by international markets. Australian soaps like *Neighbours* and *Home and Away* have been held responsible for British pensioners' inability to understand their grandchildren, but linguistic difference has also been a selling point. When the BBC exported *Eastenders* to the United States, they drew attention to its unfamiliar language as a mark of its authenticity:

> Unfortunately for American viewers, a fair amount of the dialogue is in British slang — "legless" for drunk, "naff off" for get lost, "short of the readies" for broke. And the inhabitants of Albert Square are prone to break into the less comprehensible Cockney rhyming slang, in which "dog and bone" equals telephone.... Not to worry. The British Broadcasting Corp. will try to

make it clear for you. Saturday night's introductory program…includes a glossary of the slang, and viewers will be able to write and get a phrase book to help understand the lingo.

Legless "drunk" (1976—, abbreviated from *legless drunk* (1926—)) is common in British slang, as is *readies*, which we've already seen. *Naff off* "get lost" (1959—) originated as a euphemistic substitution, largely used on stage and television, where censorship didn't permit *fuck off*. *Dog and bone* "telephone" (1961—) is among the most frequently cited of rhyming slang terms. Although this article refers to slang, the phrase book largely listed British colloquialisms. Hearing spoken English from around the world doesn't enable viewers to make fine distinctions between different levels of language.

Popular culture

Intertwined with the development of cinema, radio, and television is the music industry. Record promoters relied on radio presenters for airtime; radio presenters needed records that would deliver listeners for their advertisers. Musicians made films; actors made records. The entertainment industry was able to spread slang around a country and even around the world. Radio, the record industry, television, and film, were essential components in the development of various strands of youth culture and the slang that goes with them. Because all of these industries rely on novelty and innovation, they've fed into and fed on a faster turnover of slang terms. This has exacerbated communication problems between teenagers and their parents, leading some parents to suspect that their children were using slang to conceal illicit activities.

Let's return, finally, to the issue of the dissemination of slang in the media, using a number of key cultural terms from the late nineteenth to the twenty-first century, all of which began as slang but entered into general usage, often giving rise to derived forms that were never slang. *Ragtime* described a style of popular African American music in the 1890s. Its earliest documented use with this sense is from 1896.

By 1901, it was being used in the mainstream press in the United States, giving rise to derived forms such as *ragtimer* (1901), *to ragtime* (1908), and *ragtiming* (1912). The first use I've been able to find in the British mainstream press is from 1913, giving a transatlantic transmission period of seventeen years.

Jazz is first recorded with reference to music in 1915, appearing in the mainstream press in the United States in the same year, along with *to jazz* (1915), *jazzy* (1916), *jazzer* (1917), *jazzman* (1919), *jazzist* (1921), *jazzification* (1924), and *jazzophile* (1926).[8] With a first citation from the British press in 1919, the transmission period had come down to four years, a reduction probably attributable as much to the movement of people during WWI as to early developments in recording technology. The interwar period saw a further reduction in transmission time: *swing* is first recorded with reference to a musical style in 1936, giving rise to the adjective *swinging* (1955) and predated by the noun *swinger* (1934). It's found in the British mainstream press by 1938: a transmission time of only two years. Similarly, *funk*, first documented with reference to music in 1959, reached the British press in 1961. However, an explosion of derived forms, including *funky* (1972), *funk oriented* (1977), *jazz funk* (1977), *funk rock* (1977), *funk out* (1978), *funkadelic* (1978), *punk funk* (1979), *funk fushion* (1979), *funkless* (1979), *neo-funky* (1980), *neo-funk* (1982), *funkiness* (1983), and *funkify* (1989), suggest that *funk* remained a specialist interest for at least a decade.[9] Its later spread is connected with *disco*, abbreviated from French *discothèque*. *Disco* was first documented in 1964, giving rise to *disco beat* (1965), but it took a while to reach the mainstream press in the United States (1974), making the transition to the British press in 1975. Later derived terms include *disco mania* (1977), *to disco* (1979), *ex-disco* (1981), and *neo-disco* (1983). By this time, the combination of improved

---

[8] Cassidy, *How the Irish Invented Slang*, 59–73, offers an Irish etymology for *jazz*. You can take part in the debate on <http://en.wikipedia.org/wiki/Talk:Jazz>.
[9] The *neo-* forms demonstrate that fashion quickly moved on.

technology and marketing had ensured that mainstream American trends reached the British mainstream within a year or two, although sometimes it took longer for the American mainstream to embrace and exploit new African American musical developments.

Let's see whether this rate of transmission has changed in more recent years. *Bling (bling)* "ostentatious jewellery or other displays of wealth", also used as an adjective "ostentatious; flashy" (1999—), appeared in the title and chorus of a song on B.G.'s rap album *Chopper City in the Ghetto* (released in April 1999). It was used in a similar way in the chorus of 'Ice on my Wrist' by Magic and Master P in August of the same year and its appearance in some online versions of the lyrics of Tupac's 'Fuck Friendz' (recorded 1995–6) suggests that this and similar sounds may have been in circulation in the hip hop community before the written form became fixed. By November 1999, American newspapers were using *bling bling* with jocular reference to B.G.'s wealth and with reference to African American sportsmen with similar taste in jewellery by January 2000. In November 2000 it was used with reference to chunky gold jewellery in the fashion pages of Australian and British newspapers, reaching Canada by December of the same year. Having quickly become an international term, *bling* was also highly productive, giving rise to several frequently used derivatives, including *(bling-)blinging* (March 2000), *(bling-)blinger* (June 2001), *to bling* (July 2001), *(bling-)blinged* (October 2001), *(bling-)blingy* (June 2002), *blinged out* (August 2002), and *blinged up* (July 2003). Although *bling* retained its association with African American street fashion, it became a journalistic buzzword, and writers all around the world felt able to create new derivatives, including *anti-bling(-bling)* (August 2000), *non-bling* (September 2002), *non-blinger* (October 2002), *de-blingification* and *euro-bling* (both June 2003), *(bling-)bling master* (July 2003), *(bling-)blingify* (January 2004), *eco-bling* (July 2005), *cyber-bling* (July 2006), *blingification* (September 2006), *blingee* (May 2007), *non-blingy* and *blingette* (both June 2007), *blinginess* (July 2007), *blingily* (November 2007), and *unbling* (January 2008). The difference between *bling* and the earlier terms lies not so much in the speed of transmission, although that has continued to shorten: it lies in the rate of naturalization. This was enhanced by the combined powers of the music and fashion industries, as well as the early development of the Internet, which is the subject of the next chapter.

Conclusions

What we see in newspapers, on television, and in films isn't slang. With the possible exception of 'reality' television, what we see in the media are representations of slang. Like frogs in the media, some are carefully observed and true to life, while others (fairy-tale frogs, Kermit, Crazy Frog) behave in predictably endearing or annoying ways. The media and entertainment industries have raised the profile of slang, allowing us to pick up slang from around the world and to learn about other people's attitudes towards it, but studying representations of slang can be misleading.

These industries may have been the first to realise that slang could help to sell their products, but other industries soon caught on, and slang (genuine or manufactured) has become a staple feature of advertising (see p. 64). The forces of individualism and commerce are now inextricably linked in the development and spread of slang. The mass media has also shaped and expressed changing attitudes towards slang. Those who object to slang remain convinced that it devalues its users by making them seem both unattractive and uncultured, and that it contaminates whoever comes into contact with it, particularly the young. We've also seen, from around the English-speaking world, a growing sense that American slang has encroached not only on the territory of national slangs, but also on to ground that ought to be preserved for Standard English.

Endnotes

An example of the coverage of a recent newspaper slang controversy is provided by Max Davidson's 'Emma Thompson's Attack on Slang: the Pedants' Battle may be Lost', *Telegraph* 29 Sept. 2010, n.p., available online at <http://www.telegraph .co.uk>. Also quoted in this chapter are Finley Peter Dunne's *Mr. Dooley in Peace and War* (Boston: Small, Maynard & Co., 1898, repr. Urbana: University of Illinois Press, 2001), 'Mr. Dooley on Diplomacy', 1–5 (1), and J. R. McReynolds Banks's 'An Unabridged Collegiate Dictionary', *Columbia Jester* 27 (Dec. 1927), 10; (Jan. 1928), 19; (Feb. 1928), 14; (Mar. 1928), 12. 'The Tichborne Case', *The Times*, 25 Jun. 1880, 4, provides information about Orton's deception and trial. Harrigan orders tea in 'Rhyming Slang', *Penny Illustrated Paper*, 20 Aug. 1910, 248, and two extracts were provided from Walter Anthony's interview with Bert Little: 'Leslie on English as she is Spoke', *The San Francisco Call*, 20 Feb. 1910, 63. Anthony is also quoted celebrating America's slang victory in 'Our Cousin's Slang', *The San Francisco Call*, 21 Nov. 1909, 27. The review of *The Degenerates* is from 'Mrs Langtry at the Prince's Theatre', *The Times*, 21 Jan. 1885, 5. The glossary was published in 'Society Slang', *Bristol Mercury and Daily Post*, 20 Nov. 1899, n.p., and 'Degenerates' Slang Glossary', *Chicago Daily Tribune*, 8 Mar. 1900, 7. Other newspaper articles cited are 'Translated for English Use', *Boston Daily Globe*, 17 Aug. 1913, 45; 'American Slang', *The Argus* (Melbourne), 21 Mar. 1918, 5; 'Australian Speech and American Slang', *The Sydney Morning Herald*, 18 Jun. 1932, 9; and Stephanie Schorow, 'Brit-slang Invasion; Blimey!', *The Boston Herald*, 11 Jun. 1999, Arts & Life, 63. I haven't been able to trace the *Daily Mail* article about 'mental indiscipline', but it's cited in 'Yankee Slang Increasing', *The Argus* (Melbourne), 19 Jul. 1913, 8. The *Fast Life* glossary is from 'Use This Dictionary of Slang in Exploitation', *Film Daily* 49, 22 Aug. 1929, 15, based on James J. Finerty's *Criminalese: a Dictionary of the Slang Talk of the Criminal* (Washington, DC: [self-published], 1926), itself not an entirely original compilation.

Peter Faiman's *Crocodile Dundee* (Hollywood: Paramount, 1986) was followed by sequels in 1988 and 2001. The extract from *Round the Horne* is from series 3, programme 20, first broadcast on 25 Jun. 1967, from Barry Took and Marty Feldman's *Round the Horne* (London: Woburn Press, 1974), 145. Hy Lit's style is based on a later representation quoted on his web site <http://www.hylitradio.com/index.php?page=6>, though he also produced *Hy Lit's Unbelievable Dictionary of Hip Words for Groovy People* (Philadelphia: Hyski, 1968). Vout is best exemplified by Slim Gaillard's *Vout-O-Reenee Dictionary* ([?Hollywood: Atomic Records], 1946). The influence of *Neighbours* on British speech is discussed in Tracey Harrison's 'It's True. Kids Don't Talk the Same Language; Slang Takes Over From English', *Daily Record*, 29 Jul. 1999, 26, and Larry Thorson promotes the introduction of *EastEnders* to American audiences in 'Cockney Soap Opera on the Telly in United States', Associated Press, 8 Jan. 1988. American viewers were encouraged to refer to *How to Speak EastEnders: A Brief Glossary of Cockney Expressions* (n.p.: Lionheart, 1988).

11 Leet to Lols: The Digital Age

Building on the technological advances discussed in Chapter 10, developments in computer technology have, once again, revolutionized the way we communicate. Until only a few decades ago, emigrants kept in touch with family and friends back home with letters sent by ship or air, and then anxiously counted the days until a reply could be expected. Expensive phone calls were reserved for really bad news. Now we learn about daily routines alongside newsworthy world events from the people experiencing them and (crucially for our purposes) in their own words. Even people who still rely on newspaper and television for their news are exposed to extracts from blogs and tweets. News of the latest celebrity gossip or stage-managed media event is available within the hour, sometimes instantaneously, rather than in magazines weeks later. We engage with and participate in products and events created by the media online, and we can reveal and observe changes taking place in slang around the world. Connections between media types increase our exposure to new slang: interrelated blogs, books, films, games, podcasts, apps (and so on) reinforce new terms which sometimes feed into our face-to-face conversations. But we're not passive consumers: amateur reviewers now lambast lazy slang stereotypes within hours of a film's release. Books and articles on contentious topics (like slang) receive immediate scrutiny online (see p. 239 n).

Scholarly accounts of computer-mediated communication tend to have little to say about the use of slang. They may have found (and it's my impression too), that slang used in many contexts online is pretty similar to the slang used in speech. For people with a primary interest in online communication, slang isn't particularly interesting; but for those of us with a primary interest in slang, online communication is very interesting indeed.

The Internet builds connections between people, and these connections generate new networks of slang. Spending time online isn't a substitute or alternative to 'real life': it is an integral part of it, often interwoven with face-to-face social contact. Computer users who come across unfamiliar slang terms may start to use them both online and in speech if they're exposed to them often enough. In this chapter, I'm going to look at three interrelated topics: the influence of computers and the Internet in disseminating slang, the increased availability of information about slang, and developments in the nature of slang itself.

What is slang?

Definitions of slang that emphasize its use in spoken language are now outdated. Conversations between the same two individuals can take place in person, by phone, using text messages or email, in blogs, by instant messaging, or via webcams. Friends who use slang terms in writing will probably also use at least some of the same slang in their conversations (and vice versa), so the line between terms used in writing and those used in speech is now more uncertain than ever. Online communication is a hybrid between speech and writing. It's much more speech-like than formal written English and provides representations of non-verbal features of face-to-face communication, such as facial expressions and laughter. It can also be speech-like in signalling group

"It helps him realise I'm being serious."

21   Crossed wires II: Clive Goddard, 'It Helps Him Realise I'm Being Serious'.

membership and attitude: functions we've identified as belonging to slang in speech. Of course, nobody speaks exactly as they would type, but the barrier between written and spoken English has become more permeable: it no longer represents a reliable basis for deciding what is or isn't slang.

Hackers and gamers

I'll begin by considering the development of computer slang chronologically. *Hackers* "computer enthusiasts (who gain unauthorized access to files or networks)" (1976—) were originally concentrated in research institutions and universities, where mainframe computers were sometimes available without too many questions being asked, as long as amateur users didn't interfere with the access required for serious research. Hackers tended to congregate in university computing rooms in the evenings and at weekends, so their virtual communication was supplemental to face-to-face conversation. It's likely that individuals with such a specialized and esoteric interest would've found one another on campus in any case (nerds of a feather, and all that), but being able to communicate online will have facilitated their social connections. Links between mainframes became possible during the late 1960s, but the first substantial attempt to document the slang of computer users was the Jargon File, compiled collaboratively at Stanford University from 1975, with later input from other universities. The earliest version includes plenty of terms that didn't originate in this context, including:

diddle "to work ineffectually; to mess about" (1826–), but probably influenced by *diddle* "to masturbate" (1934–, US)

zero "to set to zero" (1949–, originally engineers)

spaz "to behave erratically; to make a serious mistake" (1957–)

glitch "a temporary malfunction" (1962–, originally astronauts)

grungy "extremely dirty" (1964–, originally students)

moby "large; complicated; exciting" (1965–, originally students)

tweak "to adjust slightly" (1966–, originally engineers)

vanilla "ordinary" (1972–, originally gay)

Computer programmers had come up with some of their own terms too, including some that were already quite well established by this date, such as *klu(d)ge* "a makeshift system or repair" (1962–), *down* "out of action" (1965–), *number-cruncher* "a computer; an unimaginative human analyser of data" (1968–), *flame* "to rant" (1968–), now usually "to send an abusive message about or to someone" (1983–), and *bells and whistles* "appealing but unnecessary features" (1975–).

As well as documenting the use of new words and senses, the Jargon File also explores the creation of words from among the existing resources of English, such as *bogosity* "the state or quality of being bogus", *mumblage* "indistinct or unclear speech or information", *softwarily* "in a manner appropriate to software", and *winnitude* "the quality of winning", none of which is listed in the *OED* although all are still current. Even the compilers of this list felt it necessary to advise against the use of some computing slang, and three usages are labelled as 'silly': *aos* "to increase; to turn up", *cdr* "to trace", and *What's the state of the world-p? "What's going on?"*

From the late 1970s, computer users were able to engage in real-time competitive or collaborative play in games that came to be known as MUDs (*multi-user dungeon(s)*, 1983—). Because of the speed of play and the relatively limited range of likely topics, acronyms and initialisms became commonplace, including *MMG* "massively multiplayer game" and *RTS* "real-time strategy game". Some of the vocabulary used by computer gamers was borrowed from military slang, such as the Vietnam-era *frag* "to kill (a superior officer) (with a fragmentation grenade)" (1970—). The language of table-based role-playing games contributed jargon like *player character* and *non-player character*, and probably also a tendency towards hyperbole and the use of archaic vocabulary, such as *sirrah, my lady,* and *methinks*.

Alongside these changes, a new way of representing the spoken language developed among computer gamers. Called *leetspeak* or *leet*,[1] it involves the replacement of letters with numbers or other characters that resemble them. For example, <l> can be represented by <1>, <e> by <3>, and <t> by <7>, so that *leet* can be spelt <1337>. Letters are sometimes replaced by approximate representations: <|-|> for <h>, <|\|> for <n>, and <|3> for <b>, and so on. Letters and other symbols also began to be substituted for sounds: <l8> for *late*, <sux> for *sucks*, <c#> for *cash*, and <c@> for *cat*.

---

[1] *Leet* is derived from *elite*, a status on bulletin boards and games that gave various privileges, including editing access to file folders.

Plurals are commonly formed with <z> rather than <s>, as in <d00dz> for *dudes*. These disguised spellings are sometimes found alongside deliberate typos such as *teh* (*the*), *pr0n* (porn), and *pwned* (*owned*), as well as initialisms like *HPB* "high-ping bastard: a player with a bad connection", *BFG* "big fucking gun", and *NPC* "a non-player character". *Leetspeak* isn't just about weird spelling and abbreviations, though: there are also grammatical features, largely involving simplification. For instance, object pronouns can be used as subjects and present tenses predominate:

Me g0 gr4b s0Me k0ph33
I am going to grab some coffee

Leetspeak is also characterized by distinctive patterns of word formation, particularly the addition of <-or> to verbs, creating forms like *suxor* and *roxor* for all forms of *suck* "to be contemptible, disgusting, or boring" (1971—) and *rock* "to be excellent" (1969—). Nouns, like *cuntor* "despicable person", are also found, alongside continued use of the hacker suffix <-age> to create nouns like *ownage* "ownership; domination" (since at least 2000—).

Leetspeak provided users with a way to evade text filters and discuss outlawed topics, but it was probably more useful as a method for signalling their position in the hierarchy. Only experienced gamers would be fluent, which enabled them to exclude, tease, or confuse new users by using terms such as *n00b* "a novice" (since at least 2000—) or *llama* "a novice" (since at least 2004—) and *w00t* "hurray" (since at least 2000—). However, by the late 1990s, these conventions had become so widely used that they no longer functioned as a signal of elite knowledge, and serious computer enthusiasts began to avoid them.

The decline of leetspeak hasn't meant that computer gamers now type in Standard English. Here, for example, is an exchange from a *World of Warcraft* forum from April 2010, with the subject 'tiny abom vs reg wfs', containing very little evidence of leetspeak:

Bilbo939: tiny abom vs reg whispering fanged? mut spec.. other trink is war token so i dont think i wana lose that to use both :P
Storkchild: Tiny Abom = win.
Unless they've nerfed it recently and I haven't read about it.
But from info I know from a month or two ago it went
H Tiny Abom > War Token > H Whisper > Reg Tiny Abom
Kopik: My Combat spreadsheet has it below both Heroic DV/DC and WFS (normal).
Depressing, because it looks like a fun trinket.
Unb3table: Cept he asked about mut, failboat.

The chances are that this exchange either makes perfect sense to you or very little. I belong to the second camp, but some familiar abbreviations include *don't* for *do not* (1670—), *cept* for *except* (1851—), *vs* for *versus* (1889—), *wana* (more usually *wanna*) for *want to* (1896—), *info* for *information* (1907—), and *spec.* for *specification* (1956—). From the context, I worked out that *trink* was short for *trinket* and *reg* for *regular*. *Abom* is short for *abomination* and *H* for *heroic*, both words used with specific reference to features of the game. :P is a tongue-in-cheek emoticon. The *World of Warcraft* glossary tells me that *nerf* means "to downgrade", which may be related to the proprietary name of a foam rubber used in making children's play equipment (1970—) which could, in its turn, be related to drag-racing, where *nerf* means "to bump (another car)" (1952—) and a *nerf bar* (1955—) or *nerfing-bar* (1949—) protects from minor bumps. *Urban Dictionary* helped me with *failboat*, which originally meant "a boat doomed to failure" (since at least 2004—), but can also refer to people. Many of the abbreviations are found in general speech or informal writing, with those that are specific to the game being jargon rather than slang. Evidence from elsewhere suggests that *nerf* and *failboat* are more widely used as slang.

Understanding the words isn't the same as understanding what they're talking about, though: what I would need to do is invest 20 hours (or more) in playing *World of Warcraft* so that I could learn the words in a meaningful context. But why is that necessary? Why can't players talk about the game in Standard English? After all, there are players from around the world, and they aren't all native speakers of English. Wouldn't it make sense to write in a more accessible way?

There are a number of reasons why this mixture of slang and jargon is preferable in specialized online contexts. First, these terms are often quicker to type, which is particularly important in the middle of a battle, where superfluous key strokes could be a matter of virtual life and death. Second, there aren't Standard English synonyms for all of these terms. The ones that refer to specific features of *World of Warcraft* are likely to remain as jargon rather than spreading to more general slang usage. Third, these words often play a social as well as a communicative function: they allow users to demonstrate their knowledge to other game-players, either to gain approval from those with more experience, or to inspire admiration and imitation from those with less. Finally, as we've already observed, the individual who fails to use or understand these terms correctly is quickly identified as a *failboat*. The slang and jargon act as a kind of initiation rite: anyone who's serious about playing the game is going to have to show willing by learning to talk (ok, write) appropriately. One of the reasons for using slang and jargon in this context is precisely that they don't make sense to those outside the group. They (or possibly you) don't want us (or maybe it's only me) to understand. This type of jargon shades into cant when narrowly defined and fixed meanings are used to prevent rather than to facilitate understanding.

The Internet, the Web, social networking, and blogging

By the late 1980s, individuals at geographically separate institutions were able to exchange emails and other files using the Internet. The cost of home computing was also dropping to affordable levels for the mass market. The World Wide Web was developed as a tool for navigating the Internet in the early 1990s, and it was at this point that the mainstream press began to comment on the effect of computing on the English language, noting the use of slang derived from the earlier university-based hackers, as well as some newer terms:

log on "to access one's computer (account)" (1963–)

phone-phreaker "a person who fraudulently accesses a telephone line" (1977–)

chiphead "a computer enthusiast" (since at least 1982–)

cyberspace "the virtual environment in which online communication takes place" (1982–)

netiquette "accepted standards of behaviour online" (1982–)

lurker "a person who reads bulletin boards but doesn't contribute" (1984–)

nethead "a habitual Internet-user" (1984–)

cyberpunk "a person who gains unauthorized access to computer files or networks" (1989–)

FAQ "frequently asked questions" (1991–)

bio-break "a toilet break" (since at least 1994–)

net-surfer "a casually inquisitive user of the Internet" (since at least 1994–)

thumb-candy "a computer game that isn't intellectually challenging" (since at least 1994–)

mouse potato "a habitual Internet-user" (1994–)

betamax "to supersede a superior technology; to defeat a superior opponent" (since at least 1997–)

Terms like these began as the professional slang of computing, but some would now pass unnoticed in formal writing, offering a powerful demonstration of the expansion and influence of online communication.

Blogs fulfil the functions of product- or self-promotion, personal journal, group therapy, confessional, journalism (and many others), and allow individuals to express their thoughts and record their language use online. Many blogs use standard or colloquial English, with more or less standard punctuation and spelling, even those addressing specialized groups like online gamers, *Star Trek* fans, and sports enthusiasts. This may be because many bloggers either are or aspire to be professional writers, and using unconventional typography and slang would undermine their credibility. However, some bloggers do make use of slang, perhaps deliberately, to signal their connection with the realities of the life they represent. A blogger's slang isn't necessarily a reflection of their own (or anyone's) spoken usage, but where we see slang terms reoccurring in blogs and other contexts, they provide useful supplementary evidence. This extract, written by 'prison journalist and gangster chronicler' Seth Ferranti, is from an American blog called *Gorilla Convict*:

> Fray's attitude toward outsiders, especially the dudes from New York, was to lean on them. He put his muscle game down and dared the New Yorkers to make a move. Fray felt secure in his city and he put his mentality in effect. When Alpo came into town flossing and fronting that gangster shit, Fray called his bluff, got shit off him and didn't even pay him. He treated Alpo like a sucker. He was leaning on the New Yorker and saw him as a coward even before he started snitching. Fray had the 411 on Alpo from the jump, before he knew him he saw the snake for what he was. In retrospect Fray played Alpo for the buster he was.

lean on "to put pressure on" (1955–)
put down "to perform; to do; to say" (1943–, originally African American)
mentality "mental ability; intelligence" (1856–, slang in later use)
floss "to flirt; to show off; to flaunt one's wealth or possessions" (1938–, originally African American)
front "to show off; to pretend to be something one is not" (1971–, originally African American)
shit "rubbish; nonsense" (1927–)
call someone's bluff "to accept a challenge or invite a showdown" (1876–, originally poker)

shit "drugs" (1950–)
sucker "a gullible fool" (1831–)
snitch "to turn informer" (1718–, originally British)
411 "information" (1985–)
the jump "the start" (1831–)
snake "a treacherous person" (1593–)
play for (a fool, sucker, or, as in this case, *buster)* "to deceive; make a fool of; cheat" (1869–)
buster "a loser; a failure; a coward" (1991–) or "an informer" (1994–), both originally African American

For the slang lexicographer, what's really interesting about blogs is that, unlike conventional publishing, they don't marginalize the everyday language of normal (or unusual) people. Bloggers think about their audience, of course, and they might modify their language to create particular effects, but we do that when we speak as well: if we didn't, there wouldn't be any slang. Bock the Robber has blogged from Limerick in Ireland since March 2006, when he began with a complaint about political correctness. His entertainingly ranty blog is written with an international audience in mind, and is colloquial in tone rather than being packed with slang like the last extract. Nevertheless, slang terms do occur:

guff "lies; nonsense" (1880–)

bollocks "a stupid or contemptible person" (1916–), often <bollix> or <bollox>

half-assed "ineffectual; inadequate" (1932–)

gobshite "an idiot; a disliked person" (1946–)

give a rat's arse "to be indifferent" (1953–), usually <ass>

shitload "a lot" (1962–)

slag (off) "to criticize" (1965–)

skobe (from *skobie*) "a scumbag" (2000–)

skanger "a (Dublin) scumbag" (2000–)

This blog proves not only that these terms are in current use in Limerick but also that Limerick slang includes terms originating in the US (*guff, half-assed, give a rat's ass, shitload*) and the UK (*slag (off)*), alongside distinctively Irish ones (*bollocks, gobshite, skobe, skanger*). In the past, slang lexicographers have been content to label words as 'originally US' or to cover their backs with 'originally and chiefly US', but now we can test these gut feelings. Electronic searches of other blogs confirm that these uses of *bollocks, skobe,* and *skanger* appear to be restricted to Irish English. Although *skanger* used to be restricted to Dublin, it has achieved wider recognition through a parody of MTV's *Pimp My Ride*, called *Skanger Me Banger*. *Gobshite* is used on the UK mainland but, along with *slag (off)*, appears not to have spread much further afield. Rat's posteriors, variously spelt, are withheld in every first-language English-speaking country I could think of, and *half-assed* (or *-arsed*), *guff,* and *shitload* are also widely used. If *skanger* does spread into wider usage, we'll be able to track when and perhaps even how this happened.

Social-networking sites began to appear in 1994, but by the end of the decade they tended to build on existing real-world relationships (which would tend to involve slang) rather than creating new links based on common interests (which would tend to involve jargon). After a few false starts, Facebook was launched in 2004. Originally based at Harvard, it enabled students to find out about and contact each another. Though it's far from being the only social-networking site, it's widely used among English speakers and now has hundreds of millions of registered users around the world. Users will be familiar with terms such as *unfriend* "to remove someone from one's 'friend' list" (since at least 2001— with reference to other social-networking applications and also to real life), *facebook* "to log into, be on, or check someone's profile on Facebook" (2004—), and *facebook stalk* "to monitor someone on Facebook surreptitiously, and with an unhealthy level of interest" (2004—). Facebook is referred to informally as *FB* (2004—), *Fbook* (since at least 2005—), *Fuckbook* (since at least 2005—), *Facey B* (since at least 2006—), *Facey* (since at least 2007—), and *Facefuck* (since at least 2007—). Many well-established terms have also acquired senses specific to Facebook and similar sites, including *poke, post, like, friend, status, news, tag,* and *profile.*

My Facebook *friends* tend to post in more or less Standard English, though they sometimes use colloquialisms and slang. They generally employ conventional spellings, though they occasionally take liberties with the usual rules for capitalization and punctuation. This is probably because most of my *friends* are around my own age (i.e. they're no *spring chickens* (1910—, originally US, now colloquial)). However, comments recently posted on Facebook sites belonging to the University of Leicester Students' Union and Fraternity & Sorority Life at Indiana State University both regularly included the following features, which are evidently transatlantic:

- messages entirely in lower case
- block capitals for emphasis
- omission of apostrophes, e.g. *Im* (more usually *im*)

- exclamation marks in place of full stops
- duplication of exclamation marks for emphasis, e.g. *!!!!*
- combinations of punctuation, e.g. *?!, ??!!*
- typographical expressions of emotion and attitude, e.g. *:) :D ;P lol, haha*
- duplication of letters for emphasis or to express enthusiasm, e.g. *yooooou, soooo, urrghhh, easyyy*
- abbreviations, e.g. *u* for *you*, *4* for *four*, *pic* for *picture*, *tix* for *tickets*.

These typographical features are unlikely to cross over to spoken English, although a few of the abbreviations can be represented in speech. The slang terms found in the students' comments tend to be the ones they would use in face-to-face conversation, so there are differences between how British and American students expressed themselves. In this small sample, Indiana State students used *awesome* and *sweet* (1821—, originally British criminals) to express approval, alongside *dork* "fool" (1967/8—) and *bump dat!* "forget it" (since at least 1989). Leicester students used *prick* "a stupid or contemptible person", *roomie* "a room-mate" (1911—, originally US), *yo* to express approval (1918—, originally US; also used to attract attention since at least 1958), *dreamy* "attractive" (1941—, originally US, also used ironically), *classic* to express approval (1944—), *rocking* "excellent" (1953—, originally US), *holy shit* to express surprise (1966—, originally US), and *hanging* "hung-over" (1971—, originally US). There are overlaps in slang usage, but national differences remain.

However, these students didn't always post their comments using slang and unconventional typography. In debates about increasing student fees and about the rules of fraternity and sorority membership, student posters on Facebook tended to use Standard English, and to spell and punctuate in a much more formal style than when they were discussing social events. As in speech, context is all.

Slang dissemination in the IT age

Many social-networking sites include microblogs in the form of status updates, whereby users can post brief observations about their current feelings and activities. The best known microblogging site is Twitter (launched in 2006). Users now post almost a hundred million *tweets* of up to 140 characters every day. Users can *follow* one another by arranging for tweets by particular individuals or organizations to be sent to them. Posts can be sent publicly or privately, and many organizations and individuals who tweet do so using Standard English. However, because of the limited characters available, microblogging is characterized by much more compressed language use than blogging, including all the typographical features found on Facebook. Slang and colloquial terms in posts on trending topics on 5 November 2010, included *scrub* "to cancel" (1828—, originally British), *peeps* "people: close friends" (1847—), *freaking* "utterly" (1928—), *top dollar* "a high price" (1970—), *holy crap* [to express surprise] (since at least 2000—), and *pimp* "to customize in an ostentatious style" (2000—, originally US), all of which originated in and are frequently used in speech. Individual posters do indicate their location, but it isn't possible to verify this or use it as the basis for searching. Twitter provides a general impression of slang usage, but isn't much help with distribution. The international intimacy promoted by tweeting may lead to increased awareness of national differences in slang, but it's very unlikely to spell the end of national or regional difference in use.

Even where the same words are used around the world, there are differences in how they're used and how often. Like earlier social and technical innovations that we've already seen, Twitter has introduced its own terms, and Nexis newspaper searches allow us to track trends in their use. Even people who aren't Twitter-users will probably be familiar with *tweet* "a message posted on Twitter", voted the American Dialect Society Word of the Year in 2009, and *twitter* "to post a message on Twitter". Although neither is yet included in the *OED*, they're commonly used in the press, along with various related forms. Figures 22 and 23 trace the use of *twitter* and *tweet* in *The San Francisco Chronicle*, from Twitter's home city, *The New York Times*, *The Guardian* (London), and *The Australian*. There was a background level of use with reference to birds, singers, and sound systems, but the

San Francisco Chronicle began to use these words with reference to Twitter in 2006, an increase that's barely visible here. The main increase, in San Francisco and elsewhere, was during 2009.

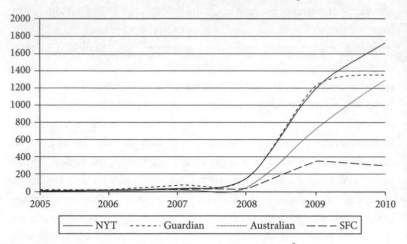

22 Newspaper articles including *twitter*, and related forms.[2]

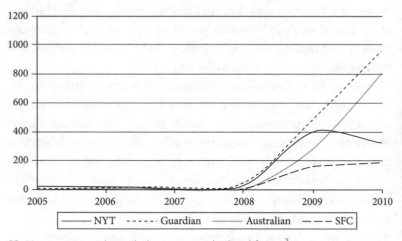

23 Newspaper articles including *tweet*, and related forms.[3]

[2] *twittered, twitters, twitterer, twitterers, twittering, twittersphere, twitterholic, twitterholics, twitterati.*

[3] *tweets, tweeted, tweeter, tweeters, tweeting.*

Twitter's official guide to terminology recognizes *tweet* as a noun and verb, and *Twitter* only as a trade name and in the form *twitterer*.[4] The newspapers don't follow these guidelines, with the *New York Times* developing a marked preference for *twitter*, while the *Guardian* and (perhaps) the *San Francisco Chronicle* appear to be moving towards a preference for *tweet*.

Newspaper searches for less frequent Twitter terms provide more varied results, shown in Figure 24. Before Twitter was launched, *trend* (top left) was already being used as a verb in the American and Australian newspapers, usually with reference to economic developments. In 2008, the *Guardian* began to use it in the same way, and then led the way with its increasing use with the sense "to be popular on Twitter", in 2009. The *Guardian* and *New York Times* made steadily increasing use of *hashtag* "the # symbol, used to mark keywords in a message" from 2009 (top right), with the *Australian* racing to catch up in 2010, at which point the *San Francisco Chronicle*'s use declined. *Retweet* "to resend someone else's tweet" (bottom left) sees a steady increase from 2009 in all the newspapers, except for the *New York Times*, where there's a marked decrease in 2010. This decrease is matched by that of *unfollow* "to cancel a request to see messages from a particular twitterer" (bottom right) in both the *New York Times* and the *San Francisco Chronicle*, though its use in the *Guardian* and the *Australian* continues to rise. British journalists' fascination with Twitter is fed by the activities of high-profile political and celebrity tweeters. On a larger scale, American journalists may be overwhelmed by the quantity of material available.

A by-product of these developments has been the increasing use of *twit* "a fool". Although used at a very low rate in all of these newspapers, the *Guardian* saw an increase from 25 to 59 instances (136%) between 2008 and 2009, and the *Australian* saw an increase

---

[4] Both *Twitter* and *Tweet* are trademarked, and although the company ask that they be capitalized to emphasize this, most newspapers use lower case. In an attempt to maintain clarity, I'm using upper case for references to the company and lower case for lexical items.

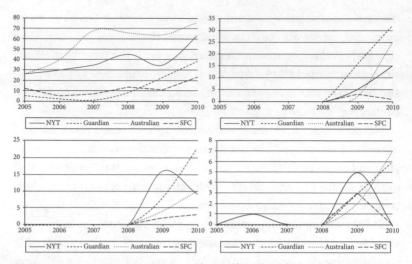

24 Newspaper articles including *trend* (top left), *hashtag* (top right), *retweet* (bottom left), *unfollow* (bottom right), and related forms.[5]

from 25 to 41 instances (64%) between 2009 and 2010, in each case corresponding with the increase in Twitter terms. *Twit* may be coming to mean "an opinionated or garrulous fool" as a result of its association with Twitter. In the American newspapers, where *twit* was less frequently used in any case, there was no change in frequency.

These Twitter terms began as jargon, with a fixed, precise, and narrowly constrained meaning. If Twitter is superseded by another technology with its own terminology, the wider use of Twitter terms may be short-lived and future lexicographers will probably consider them to have been slang. Perhaps in twenty or thirty years' time these Twitter terms and conventions will have become a fond memory, like

---

[5] *unfollow, unfollowed, unfollowing; retweet, retweets, retweeted, retweeting; hashtag, hashtagged; trended, trending.* The agent nouns (*unfollower*, etc.) didn't occur. *Trend* was already so common as a noun that the inclusion of *trend* and *trends* would have obscured developments in the verb.

the terms now used only by a restricted number of Citizens' Band radio enthusiasts, such as *ten-four* "message received; ok; excellent" (1962—), *breaker* "one who interrupts a CB radio conversation; any CB radio user" (1963—), *smokey (bear)* "a state policeman" (1974—), and *ears* "a CB radio or antenna" (1976—). However, if Twitter terms continue in their current use over a longer period, they might come to be viewed as colloquial or even standard, and perhaps they already are in some circles. If Twitter terms extend in reference to other micro-blogging or social-networking sites, or to conversations taking place in the real world, those usages will each follow their own path into slang, colloquial, or standard usage.

Twitter terms offer unusually high-profile examples of the spread of new words and new usages through technological means. However, because many computer professionals start out as computer enthusiasts, there's a fluid line between amateur and professional. Computer users adopt and adapt manufacturers' jargon, and slang developed by computer users is often adopted by the commercial organizations catering to them. There have been computer *applications* since 1959, for example, but computer enthusiasts have used *app* since at least 1984. Voted American Dialect Society Word of

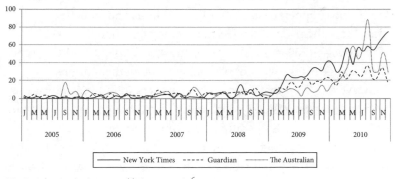

25 Articles including *app(s)*, by month.[6]

---

[6] Peaks before 2008 are caused by individuals whose last names are *App* or *Apps*, but the IT sense is used, at a low level, throughout this period.

the Year in 2010, *app* was used at a relatively low rate in mainstream newspaper coverage until July 2008, when Apple launched their *App Store* (see Figure 25). The time lag in the international adoption of commercialized slang in the mainstream press is now a matter of months rather than years, and there's no reason why it shouldn't be more or less instantaneous among the keenest purchasers of new technology. The movement from specialized slang to the mainstream can take rather longer.

Developments in the documentation of slang

When Partridge compiled his slang dictionary, his only evidence for Irish slang or the slang of American prisoners was its appearance in fiction, a small number of glossaries, and letters sent to him by correspondents. As you've seen throughout this book, the digitization of books and newspapers allows much easier access to historical evidence of slang usage and of attitudes towards it. Social-networking sites, chat rooms, games, and blogs can also be harvested for evidence of contemporary slang usage—often conveniently dated and some-times accompanied by all kinds of personal information about the writer, providing a whole new challenge to university ethics commit-tees. Lexicographers of slang now have far more and far better evidence available to them, but it can feel like looking for a noodle in a haystack. If you *google* (2000–) a slang term now, you might find thousands of hits, but then the work of ploughing through them begins.

We've also seen that early computer users found innovative ways to document their slang collaboratively. Although early computer users sat at terminals operating from university mainframes, *bulletin boards* "systems giving computer users access to text and files con-tributed collectively and stored centrally" (1979–) enabled them to form groups and discuss specialist interests using telephone lines, but connection charges tended to ensure that these remained relatively local. The Jargon File, discussed above, existed first as a text file that

THE GREAT THING ABOUT
THE INTERNET IS THAT NO ONE
KNOWS YOU'RE A NERD!

COMIC BOOK
CHAT ROOM

CHRIS MADDEN

26 Talking the talk: Chris Madden, 'Internet Nerd'.

could be edited by anyone who had access to it at Stanford and, later, at MIT (the Massachusetts Institute of Technology), where a backup was stored. These variant versions, with separate updates by multiple contributors, were periodically combined to produce a new master document, which is now numbered 4.4.8 and updated by a single editor. Numerous updated versions of the Jargon File are preserved as html and text files in various online locations and several book-editions have been published.

Bulletin boards were superseded by newsgroups, which performed much the same function. In the early 1990s, users of a newsgroup called *alt.rap* found themselves having regular and increasingly repetitive discussions about the meaning of terms heard in rap music, and a glossary was compiled and updated by Patrick Atoon and (later) Niels Janssen. *The Rap Dictionary* became accessible to many more people when it migrated to the Web in 1994, and has been user-edited since it became a wiki in 2004. It's now possible to trace changes made to an entry, and to undo changes made by other people. For example, in July 2004 one user posted the following definition for the verb *front*:

> Pretend to be that which you are not; act tough. "You can't front on that" – Beastie Boys (So what'cha want [1992]).

In January 2005, another user added a query:

> What about how Ghostface's usage of the term in Theodore Unit's song "Wicked With Lead"? "In those Coca-Coal rugbys, 2 bitches with a front in my mouth" What does 'front' mean in this context?

This was quickly moved to the 'Discussion' section, where it still languishes unanswered, but over the next few years three additional senses were added, numbered 2–4 in the current version:

> 2. To bluff or to be a coward. [added March 2006]
> 3. To pretend to not be interested; as in "why you frontin' on my boy for?" [added April 2006]
> 4. To give something away for a certin amount of time, and get paid back later. (Yo, front me a dime bag..) [added April 2007]

The Rap Dictionary now has almost 5000 content pages, each of which defines a slang term or provides information about rap music and artists. As in all wikis, the quality is variable, but the dictionary is still overseen by Atoon, and other users edit one another's entries and reinstate earlier versions where necessary. Worth an estimated $11,607, it receives approximately 4500 page views per day.

Other online slang dictionaries originated in the Internet era, and always existed as web pages. Some are entirely static and text-based; others are updated by an editor or editorial term. Chris Lewis's *Online Dictionary of Playground Slang* allowed its users to contribute slang terms by email, and these were mediated by its editor before they went online, although they weren't heavily edited or carefully checked. For example, *wicked* appears in the following definitions:

bostin' *n.* Wicked, brilliant, good, favourable, best. Source: UK (NW)

cushty *num.* Nice. Appropriate for needs. Cool or 'wicked'. Made popular by David Jason playing Derek Trotter in the famous TV series "Only Fools and Horses". Cockney's assume this is one of 'their' words, but in fact it derives from Romany!... Source: circa 1980's +, UK

nang *adj.* Means 'wicked', 'good'. Used as "Cor, that's nang." or, more phonetically, (cor, dass nang). Heard spoken by a white child, but possibly influenced by Black London English. Source: circa current, UK (S)

oudish *adj.* Very good, excellant, top hole, spiffing. Basically wicked good! Source: circa 1990's, UK

sed *adj.* (1) Great, magic, wicked good. Used as (That MP3 was sed!"... Source: circa 1990's, USA (Minn)

Although some of the additional information is correct (*cushty* is from Romany), grammatical labelling is erratic. Without further information, it's hard to know what to make of the dates, but *n(y)ang* (1922—), *cushty* (1929—), and *bosting* (1974—) are well established with this sense, though *oudish* (2001—) is less common in unambiguous contexts. I haven't found any evidence for *sed* at all. Users' submissions eventually grew into nine separate lists, which can be searched collectively. The site was first listed by Yahoo in 2000, and Lewis published *The Dictionary of Playground Slang* three years later. The most recent updates appear to have been in 2007, but the site has an estimated value of $4343, and still receives over 1200 page views a day. Clearly, an online dictionary that relies on a single person to mediate and edit entries submitted by multiple users makes a heavy demand on its editor's time. An enthusiastic individual may be willing to put in the required time to begin with, but this enthusiasm is unlikely to be sustainable in the long run, particularly if it doesn't generate enough income to free them from paid work.

The *Online Slang Dictionary* has existed since 1996, and instead of relying on its editor, Walter Rader, to post updates and changes, this site allows users to edit existing definitions, record their own frequency of use, plot their position on a map, and vote on whether words are 'vulgar' or not by increasing or decreasing the proportion of a chilli pepper that's coloured red, starting from a default chilli rating of 50%. This user input is with reference to entire entries, which may include different senses and different parts of speech. Users often add definitions rather than editing existing ones. For example, the entry for *dude* reads:

To dress elaborately or flamboyantly. *got all duded up for the show.* [2002]
Used to express approval, satisfaction, or congratulations. [2002]
Can sometimes be used when something disappointing happens. *Dude, that's stupid.* [2003]
1) goes before a sentence in exclamation to get the listeners attention 2) a way of referring to someone. *Dude, I finally figured out how to play that really hard song on my guitar! Do you understand what I'm trying to say, Dude?* [2003]
an expression meaning "yes, very good, cool, hello, etc." *Dude! Good to see ya!* [2003]
Distain. *Dude.* [2004]
Greeting. *Dude!* [2004]
Is there someone in the closet with a knife? Origin: Rob Schnider stand up *Dude?* [2004]
used to obtain another persons attention, used to reference a person without using their name. *Hey dude, what are you doing?* [2004]
a man *Hi dude, waht's up?* [2006]
A friend or buddy *Dude, what's on your face?* [2007]
a male. *That dude over there is pretty cute. He's a weird dude.* [1998]
To show polite acceptance of one's presence or approval of one's suggestion. [2004]

A total of 95 users had voted in response to the question 'How common is this slang?' 78 said 'I use it', 3 'No longer use it', 11 had 'Heard it but never used it', and 3 'Have never heard it'. 28 had voted on 'How vulgar is this slang', resulting in a meaningless 11% vulgarity rating. Several users of the term had mapped their positions on the west and east coasts of the United States, with a large gap in the middle, with isolated users in Mali, Russia, India, and Singapore. No British users had mapped their usage, though *dude* is commonly used as a term of address in the UK. *D00d* is defined separately on *The Online Slang Dictionary*, with no link provided between the two spellings. If users were willing to read other definitions before posting their own, to check for other possible spellings, and to take the time to provide information about their own usage for terms that other people had posted, this could be a very useful online resource. Links to Twitter for each term provide particularly interesting evidence of contemporary use, although there's a lot of background noise. The website receives approximately 23,600 page views per day, and has an estimated value of $51,757.

An even more profitable business model was adopted by *Urban Dictionary*, founded in 1999 by a first-year computer science student at California Polytechnic State University, as a parody of *dictionary. com*. Aaron Peckham couldn't have anticipated how many definitions the site would eventually host (over 6 million at the time of writing). By 2005, he was making 'a very small profit' after covering his costs, but by 2009 he'd given up the day job. Two dictionaries in book form, *Urban Dictionary* calendars, and a wide range of products customizable with any definition from the site combine with advertisements from Google AdSense to generate income. A 'word of the day' email list, Facebook and Twitter links, a text message lookup system, and a version designed for searching by phone all ensure that the *Urban Dictionary* website receives as many hits as possible. This is clearly successful, because the website receives an estimated 1.6 million page views each day, and is worth approximately $3.47 million.

Urban Dictionary celebrates its democratic status, emphasizing that anyone can post terms and definitions and that no editorial judgements are made on the grounds of quality. A selection from among the definitions for *minger*, in which references to individuals' names are replaced here by 'XX', illustrates some of the problems with *Urban Dictionary*'s contents:

a woman u take out back and shoot *damn that chick is minger (I'd Better go take her out back and shoot her)* [2003]

Any hata. [2003]

ugly and spoty person with bad teeth and breath. may have a nice ass. XX
[2003]

a minger is a fucker. it is a very versatile word similar to fuck except you can
say it in public without getting dirty looks because no one knows what
you're talking about. *Ming off!* or *What the ming does that girl think shes
doing with my man?* or *Whatever, go ming yourself.* [2004]

someone who is the coolest person in the world. not only are they hot as
hell, they are fun to be around and put your stick in. *DAMN NUKKAH! look
at dat fine ass minger.* [2004]

Since 2005, volunteer editors have sifted through users' contributions
to filter out nonsensical submissions and personal, sexist, and
racist definitions (though racist and sexist terms can be defined).
Editors aren't permitted to reject submissions they consider to
be incorrect. A few definitions for *minger* from after this date will
allow you to judge the success of the editors' application of these
rules:

A person who is a descendant of a Mexican and Ginger. Who has black thin
hair and is white freckly skin. Mingers are also ugly as shit. One example of
a ginger is XX. *XX is a Minger.* [2008]

Someone who is ugly, fat, gross or otherwise undesirable. *XX is a minger.*
[2009]

the ugliest person i know. she is the definition of smelly and fat and is
terrible at netball. lazy and ungrateful, a minger sleeps and eats more than
anything else. You'd rather saw off your own foot than dare walking closer
to her *wow that XX girl is such a minger!* [2010]

Users can click a 'thumbs up' or 'thumbs down' symbol to indicate
whether or not they like a definition, and the definition with the highest
approval rating is presented first for each word. The last three examples
are among the lowest rated for *minger*, but thumbs up and down don't
always provide an indication of quality because insults directed towards
famous people tend to drift towards the top of the list.

In 2009, Peckham redefined *Urban Dictionary* as 'the dictionary you wrote' rather than 'the slang dictionary you wrote', in recognition that much of what it contains isn't slang. It also isn't a dictionary in any traditional sense, but it does contain raw materials that are invaluable to any serious slang lexicographer. An entry in *Urban Dictionary* doesn't prove that a word is still in use in a particular way, and much of its contents are just made up, but if an *Urban Dictionary* definition precedes other evidence, it can provide a reliable antedating. It also offers a forum for arguments about the meaning and origins of slang terms, but no definitive answers are provided.

Many online slang dictionaries have no pretensions to authority or comprehensiveness. They're intended as entertainment rather than education, and often rely on stereotypes about local and national groups. Dictionaries written from an outsider perspective often find it difficult to distinguish between dialect, colloquialisms, and slang. For example, *The Septics Companion* website purports to list British slang, but includes many terms that are standard in British English, such as *aerial* "radio antenna", *bank holiday* "a public holiday", and *car park* "parking lot". This represents a reversal of the position we saw in the nineteenth century, when British commentators considered all terms originating overseas to be slang. Professional lexicographers and lexicologists offer more authoritative sources of information about slang online, and some of these are listed in the notes.

Using online resources to document slang

I'm going to end this chapter by using online resources to trace the history of a slang word that's too new to be in any of my dictionary sources: *kettle* "to control protestors by containing them in a small area", often in the form *kettling*. Its first appearance in a newspaper with this sense was in the *Guardian* in March 2009, where *kettle* "an area surrounded by police" is also found. The BBC news website soon followed (April 2009), as did newspapers in the United States (May 2009), Ireland (December 2010), India (April 2010), Canada (May 2010), and South Africa (February 2011). Outside the UK, references were often to British policing tactics used in the UK or adopted abroad for events like the G20 summit, and *kettle* is sometimes described as a police term. This gives rise to the first hypothesis: 2009—, originally UK police slang.

However, while newspaper citations prove that journalists around the world use *kettle*, they don't prove that the police (or anyone else) use it, or that it's slang. There are several well-established police blogs and glossaries of UK police slang online, but none were using *kettle* with this sense before its appearance in the press in 2009. This doesn't prove that it wasn't police slang: it could have been restricted to a single police force. On the other hand, it might have been a convenient metaphor invented by one reporter and misinterpreted by others, leading us to a second hypothesis: 2009—, originally UK journalists.

If *kettle* is journalists' slang, we might expect it to be restricted to newspapers, but Twitter provides 20 examples of *kettling* from the last 24 hours (and that's only the first screen), which satisfies me that the term isn't restricted to journalists. Since it's evidently reasonably widely used, we now have to decide whether it might be standard or colloquial rather than slang. Of the first 20 Google blog search results, seven place *kettling* in inverted commas, and five explain its meaning: it evidently isn't used widely enough that bloggers expect their readers to understand it. It's not colloquial, then, or restricted to journalists, and it's not police slang or jargon, so what is it?

The earliest example I've found online is from 2003, written from the perspective of protestors, with two from 2005 referring to protests in Hamburg and Hong Kong. Three of the earliest examples are ultimately from Indymedia sites, which offer 'grass-roots, non-corporate, non-commercial coverage of important social and political issues'. This suggests a third hypothesis: 2003—, originally protest groups. Various websites state that the tactic of kettling was first used in response to protests in Seattle in 1999, and some assume that the term also dates from then, but online searches don't support this position at present: it's possible that 2003 could be antedated using written sources, but at least we would now know where to start looking.

Conclusions . . . and questions

Naturally, the introduction of these new technologies has given rise to new terms, both formal and informal. Commercial terms tend to be assimilated quickly by those marketing, reviewing, and using new products, sometimes spreading rapidly into general usage. Computer users also develop their own slang to supplement the technical and informal terms used by industry professionals.

Computers have also allowed people to document their own slang in innovative and interactive ways. Although the results aren't always very good, this material will continue to be invaluable to slang lexicographers, and the wealth of material online allows us to seek evidence in new ways. Online citations also raise new questions that I'll attempt to answer here, in case any budding slang entrepreneurs are reading this book.

- Can online terms be categorized as slang? I would say yes: online and spoken language aren't distinct anymore, if they ever really were.
- Do people use slang terms in the same way online as in speech? Probably not entirely: the way people use slang terms is conditioned by the context, on and offline. The way people use slang online is likely to be influenced by their anticipated audience or by the image they want to project of themselves. But it's a less distorting lens than the literary and media representations we've relied on until now.
- Can you be sure when and where an online citation was written? This depends on your source: on newspaper websites and blogs you'll be able to see the date of original posting, but for some websites you may only be able to see when it was last updated. In this case, even if you're certain a term was used before that date, you're going to have

to look elsewhere for concrete evidence. Take datings from Google Books with extreme caution: there are about 20,500 twenty-first century hits for *prithee*.

- Is the concept of national slang still sustainable? I think it is. Though the proportion of slang that's international may continue to rise, it's also possible that new terms will develop to maintain distinctiveness, as has happened with African American slang.
- Fellow Australians use this term. Can I label it 'Australian'? Before you label something as 'British', 'American', 'Canadian', or whatever, decide what you mean by that label and find out whether it's accurate. You can't rely on your own intuitions, but blogs offer really useful evidence.
- Isn't slang changing so rapidly that it's no longer possible to keep up? No. You've seen that a lot of the slang used today has been around for a surprisingly long time. If no one had documented the early uses of these terms, we'd think they were new. The same goes for current slang. Some of the slang you use will fall from use in a few years time; some will spread to wider international or colloquial usage. In either case, isn't it worth documenting that you used it?
- Have online slang dictionaries put professional slang lexicographers out of a job? Absolutely not. The more (mis)information there is online, the more necessary it becomes to have authoritative sources.
- Could slang lexicography be done to a higher standard online? Hell yes! Online slang lexicography could combine professional standards with input from slang-users around the world. A site that received enough hits could generate the money to pay for high-quality research and editorial work. How wicked would that be?

Endnotes

David Crystal, *Language and the Internet*, 2nd edn (Cambridge: Cambridge University Press, 2006), and Greg Myers, *The Discourse of Blogs and Wikis* (London: Continuum, 2010), both provide fascinating accounts of online language use, but neither has much to say about slang. In 1959, a member of MIT's Tech Model Railroad Club (TMRC), called Peter Samson, had documented terms used by model train enthusiasts at the university <http://tmrc.mit.edu/dictionary.html>. Overlaps between this list and the Jargon File are relatively few in number, but reveal hybrid social connections. The latest print version is Eric

S. Raymond and Guy L. Steele, *The New Hacker's Dictionary*, 3rd edn (Cambridge, MA: MIT Press, 1996). The unedited original file is available at <http://www.dourish.com/goodies/jargon.html>, and the current revision at <http://www.catb.org/jargon>.

'Me g0 gr4b s0Me k0ph33', like many examples from this section, is from Erin McKean, 'L33t-sp34k', *Verbatim* 27/1 (2002), 13–14. Greg Costikyan, 'Talk Like a Gamer', *Verbatim* 27/3 (2002), 1–6, provides many of the lexical examples and initialisms cited here. J3ff C4r00s0 (Jeff Carooso), 'Are you l33t?', *Network World*, 17 May 2004, Back News, 76, documents the decline of leetspeak. The exchange from the *World of Warcraft* forum <http://eu.battle.net/wow/en> (EU site) is no longer accessible online. I've changed the posters' names. Computing terms were listed as slang in Scott LaFee's 'We're Spammin' Now; So Can any Chiphead', *The San Diego Union-Tribune*, 10 May 1995, Lifestyle, E3; and Jim McClellan's 'Netsurfers [sic] Paradise', *The Observer*, 13 Feb. 1996, Life, 8.

'Alpo and Fray' by Seth Ferranti (aka Soul Man) on <http://www.gorillaconvict.com/blog> was posted on 2 Oct. 2010 and edited two days later. You can read Bock the Robber at <http://bocktherobber.com> and watch *Skanger Me Banger* on *YouTube* at <http://www.youtube.com/watch?v=tPddpNuzLn8>. I looked at the Facebook sites for the University of Leicester Students' Union site and Fraternity & Sorority Life at Indiana State University on 5 Nov. 2010, and considered posts from the past month or so. Many of the comments appeared to be from students new to the institutions who were, presumably, using slang terms they'd learnt at home. It's possible that different slang would have been used later in the academic year.

Twitter's user statistics and glossary are at <http://support.twitter.com/articles/166337-the-twitter-glossary>. The graphs showing the dissemination of Twitter terms come with a health warning. They make no distinction between grammatical forms, so *tweet* "a message" and *tweet* "to send a message" are counted together and the results are combined here. These are counts of articles containing the words rather than of word frequency, which may deflate the results. However, Nexis results sometimes include multiple editions of the same newspaper, and this will have an inflationary tendency. In short, the numbers aren't comparable between papers, though the trends should be. My final caveat is that these figures don't tell us anything about the spoken usage of these journalists, let alone their readers, but they do tell us about the rate at which regular readers of these particular newspapers were exposed to these words.

Extracts from online dictionaries are uncorrected and appear as they do online. I've referred to *The Rap Dictionary* <http://www.rapdict.org/Main_Page> (my information about the history of this dictionary is from its 'about' page) and *The Online Dictionary of Playground Slang* <http://odps.org>, which gave rise to Chris Lewis's *The Dictionary of Playground Slang* (London: Allison and Bushby, 2003), described on the website and in David Newnham's 'The Word on the Street', *Times Educational Supplement*, 31 Oct. 2003, n.p. Estimates of web traffic and value in this chapter are from *Website Outlook* <http://www.websiteoutlook.com> [25 Mar. 2011]. *The Online Slang Dictionary* can be found at <http://onlineslangdictionary.com>, The Septic's Companion at <http://septicscompanion.com>, and information about *Urban Dictionary* is from its website and the following newspaper articles that documented its development: Thuy-Doan Le, 'Urbandictionary.com Sorts out Slang from Standard Lingo', *Sacramento Bee*, 7 Jul. 2005, n.p.; Casey Phillips, 'Web Site Compiles Online "Slangtionary"', *Chattanooga Times Free Press*, 23 Jan. 2008, Life, E1; Denise Ryan, 'Teen Slang: Enter at Your Own Risk', *The Vancouver Sun*, 12 Sept. 2009, A10; and Blessy Augustine, 'Word toyour [sic] Mother', *MINT*, 26 Dec. 2009, n.p. If you're interested in keeping up with the latest developments in English vocabulary, you might try <http://www.doubletongued.org> by Grant Barrett, <http://www.dictionaryevangelist.com> by Erin McKean, or <http://languagelog.ldc.upenn.edu/nll> by Mark Liberman *et al.* On Twitter, you can follow bgzimmer, GrantBarrett, or emckean. Early examples of *kettle* are available at <http://www.doubletongued.org/index.php/citations/kettle_11>, <http://kotaji.blogsome.com/2005/12/18/satueday-in-hong-kong-eyewitness-accounts>, <http://www.indymedia.org.uk/en/2007/04/368011.html>, and <http://de.indymedia.org/2007/05/179084.shtml>. Searches in this section were performed on 18 Mar. 2011.

12 Endsville

What is slang?

If you've stuck with me this far, you'll know that I disagree with some of the ways people have distinguished slang from other types of language. It's not necessarily new, or linguistically unusual, or associated with uneducated people, or necessarily vulgar. It's not just colloquial language taken to an extreme. It doesn't include dialect or jargon, although local and professional slang do occur. It doesn't include swearing, though some swearing is slang. Neither is it restricted to the spoken language to the extent that it once was. It isn't necessarily used for deliberate effect. Slanginess isn't a quality of words or meanings: what's slang in one context wouldn't be slang in another. It isn't bad to use slang, but it isn't good to use it either. What's key is whether you use it well—in an appropriate context and in a way that achieves the result you want. Unfortunately, the judges of your success (your audience), who may not even agree among themselves, are applying ever-changing rules that no one will ever explain to you clearly.

So is *slang* a useful word? Bethany Dumas and Jonathan Lighter wrote a long article asking that very question, and concluded that it is, as long as it's used carefully. They argued that an expression that fulfilled two or more of the following criteria should be considered slang:

1. if it were used in formal speech or writing, it would lower the tone (with a jarring or comical effect)
2. its use implies familiarity with the thing being referred to and a rejection of the more conventional views of those who might not be familiar with it
3. it is a taboo word in conversations with people of greater power or higher social status
4. it is used in place of a more widely known synonym.

It is worth noting that these criteria all refer to how expressions are used rather than to the expressions themselves, which is great, but while these filters might eliminate some contenders, I'm not convinced that they'd block out all other types of non-standard English. *Mardy* "moody" (1903—, UK dialect) would fulfil 1 and 4, and probably 2 and 3, but it isn't slang. *Poo* "faeces; a lump of excrement" (*c.*1939—) would tick 1 and 4, and probably 3, but it's now colloquial in British English. Criteria 3 and 4 more or less guarantee that all swear words are categorized as slang, which makes it impossible to distinguish between widely used and restricted forms.

What these criteria don't acknowledge is the importance of slang in creating and maintaining a sense of group or personal identity. Slang isn't just about rejecting conventional values and words. It's also about fitting in: about conforming to the way your friends speak, or the people you'd like to be friends with. These four criteria also imply that slang is used with deliberate intention, but most slang is used without self-reflection. The most common slang terms are used repeatedly to express value judgements and affiliations. For example, in Pixar's *Finding Nemo*, Marlin (a clownfish) comes round after a run-in with some jellyfish to find himself riding on the shell of a turtle:

> Crush: Dude [Marlin Groans] Oh, he lives! Hey Dude!
> Marlin: [Groans.] What happened?
> Crush: Oh, saw the whole thing dude! First we were like whoa. Then we were like wooo. And then you were like woaoaor.
> Marlin: What are you talking about?

Crush: You, mini man! Taking on the jellies! You've got serious thrill issues,
    dude! Awesome!

Marlin: Ooh oh, my stomach!

Crush: Oh man, hey, no hurling on the shell, ok dude? Just waxed it.

Marlin: So, Mr Turtle...

Crush: Hey, dude, Mr Turtle is my father. Name's Crush.

Marlin: Crush, really? Ok Crush. Listen, I need to get to the East Australian
    Current. EAC.

Crush: Dude. You're riding it dude. Check it out!

Crush's repeated use of *dude* adds nothing to the content of his comments, but it tells us a lot about him (laid-back surfer) and how he feels towards Marlin (friendly and respectful). He switches to *man* when he wants to make a serious point and still defines his self-identity in opposition to his parents, even though he's 150 years old. *Dude* is an expression of Crush's identity every bit as much as his Californian accent, along with *like, check it out, hurl, ride,* and *awesome.* But Crush doesn't stop to agonize over his word choices. The turtles Crush hangs out with all say *dude,* and it's become part of their group identity: a turtle that didn't say *dude* would be marginal to this group, and it would be hard to pin down whether its *dude*lessness was cause or effect.

Representations of slang

But turtles can't talk. That wasn't real slang: like most of the quotations in this book, it was a representation of the speech of a character type rather than a sample of actual speech. In films and other forms of representation, words are chosen very deliberately with an eye to their effect on viewers, listeners, or readers. Children watching *Finding Nemo* probably pick up that there's an amusing difference between the over-anxious urban clownfish and the laid-back turtle, but they may not be able to identify the meaning of their accents or the connotations of their word choices. These additional layers of meaning are for adult viewers.

Representations of slang on screen are misleadingly convincing: we forget entirely that the characters are carefully honed products of meetings and script changes, with every word chosen for optimum effect. Their artistic merit doesn't rely on the slang being up to date or realistic: it can convey character traits and information about relationships even if it isn't an accurate representation of how people really speak. But there are also plenty of representations of slang that are just lazy reworking of stereotypes. There are documentaries about frogs and there's Kermit. What's difficult is telling the difference between the two. I think *Finding Nemo* is great and the turtles speak convincingly, but what do I know? If you were riding the waves in California in 2003, you'd be a better judge, but could you distinguish between the way you spoke in 2003 and the way you spoke in 2002? Could you be sure the way you spoke was representative of all Californian surfers? Are you sure you were quite as central to the surf scene as you'd like to believe?

We can check contemporary television and cinematic use of slang by listening to speech and looking at tweets and blogs and other online material, but representations of slang in novels and plays, which can be just as convincing, can't be verified in this way. When we come across sixteenth-century beggars or eighteenth-century socialites speaking in a particular way, we're likely to assume that this is really how that type of person spoke at that time. Maybe they (or some of them) did, but that's only likely if their author mixed in the appropriate circles, had a really good ear, *and* resisted the temptation to exaggerate for comic or dramatic effect. Slang used on stage or on the page will probably have been as unfamiliar to most of its contemporary audience as it is to us, and most of them would have been no better judges than we are. There are similar problems with all the other types of evidence available to us: journalists may report stereotype rather than reality, Old Bailey records provide us with reported speech rather than accurate transcripts, and many slang dictionaries copy earlier slang dictionaries. Letters, blogs, even autobiographies, are written self-consciously. It's next to impossible to write without imagining a reader or engaging in greater self-reflection than we use in speech.

Before (I hope) you throw your hands up in despair, let me just say that although we can't rely on any of these types of evidence on their own, they often coincide. Where playwrights, novelists, and letter-writers use or talk about the same terms, apparently independently, we can start to rely on their evidence. What we're collecting is circumstantial evidence, but if we get enough of it, it does become convincing.

Slang creation, use, and documentation

We've seen that some conditions are particularly conducive to the development of slang. Conditions conducive to the use of slang are much easier to fulfil: all you need is a standard language in a society that's big enough to break into subgroups, whether defined by social class, age, gender, or any combination of these and other factors. There has to be some movement between the groups, or at least some admiration or emulation. Until relatively recently, the people documenting slang have been the literate elite with contacts in journalism or publishing, and their personal experience of slang-creators and even slang-users has often been minimal (see Figure 27). For this reason, slang has often been attributed to groups closer to those in power: not African American musicians, for example, but beats (primary adopters), or young people in general (secondary adopters). Writers of slang dictionaries have often picked up their evidence from representations rather than slang usage, and the representation and documentation of slang have both been subject to censorship.

With increasing literacy, relaxed censorship, and greater access to publishing technologies, including the Internet, some of these boundaries have begun to dissolve. Advertisers, entertainers, the media, and Joe Blogger sometimes simultaneously create and represent 'slang' (see Figure 28). If this catches on, it may genuinely become slang

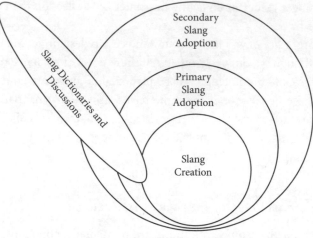

27 A model of traditional slang creation, adoption, representation, and documentation.

through use. The documentation of slang is no longer restricted to any one group: slang-creators and adopters can use and discuss their own slang in dictionaries and online discussions. Although the situation represented by Figure 28 offers the potential for more informed accounts of the origins of slang, it also generates misinformation. The transition between these two models isn't complete, and probably never will be. Commentators and dictionary-makers wanting to provide broad coverage will still have to operate under the traditional model, to some extent, though with greater access to documentation by the inner circles.

Slang and freedom

It's no coincidence that the groups considered to be particularly creative makers and users of slang have generally been oppressed (African Americans, gay men, the working classes, etc.) or marginalized (young people, criminals, drug-users, etc.). If you're a member of a

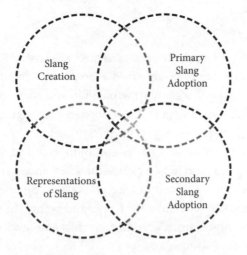

Slang Dictionaries and Discussions

28   A model of contemporary slang creation, adoption, representation, and documentation.

group that isn't oppressed or marginalized, you don't have much reason to undermine the hierarchy. But why the repeated pattern in which the dispossessed create slang terms and the privileged adopt them? Why did upper-class British men emulate working-class men in the nineteenth century? Why do middle-class white teenagers emulate inner-city African Americans today? The answer must surely lie in the freedoms that come with being marginalized and the restrictions that come with being a member of polite society. No one would expect a working-class man to spend his leisure time drinking tea in a drawing room, so the upper-class young man rebelled against the constraints of respectability by using working-class slang. We don't expect black rap artists to have progressive attitudes towards gender or sexuality, and white teenagers (white rap artists) feel free to adopt the sexual politics of rap along with its slang. By identifying with disadvantaged minorities, slang-users can show their disdain for the standards and traditions of mainstream society without actually having to give up their privileges or go to the trouble of being creative in their own right.

Slang and gender

Slang has often been about gender as well as class and ethnicity. In 1922, Otto Jespersen (who deserved a better fate than to be quoted mainly for the sake of argument) wrote that women exert a 'great and universal influence on linguistic development through their instinctive shrinking from coarse and gross expressions', in contrast with men, who 'want to avoid what is commonplace and banal and to replace it by new and fresh expressions'; to men 'are due those changes by which we sometimes see one term replace an older one, to give way in turn to a still newer one, and so on'. In other words, women create euphemisms and men create slang. Jespersen went so far as to say that using slang 'is undoubtedly one of the "human secondary sexual characters"', though presumably in the same way that a well-paid job is: slang use is a product of social structures and rules, not of inherent physical or psychological difference.

Women have played a vital, though probably involuntary, role in the development of slang. Rebellion is less rewarding if no one is upset by it, and we've seen that the restriction of women's talk has been intertwined with the development of slang around the world. For much of the period covered in this book, middle-class young women with a rebellious streak have only been able to adopt young men's slang, having been forced into the position of secondary adopters by the restrictions of their own lives. Now that young women have more freedom, they both use and develop more slang of their own. Fortunately, there are still plenty of people willing to supply the necessary disapproval.

National slang

Slang is also associated with the question of national identity, though the nationality of slang terms can be a complicated business. Figure 29 contains parallel subcategories of slang terms (it's impossible for

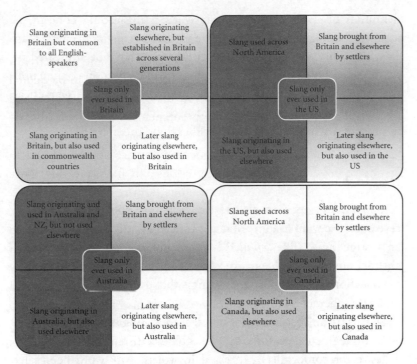

29 Slang nationalities.

them to be identical because of the historical differences), showing that different definitions of 'national slang' operate in different contexts. Putting aside the complications caused by national colloquialisms, solid grey boxes indicate categories of slang that are usually considered national slang. Gradated grey indicates categories of slang only sometimes considered national. Those categories of slang that aren't claimed as national are left white. Only 'American slang' encompasses terms originating elsewhere, sometimes on the assumption that all slang used in America is American in origin. Conversely, 'Canadian slang' is defined most narrowly, in opposition to both British and American slang.

Any dictionary of national slang that doesn't explain what it includes and excludes isn't worth buying, but there isn't a definitive definition of national slang because it's a misleading concept: it assumes both greater conformity and greater distinctiveness than exist in reality. A particular slang usage may have been created in Australia and only ever used there, but it will be used in conjunction with slang with various other origins and distributions. A practical account of 'Australian slang' would need to include all these other terms, but a symbolic account would exclude them.

One last metaphor

The metaphors used to discuss slang, in this book and elsewhere, reveal that we want to think of it as a concrete entity, although *slang* is an abstract noun (like *defiance*, *solidarity*, or *evaluation*). Even as an abstract noun, it's problematic. When *slang* is used to refer to a word or collection of words, it seems to imply that they are *slang*, or that it's a quality inherent in them.

So let's try an abstract metaphor, if such a thing is possible. Slang is an attitude (insolence, for example, coolness, disdain, admiration, or a desire for conformity) expressed in words. Any word habitually used with one of these slangy attitudes retains the association, but the association wears off when the word is used by people who don't share or are only pretending to share the attitude. When a group of people are stereotyped by their attitude, outsiders will find signs of it even where it isn't being expressed. Words associated with the attitude will come to be used in representations of the group. Most of us don't analyse our attitudes while we're expressing them, but members of the group may find pleasure or take pride in their attitude, and wish to represent it to the world or encourage other people to adopt it. Others will guard their attitude fiercely against intruders and feel resentful when people they see as members of their own group express a different attitude.

Attitudes are exported along with political and economic influence. Britain's attitudes were influential in the eighteenth and nineteenth centuries. American attitudes have been influential since WWII. We all have attitudes, but if we're in line with the majority, we tend not to acknowledge our own. Attitudes don't have an independent existence: they're products of people, relationships, and contexts.

THE END
"the last straw" (1919-1975, originally Australian)
"perfection" (1950-1996, US jazz slang)

Endnotes
Bethany K. Dumas and Jonathan Lighter asked 'Is *slang* a Word for Linguistics' in *American Speech* 53 (1978), 5–17. Otto Jespersen is quoted from *Language: Its Nature, Development and Origin* (London: Allen & Unwin, 1922), 247–8. Marlin encounters the turtles in Andrew Stanton and Lee Unkrich's *Finding Nemo* (Burbank/Emeryville, CA: Walt Disney/Pixar, 2003). In a *60 Minutes* interview (broadcast 10 Oct. 2010), Eminem complained that his sexism is unfairly singled out for criticism because he's white. Any dictionary of 'American slang' will include numerous terms that originated in the UK, but Paul Dickson's *War Slang* (Darby, PA: Diane Publishing, 1994), allegedly listing 'slang expressions created by, for, or about American fighting men and women' (x), now in its third edition, provides a clear demonstration of the elasticity of the concept.

Acknowledgements

· ·

Figures 1, 3, and 17 are reproduced by permission of <http://www.offthemark.com>. Figure 2 was scanned by Philip V. Allingham, and is reproduced with permission from <http://www.victorianweb.org>. Figures 4, 8, 11, 20, and 21 are reproduced by permission of <http://www.cartoonstock.com>, and Figure 6 with the permission of Charley Krebs. Figure 12 is reproduced with permission from the British Library Board (© All Rights Reserved. The British Library Board. Licence Number: UNILEI22), and Figure 15 courtesy of the Library of Congress. Figure 19 is reproduced by permission of Ohio State University Libraries, and Figure 26 by permission of <http://www.chrismadden.co.uk>. Figures 5, 7, 13, 14, 15, and 18 were scanned by the University of Leicester Design Services. Greg at <http://bocktherobber.com> and Gorilla Convict at <http://www.gorillaconvict.com/blog> kindly gave me permission to use material from their blogs. Except where it has expired, copyright remains with the original holder. I would be glad to hear from the copyright holders for Figures 5, 7, and 18, which are reproduced without prejudice.

Work on this book was completed during study leave from the University of Leicester. I'm very grateful to my Head of School, Martin Halliwell, for his continued support, to Ruth Page for giving me the benefit of her much greater knowledge of online communication, and to Ben Parsons for his expertise on Early Modern contact with the Netherlands. I've also learnt a tremendous amount from my students, as will be apparent. I've enjoyed it too. Thanks very much. Michael Adams, Paul Denton, Jonathon Green, Alan Kirkness, Tim

Machan, and Sarah Ogilvie (in alphabetical order) were all incredibly generous in reading drafts and offering countless useful suggestions for their improvement. They have enhanced and enriched this book no end, and I'm enormously grateful to them. I'd also like to thank Julia Steer, Elmandi du Toit, and Jenny Lunsford at OUP, as well as Jack Whitehead and Michael Sheppard. The remaining faults are entirely my own.

Explanatory Notes

Abbreviations and typographical conventions

a.	preceding a date = ante (before)
	e.g. *a.*1590 = before 1590
AAVE	African American Vernacular English
AND	*Australian National Dictionary*
c.	preceding a date = circa (around)
	e.g. *c.*1590 = around 1590
HDAS	Lighter, *Historical Dictionary of American Slang*
MED	Kurath, *et al.*, *Middle English Dictionary*
n	noun; (in references) note
n.p.	no place of publication; no publisher; no page numbers
	e.g. (n.p.: Hemlock Press, 1910) = no place of publication given
	e.g. (London: n.p., 1910) = no publisher named
	e.g. (London: Hemlock Press, 1910), n.p. = no page numbers provided
NZ	New Zealand
OE	Old English (as used by the Anglo-Saxons)
OED	*Oxford English Dictionary*
r	after a page number = recto (the front of a page)
	e.g. 8r = the front of the sheet numbered 8
RAF	Royal Air Force
UK	United Kingdom
US	United States (of America)
v	after a page number = verso (the back of a page)
	e.g. 8v = the back of the sheet numbered 8
WWI	World War One
WWII	World War Two
+	in dates: indicates discontinuous evidence
	e.g. 1517+1972 = only two citations, with one from each of these years
-	in dates: indicates continuous evidence
	e.g. 1517⊠1972 = numerous citations spanning this period
—	in dates: indicates evidence of current use
	e.g. 1517— = used since 1517 and still in use

/   in dates: indicates the date range of a source

        e.g. 1888/94 = cited in a source published between 1888 and 1894

[ ]   in dates: indicates that the OED marks this citation as a dubious or marginal example

        e.g. [1941]+1952—

?   indicates an uncertain date or derivation

        e.g. ?1517 = the date of the source is debateable, but 1517 is based on the best evidence available

italics used for cited terms

" "   used for definitions

( )   indicate optional elements of definitions

        e.g. "a (fat) man" = "a man" or "a fat man"

[ ]   contain indications of meaning where a definition would be unhelpfully long

        e.g. [a type of whisky]

:   in definitions: indicates that the preceding element also explains the term's etymology

        e.g. *peeps* "people: close friends"

< >   contain spellings or URLs

A note on spelling

Slang words often vary in spelling, particularly when they are first written down. When I cite slang terms, I have used the spelling preferred by my dictionary sources, but the spellings in quotations will sometimes be different.

A note on dates: 'That's still in use'

For each of the slang words mentioned in this book, and for some of the colloquial and standard ones too, I've given dates of use in brackets. These are based on citations (verifiable examples of use) from the *Oxford English Dictionary* (*OED*), *Green's Dictionary of Slang*, the *Historical Dictionary of American Slang* (*HDAS*), and the *Australian National Dictionary* (*AND*), occasionally supplemented by my other cited sources. Qualified dates (e.g. 'since at least 2000—') are based on online searches and could probably be antedated. None of my dates indicates the whole period during which a word was used: only the time during which there's evidence of its use with the definition given. I'm using the dictionaries critically, and where I don't feel that a dictionary citation illustrates the meaning I'm talking about, I've excluded it.

Final dates are even more contentious than first dates of use. I decided not to give last dates where I have evidence of use in or after 2000 (e.g. 1966—). When the dictionaries didn't have contemporary citations for a term that I thought might still be current, I used Nexis newspaper searches, Google Blogs, and Google Books to determine whether or not it was. In each case, I looked for examples of people using the term rather than just talking about it, so 'He's what the earliest settlers might have called "a right minger"' and 'He's what we call a right minger round here' don't prove continued use, but 'He's a right minger' does. For most words there are plenty of examples of use, but if they're all of the first or second type, I haven't recorded them as current. I've also excluded later citations from dictionary sources from the dates given.

It's very hard to pin down when a word falls from use altogether, because anyone who remembers using it themselves, remembers someone talking about it, sees it written down, hears it in a song or a film, or comes across it by any other means, might use it again at any time. It's probable that some of the terms with last dates are still in use, but at a (perhaps temporarily) low frequency. Contemporary examples of slang senses for words frequently used in Standard English have been particularly hard to locate.

All the dates cited here should therefore be understood as statements of the best evidence available to me at the time of writing. They could be proved wrong by additional evidence at any time, but if you disagree with them, please look first at my dictionary sources to see if they explain the difference of opinion.

A note on definitions: 'That's not what it means'

Most words have more than one meaning, and they're often only subtly different. For example, *animal* can refer to:

1. "any living creature"
2. (by narrowing of 1) "any living creature other than a human"
3. (by narrowing of 1 or 2) "any mammal"
4. (a figurative use of 2) "a human who behaves like an animal"
5. (by extension of 2) "a toy in the shape of a living creature"
6. (by narrowing of 4) "a passionate sexual partner".

There aren't any hard and fast rules about when these developments should be treated as separate meanings in a dictionary, though decisions are often influenced by the amount of evidence available. A dictionary-maker with dozens of examples of usage 6, for example, might treat it under a separate definition, but if it occurred only once, 6 could be listed in combination with 4, with the addition of "specifically a passionate sexual partner" if necessary.

Definitions in this book are generally based on my dictionary sources, and they reflect the divisions in meaning found there. If you feel that any of my definitions are too specific or just plain wrong, it may be that these are high frequency words for which closely related meanings have been split into separate definitions by the dictionaries I'm using. My evidence that a slang term has been used in a particular way isn't intended to exclude the possibility that you use it differently. I've had to resist the temptation to mention all the other meanings of the words listed here, some of which are only subtly different, to avoid getting bogged down in detail. Luckily, if you're not convinced by my definitions, you can usually check the evidence provided in the dictionaries I've used.

By saying that a word has one meaning, I'm not implying that it doesn't have other meanings. In Britain, *fanny* has been used to refer to the female genitals since 1835; in the United States it has been used to refer to the buttocks since 1919. An unrelated *fanny* was used at sea to refer to a mess-kettle (1904⊠1952). It would be nonsensical for me to tell you that *fanny* "buttocks" is wrong because the word really means "female genitals", and it would be nonsensical for you to tell me that the "female genitals" sense is wrong. Neither of us would pay much attention to Captain Birdseye insisting that *fanny* meant "kettle". These senses aren't mutually exclusive. The fact that one or more of us is right doesn't prove that the others are wrong, but we would all be justified in wanting evidence for meanings we're unfamiliar with. This is why I've provided the dates.

A note on sources

It wouldn't have been possible to write this book if so much work hadn't already been done in this area, and I don't want to take credit for other people's labours. Rather than peppering the discussion with bibliographic footnotes, I've listed my sources for each chapter in the endnotes

Bibliography

ADAMS, MICHAEL, *Slang: The People's Poetry* (Oxford: Oxford University Press, 2009).

ADE, GEORGE, *Fables in Slang* (Chicago & New York: Stone, 1899).

ALCOTT, LOUISA MAY, *Little Women* (Boston: Roberts, 1868).

'American Slang', *The Argus* (Melbourne), 21 Mar. 1918, 5.

'American Slang', *The Weekly Standard and Express*, 19 Aug. 1899, 3.

ANTHONY, WALTER, 'Our Cousin's Slang', *The San Francisco Call*, 21 Nov. 1909, 27.

—— 'Leslie on English as she is Spoke', *The San Francisco Call*, 20 Feb. 1910, 63.

'Anzac Slang', *The Argus* (Melbourne), 25 Dec. 1915, 4.

AUGUSTINE, BLESSY, 'Word toyour [sic] Mother', *MINT*, 26 Dec. 2009, n.p.

The Australian: <http://www.theaustralian.com.au>.

'Australian Speech and American Slang', *The Sydney Morning Herald*, 18 Jun. 1932, 9.

AVIS, WALTER S., *A Dictionary of Canadianisms on Historical Principles* (Toronto: Gage, 1967).

AWDELAY, JOHN, *The Fraternitye of Vacabondes* (London: John Awdelay, 1575).

BAKER, PAUL, *Fantabulosa: A Dictionary of Polari and Gay Slang* (London: Continuum, 2002).

BAKER, SIDNEY J., *A Popular Dictionary of Australian Slang* (Melbourne: Robertson & Mullens, 1941).

—— *New Zealand Slang: A Dictionary of Colloquialisms* (Christchurch: Whitcombe & Tombs, 1941).

BARKER, RONNIE, *Fletcher's Book of Rhyming Slang* (London: Pan, 1979).

'Barrack-Room Slang', *Pall Mall Gazette*, 17 Dec. 1896, n.p.

BARRETT, GRANT: <http://www.doubletongued.org>.

BAYARD, DONN, 'New Zealand English: Origins, Relationships, and Prospects', *Moderna Språk* 94/1 (2000), 8–14.

BBC News: <http://news.bbc.co.uk>.

'Betrayed by Slang', *Alderson News*, 11 Apr. 1918, 3.

BOCK THE ROBBER: <http://bocktherobber.com>.

BOLDERWOOD [*sic*], ROLF, *Robbery Under Arms* (Leipzig: Tauchnitz, 1889).
BOYLE, DANNY, *Trainspotting* (London: PolyGram, 1996).
BRANDON, HENRY, *see* W. A. Miles.
British Newspapers 1600–1900: <http://www.bl.uk/eresources/newspapers/colindale2.html>.
BROADUS, E. K., 'Campus English', *The Gateway*, 12 Feb. 1932, 5.
BROME, RICHARD, *A Jovial Crew, or, The Merry Beggars* (London: E.D. and N.E., 1652).
BROWNE, THOMAS, *see* Rolf Bolderwood.
BURCHFIELD, ROBERT (ed.), *The Cambridge History of the English Language, Vol. 5: English in Britain and Overseas* (Cambridge: Cambridge University Press, 1994).
'BUSHMAN', 'The Prevalence of Slang', *The West Australian*, 21 Aug. 1897, 6.
CAGE, KEN, *Gayle: The Language of Kinks and Queens* (Houghton, SA: Jacana Media, 2003).
CAROOSO, JEFF (J3ff C4r00s0), 'Are you l33t?', *Network World*, 17 May 2004, Back News, 76.
CASSIDY, DANIEL, *How the Irish Invented Slang* (Oakland, CA: CounterPunch, 2007).
CATTANEO, PETER, *The Full Monty* (Los Angeles: 20th Century Fox, 1997).
'A Chapter on Slang', *Caledonian Mercury*, 8 Jul. 1859, n.p.
CHAUCER, GEOFFREY, *The Canterbury Tales*: <http://www.librarius.com/cantales.htm>.
'A Chicago Girl's Slang', *Hampshire Telegraph and Sussex Chronicle*, 7 Nov. 1885, 1.
Chronicling America: Historic American Newspapers: <http://chroniclingamerica.loc.gov>.
COLEMAN, JULIE, *A History of Cant and Slang Dictionaries. Volume I: 1567–1784* (Oxford: Oxford University Press, 2004).
—— *A History of Cant and Slang Dictionaries. Vol. II: 1785–1858* (Oxford: Oxford University Press, 2004).
—— *A History of Cant and Slang Dictionaries. Vol. III: 1859–1936* (Oxford: Oxford University Press, 2008).
—— *A History of Cant and Slang Dictionaries. Vol. IV: 1937–1984* (Oxford: Oxford University Press, 2010).
'College Colloquialisms are a Mystery', *The Gateway*, 7 Nov. 1939, 2.
'Conversations in Slang', *The Advertiser* (Adelaide), 27 Jun. 1906, 8.
COPLAND, ROBERT, *Hyeway to the Spital-House* (London: Copland, *c*.1536).
COSTIKYAN, GREG, 'Talk Like a Gamer', *Verbatim* 27/3 (2002), 1–6.
CRANE, STEPHEN, *Maggie: A Girl of the Streets* (New York: Appleton, 1896).
CROWE, CORNELIUS, *Australian Slang Dictionary: Containing the Words and Phrases of the Thieving Fraternity, Together with the Unauthorised, though*

Popular Expressions Now in Vogue with All Classes in Australia (Fitzroy: Barr, 1895).

CRYSTAL, DAVID, *Language and the Internet*, 2nd edn (Cambridge: Cambridge University Press, 2006).

D., E. E., 'Of Some Australian Slang', *The Sydney Morning Herald*, 6 Oct. 1894, 5.

D., J., 'Slang', *The Newcastle Weekly Courant*, 23 Jan. 1892, n.p.

D., K. S., 'Slang and Accent', *The West Australian*, 12 Sept. 1892, 3.

DALZELL, TOM, *Flappers 2 Rappers: American Youth Slang* (Darby, PA: Diane Publishing, 1996).

DAVIDSON, MAX, 'Emma Thompson's Attack on Slang: the Pedants' Battle may be Lost', *Telegraph*, 29 Sept. 2010, n.p., available online at <http://www.telegraph.co.uk>.

'Degenerates' Slang Glossary', *Chicago Daily Tribune*, 8 Mar. 1900, 7.

DE HEK, DANNY, *New Zealand's Information Pack*: <http://www.nz-immigration.co.nz/lifestyle/slang-words.html>.

DEKKER, THOMAS, *O Per Se O, or A New Crier of Lanthorn and Candlelight* (London: John Busbie, 1612).

DENNIS, C. J., *The Songs of a Sentimental Bloke*, reprinted edn (Sydney: Angus & Robertson, 1915).

DICKENS, CHARLES, *The Posthumous Papers of the Pickwick Club* (London: Chapman & Hall, 1836).

—— *American Notes* (London: Chapman & Hall, 1842).

DICKSON, PAUL, *War Slang* (Darby, PA: Diane Publishing, 1994).

DILL, STEPHEN H. and CLYDE BURKHOLDER, *Current Slang: A Biennial Cumulation* (Vermillion: University of South Dakota, Department of English, 1969).

—— and DONALD BEBEAU, *Current Slang: A Biennial Cumulation* (Vermillion, University of South Dakota, Department of English, 1970).

DOYLE, RODDY, *The Commitments* (London: King Farouk, 1987).

DUCANGE ANGLICUS, *The Vulgar Tongue: Comprising Two Glossaries of Slang, Cant, and Flash Words and Phrases used in London at the Present Day* (London: Bernard Quaritch, 1857).

DUMAS, BETHANY K. and Jonathan Lichter, 'Is *Slang* a Word for Linguists?', *American Speech* 53 (1978), 5–17.

DU MAURIER, GEORGE, 'The Slang of the Day', *Punch*, 5 Aug. 1871, 44.

DUNNE, FINLEY PETER, *Mr. Dooley in Peace and War* (Boston: Small, Maynard & Co., 1898, repr. Urbana: University of Illinois Press, 2001).

E., B., *A New Dictionary of the Terms Ancient and Modern of the Canting Crew* (London: W. Hawes, *c*.1698).

Early English Books Online: <http://eebo.chadwyck.com/home>.

EBLE, CONNIE C., *Slang and Sociability: In-group Language among College Students* (Chapel Hill: North Carolina University Press, 1996).

'Editorial Notes', *Red Deer News*, 3 Apr. 1906, 4.

EGAN, PIERCE, *Life in London* (London: Sherwood, Neely & Jones, 1821).

Facebook: <facebook.com>.

FAIMAN, PETER, *Crocodile Dundee* (Hollywood: Paramount, 1986).

FINERTY, JAMES J. *Criminalese: a Dictionary of the Slang Talk of the Criminal* (Washington, DC: [self-published], 1926).

'Flapper Filology', *Philadelphia Evening Bulletin*, 8 Mar. 1922, 9.

FRENCH, PHILIP, 'Leaving', *The Observer*, 11 Jul. 2010, New Review, 26.

GAILLARD, SLIM, *Vout-O-Reenee Dictionary* ([?Hollywood: Atomic Records], 1946).

GALSWORTHY, JOHN, *To Let* (London: Heinemann, 1921).

GAMES, ALEX, *Balderdash and Piffle* (London: BBC Books, 2006).

Gay Girl's Guide to the U.S. and the Western World (n.p., *c.*1955).

Glossary of Eton Expressions: <http://www.etoncollege.com/glossary.aspx>.

GOLDSMITH, OLIVER, *She Stoops to Conquer, or The Mistakes of a Night* (London: F. Newbery, 1773).

Google Blog Search: <http://blogsearch.google.com>.

Google Book Search: <http://books.google.com>.

Gorilla Convict Blog: <http://www.gorillaconvict.com/blog>.

GRANVILLE, WILFRED, *Sea Slang of the Twentieth Century* (London: Winchester, 1949).

GREEN, JONATHON, *Green's Dictionary of Slang* (London: Chambers, 2010).

GREENE, ROBERT, *A Disputation between a He Coney-Catcher and a She Coney-Catcher... Discovering the Secret Villainies of Alluring Strumpets* (London: T.G., 1592).

GROSE, FRANCIS, *A Classical Dictionary of the Vulgar Tongue* (London: Hooper, 1785).

The Guardian: <http://www.guardian.co.uk>.

HARMAN, THOMAS, *Caveat or Warning for Common Cursitors* (London: William Griffith, 1567).

HARRISON, TRACEY, 'It's True. Kids Don't Talk the Same Language; Slang Takes Over From English', *Daily Record*, 29 Jul. 1999, 26.

Hell upon Earth (n.p.: n.p., 1703).

HITCHIN, CHARLES, *The Regulator or, A Discovery of the Thieves, Thief-takers and Locks* (London: T. Warner, 1718).

HORNE, ALEX, *Wordwatching* (London: Virgin Books, 2010).

HOTTEN, JOHN CAMDEN, *A Dictionary of Modern Slang, Cant, and Vulgar Words*, 2nd edn (London: Hotten, 1860).

How to Speak EastEnders: A Brief Glossary of Cockney Expressions (n.p.: Lionheart, 1988).

'INDIGNANT', 'Slang Teaching in State Schools', *The Argus* (Melbourne), 20 Mar. 1896, 3.

Indymedia: <http://de.indymedia.org> and <http://www.indymedia.org.uk>.

The Jargon File (original version): <http://www.dourish.com/goodies/jargon.html>.

The Jargon File (current version): <http://www.catb.org/jargon>.

JESPERSEN, OTTO, *Language: Its Nature, Development and Origin* (London: Allen & Unwin, 1922).

JOHNSON, SAMUEL, *A Dictionary of the English Language* (London: J. & P. Knapton, 1755).

JONES, JACK, *Rhyming Cockney Slang* (Bristol: Abson, 1971).

JONSON, BEN, *The Alchemist* (London: John Stepneth, 1612).

JORY, REX, 'Aussie Slang is on the Endangered List Like Animals and Plants Facing Extinction', *The Advertiser*, 10 Aug. 2009, Opinion, 18.

KENDALL, PARK, *Dictionary of Service Slang* (New York: Mill, 1944).

KIPLING, RUDYARD, *Barrack-Room Ballads and Other Verses* (London: Methuen, 1892).

KOALA NET, *Australian Slang Dictionary*: <http://koalanet.com.au/australian-slang.html>.

KURATH, HANS *et al.*, *Middle English Dictionary* (Ann Arbor: University of Michigan Press, 1952-2001): <http://quod.lib.umich.edu/m/med>.

LAFEE, SCOTT, 'We're Spammin' Now; So Can any Chiphead', *The San Diego Union-Tribune*, 10 May 1995, Lifestyle, E3.

LANEHART, SONJA L. (ed.), *Sociocultural and Historical Contexts of African American English* (Amsterdam: John Benjamins, 2001).

LAUGESEN, AMANDA (ed.), *Glossary of Slang and Peculiar Terms in Use in the A.I.F. 1921-1924* <http://andc.anu.edu.au/australian-words/aif-slang>. See also A. G. PRETTY.

LAY, MAY AND NANCY ORBAN, *The Hip Glossary of Hippie Language* (San Francisco: [self-published], 1967).

LE, THUY-DOAN, 'Urbandictionary.com Sorts out Slang from Standard Lingo', *Sacramento Bee*, 7 Jul. 2005, n.p.

LEECH, JOHN, 'The Great Social Evil', *Punch*, 10 Jan. 1857, 114.

LEGMAN, GERSHON, 'The Cant of Lexicography', *American Speech* 26 (1951), 130-7.

Leicester Online Slang Glossaries: <http://www.le.ac.uk/ee/glossaries>.

LEVERAGE, HENRY, 'Flynn's Dictionary of the Underworld', *Flynn's* 3-6 (3 Jan.-2 May 1925), Vol. 3: 690-3, 874-7, 1056-7; Vol. 4: 118-9, 488-9, 664-5, 868-9, 1150-1; Vol. 5: 191-2, 280-1, 511-12, 660-1, 818-19, 968-9; Vol. 6: 116-17, 211-12, 426-7.

LEWIS, CHRIS, *The Dictionary of Playground Slang* (London: Allison and Bushby, 2003).

LIBERMAN, ANATOLY, *Analytic Dictionary of English Etymology: An Introduction* (Minneapolis: University of Minnesota Press, 2008).

LIBERMAN, MARK *et al.*: <http://languagelog.ldc.upenn.edu/nll>.

The Life and Character of Moll King (London: W. Price, 1747).

LIGHTER, JONATHAN EVAN, 'The Slang of the American Expeditionary Forces in Europe, 1917-1919: An Historical Glossary', *American Speech* 47 (1972), 5-142.

—— *Random House Historical Dictionary of American Slang* (New York: Random House, 1994–).

LIPTON, LAWRENCE, *The Holy Barbarians* (New York: Messner, 1959).

LIT, HY: <http://www.hylitradio.com/index.php?page=6>.

—— *Hy Lit's Unbelievable Dictionary of Hip Words for Groovy People* (Philadelphia: Hyski, 1968).

LITTLE, BERT, 'Prison Lingo: A Style of American English Slang', *Anthropological Linguistics* 24 (1982), 206–44.

LYNCH, JOHN, 'Oxford Costume', *Punch*, 7 May 1853, 191.

MCCLELLAN, JIM, 'Netsurfers [sic] Paradise', *The Observer*, 13 Feb. 1996, Life, 8.

MACKAY, CHARLES, 'Fashionable Slang', *North Wales Chronicle*, 18 Jan. 1879, n.p.

MCKEAN, ERIN, 'L33t-sp34k', *Verbatim* 27/1 (2002), 13–14.

—— <http://www.dictionaryevangelist.com>.

MCREYNOLDS BANKS, J. R., 'An Unabridged Collegiate Dictionary', *Columbia Jester* 27 (Dec. 1927), 10; (Jan. 1928), 19; (Feb. 1928), 14; (Mar. 1928), 12.

MAITLAND, JAMES, *The American Slang Dictionary* (Chicago: privately printed, 1891).

MALCOLM, SHERMAN, *The American Slangist* (Blenheim, Ont.: n.p., 1888).

MATHERS, ANN, *The Hip Pocket Book* (New York: Aphrodite Press, 1967).

MATSELL, GEORGE, *Vocabulum, or, Rogue's Lexicon* (New York: Matsell, 1859).

MAYHEW, HENRY, *London Labour and the London Poor* (London: Woodfall, 1851).

'May Use Native Slang But Professor Bans Americanisms', *The Courier-Mail* (Brisbane), 13 Dec. 1933, 12.

MENCKEN, H. L., *The American Language* (New York: Knopf, 1919).

MILES, W. A., *Poverty, Mendicity and Crime... to which is added a Dictionary of the Flash or Cant Language, Known to Every Thief and Beggar edited by H. Brandon, esq.* (London: Shaw and Sons, 1839).

'Military Slang', *Hampshire Telegraph and Sussex Chronicle*, 23 Jun. 1894, n.p.

'Modern American Slang', *The Queenslander* (Brisbane), 11 Jun. 1892, 1134.

MONCRIEFF, W. T., *Songs, Parodies, Duets, Chorusses* [sic] *&c. &c.: in an Entirely New Classic... in Three Acts, called Tom & Jerry, or, Life in London* (London: John Lowndes, 1821).

MOORE, BRUCE, *Speaking Our Language: The Story of Australian English* (Oxford: Oxford University Press, 2006).

MORRISON, ARTHUR, *Tales of Mean Streets* (London: Methuen, 1865).

'Mrs Langtry at the Prince's Theatre', *The Times*, 21 Jan. 1885, 5.

MÜGGE, MAXIMILIAN AUGUST, *The War Diary of a Square Peg* (London: Routledge, 1920).

'Multimedia News Release – Don't be 'Naff' – Learn to Use 'Chuffed', 'Laughing Gear', 'Half Four' and Dozens of other British Slang Words before your London Holiday', *PR Newswire US*, 4 May 2005.

MYERS, GREG, *The Discourse of Blogs and Wikis* (London: Continuum, 2010).

National Library of Australia, *Australia Trove*: <http://trove.nla.gov.au/newspaper>.

'Need of a Slang Dictionary', *The Times* (London), 23 Jun. 1919, 18.

The New Art and Mystery of Gossiping (London: n.p., ?1760).

NEWNHAM, DAVID, 'The Word on the Street', *Times Educational Supplement*, 31 Oct. 2003, n.p.

Nexis: <http://www.lexisnexis.com/uk/nexis>.

NOEBEL, DAVID A., *The Homosexual Revolution* (Tulsa, OK: American Christian College, 1977).

NYE, RUSSEL B., 'A Musician's Word-List', *American Speech* 12 (1937), 45–8.

O'FLAHERTY, H. C., *Life in Sydney*, ed. Richard Fotheringham, *Australian Plays for the Colonial Stage 1834–1899* (Queensland: University of Queensland Press, 2006).

OLIPHANT, LAURENCE, *Piccadilly* (Edinburgh: W. Blackwood and Sons, 1870).

The Online Dictionary of Playground Slang: <http://odps.org>.

The Online Slang Dictionary: <http://onlineslangdictionary.com>.

'On Slang', *The Times*, 31 Dec. 1913, 63F.

Ordinary's Account, see *Proceedings of the Old Bailey*.

ORSMAN, H. W., *Heinemann New Zealand Dictionary* (Auckland: Heinemann, 1979).

——— and DES HURLEY, *New Zealand Slang Dictionary* (Auckland: Reed, 1992).

OUTCAULT, RICHARD FELTON, 'The Yellow Kid Takes a Hand at Golf', *New York Journal*, 24 Oct. 1897, 8.

'A Parent', 'Slang Teaching in State Schools', *The Argus* (Melbourne), 23 Mar. 1896, 6.

PARKER, ALAN, *The Commitments* (Los Angeles: 20th Century Fox, 1991).

PARKER, GEORGE, *Life's Painter of Variegated Characters* (London: R. Bassam, 1789).

PARSONS, BEN, 'Dutch Influences on English Literary Culture in the Early Renaissance, 1470-1650', *Literary Compass* 4/6 (2007), 1577–96.

PARTRIDGE, ERIC, *Slang: Today and Yesterday* (London: Routledge and Kegan Paul, 1933).

——— *A Dictionary of Slang and Unconventional English* (London: Routledge, 1937).

——— *A Dictionary of Slang and Unconventional English*, 3rd edn (London: Routledge, 1949).

——— *A Dictionary of the Underworld* (London: Routledge & Kegan Paul, 1949).

PHILLIPS, CASEY, 'Web Site Compiles Online "Slangtionary"', *Chattanooga Times Free Press*, 23 Jan. 2008, Life, E1.

POULTER, JOHN, *The Discoveries of John Poulter*, 5th edn (Sherbourne: R. Goadby, 1753).

POUNTAIN, DICK AND DAVID ROBBINS, *Cool Rules: Anatomy of an Attitude* (London: Reaktion, 2000).

PRESTON, DONALD WESLEY, *A Survey of Canadian English Slang* (University of Victoria: MA thesis, 1973).

PRETTY, A. G., *Glossary of A.I.F. Slang* (typescript, Australian War Memorial). See also LAUGESEN, AMANDA.

The Proceedings of the Old Bailey: London's Central Criminal Court, 1674–1913: <http://www.oldbaileyonline.org/index.jsp>.

QUINION, MICHAEL, *Port Out Starboard Home* (London: Penguin, 2004).

RAMIREZ, J. DAVID *et al.* (eds.), *Ebonics: The Urban Education Debate*, 2nd edn (Clevedon/Buffalo/Toronto: Multilingual Matters, 2005).

RAMSON, W. S., *The Australian National Dictionary* (Melbourne: Oxford University Press, 1988). <http://203.166.81.53/and>.

The Rap Dictionary: <http://www.rapdict.org/Main_Page>.

RAYMOND, ERIC S. AND GUY L. STEELE, *The New Hacker's Dictionary*, 3rd edn (Cambridge, MA: MIT Press, 1996).

'Restaurant Slang', *Penny Illustrated Paper and Illustrated Times*, 10 Oct. 1908, 234.

'Rhyming Slang', *Penny Illustrated Paper*, 20 Aug. 1910, 248.

RODGERS, BRUCE, *The Queens' Vernacular: A Gay Lexicon* (San Francisco: Straight Arrow, 1972).

ROGERS, DAVID, 'We Know What U Mean, M8. Innit?', *Times Educational Supplement*, 12 Dec. 2008, n.p.

ROSS, ALLY, 'If You Tinkin' Ali G is Racis You Can Kiss Me, Batty Boy', *The Sun*, 12 Jan. 2000, n.p.

RUEHL, P., 'Dinkum Slang gets the Gong', *Sunday Herald Sun*, 9 Apr. 1995, News, 6.

RYAN, DENISE, 'Teen Slang: Enter at Your Own Risk', *The Vancouver Sun*, 12 Sept. 2009, A10.

SAMSON, PETER *et al.*, *Abridged Dictionary of the TMRC Language*: <http://tmrc.mit.edu/dictionary.html>.

SCHOROW, STEPHANIE, 'Brit-slang Invasion; Blimey!', *The Boston Herald*, 11 Jun. 1999, Arts & Life, 63.

SCORSESE, MARTIN, *Gangs of New York* (New York: Miramax, 2002).

Sea Cadets Training and Administration Website: <http://www.sccheadquarters.com>.

SEBASTIAN, HUGH, 'Negro Slang in Lincoln University', *American Speech* 9 (1934), 287–90.

'The Sentimental Bloke', *The Advertiser* (Adelaide), 10 Apr. 1918, 7.

The Septic's Companion: <http://septicscompanion.com>.

SHADWELL, THOMAS, *The Squire of Alsatia* (London: James Knapton, 1688).

SHAKESPEARE, WILLIAM, *The History of Henry the Fourth, Part I*. The Arden Shakespeare, ed. David Scott Kastan (London: Thompson Learning, 2002).

SIMPSON, J. A. AND WEINER, E. S. C. (eds.), *OED Online*, 3rd edn (Oxford: Oxford University Press, 2000–): <http://www.oed.com>.

Skanger Me Banger: <http://www.youtube.com/watch?v=tPddpNuzLn8>.

'Slang', *Daily News*, 25 Sept. 1868, n.p.

'Slang', *The Sheffield and Rotherham Independent*, 9 Nov. 1869, 7.

'Slang', *The Star*, 3 Apr. 1875, n.p.

'Slang in the Salon', *Glasgow Herald*, 22 May 1865, n.p.

'Slang in Women's Colleges', *New York Tribune*, 19 Jan. 1901, 7.

'Slang Not Slander', *The Queenslander* (Brisbane) 21 Apr. 1888, 628.

'Slang Words and Phrases', *The Times*, 3 Apr. 1858, 5F.

'A Society for the Suppression of Slang', *The Penny Illustrated Paper and Illustrated Times*, 22 Feb. 1873, 115.

'Society Slang', *Bristol Mercury and Daily Post*, 20 Nov. 1899, n.p.

South African Dictionary Unit: <http://www.ru.ac.za/dsae>.

SPENSER, EDMUND, *The Faerie Queene* (London: William Ponsonbie, 1590).

STANTON, ANDREW AND LEE UNKRICH, *Finding Nemo* (Burbank/Emeryville, CA: Walt Disney/Pixar, 2003).

STEELE, GUY L., *The Hacker's Dictionary: A Guide to the World of Computer Wizards* (New York/London: Harper & Row, 1983).

'A Study in Current Slanguage', *The San Francisco Call*, 31 Oct. 1897, 23.

SWIFT, JONATHAN, *Polite Conversation in Three Dialogues* (1738), ed. George Saintsbury (London: Chiswick, 1842).

'TEACHER', 'Slang Teaching in State Schools', *The Argus* (Melbourne), 27 Mar. 1896, 6.

THORSON, LARRY, 'Cockney Soap Opera on the Telly in United States', *Associated Press*, 8 Jan. 1988.

'The Tichborne Case', *The Times*, 25 Jun. 1880, 4.

The Times Digital Archive: <http://archive.timesonline.co.uk/tol/archive>.

Times of India: <http://timesofindia.indiatimes.com>.

TOOK, BARRY AND MARTY FELDMAN, *Round the Horne* (London: Woburn Press, 1974).

TOTTIE, GUNNEL, *An Introduction to American English* (Oxford: Blackwell, 2002).

'Translated for English Use', *Boston Daily Globe*, 17 Aug. 1913, 45.

TRUMBLE, ALFRED, *Slang Dictionary of New York, London and Paris* (New York: National Police Gazette, 1881).

TUFTS, HENRY, *A Narrative of the Life, Adventures, Travels and Sufferings of Henry Tufts* (Dover, NH: Samuel Bragg, 1807).

TWAIN, MARK, *Adventures of Huckleberry Finn* (New York: Century, 1884).

Twitter: <http://twitter.com>.

Urban Dictionary: <http://www.urbandictionary.com>.

'Use This Dictionary of Slang in Exploitation', *Film Daily* 49, 22 Aug. 1929, 15.

VAN PATTEN, NATHAN, 'The Vocabulary of the American Negro as Set Forth in Contemporary Literature', *American Speech* 7 (1931), 24–31.

VAUX, JAMES HARDY, *Memoirs of James Hardy Vaux* (London: W. Clowes, 1819).

Voices from the Days of Slavery: <http://memory.loc.gov/ammem/collections/voices>.

WALKER, GILBERT, *A Manifest Detection of the Most Vile and Detestable Use of Diceplay, and Other Practices Like the Same. A Mirror Very Necessary for all Young Gentlemen [and] Others Suddenly Enabled by Worldly Abundance, to Look in* (London: Abraham Vele, c.1555).

WASHINGTON, BOOKER T., *Up From Slavery* (Garden City, NY: Doubleday, 1901).

WEAVER, PAUL et al., 'County Cricket Blog – as it Happened', *Guardian Unlimited*, 20 Jul. 2010: <http://www.guardian.co.uk/sport/blog/2010/jul/20/county-cricket-live-blog>.

WEBB, H. BROOK, 'The Slang of Jazz', *American Speech* 12 (1937), 179–84.

WebsiteOutlook: <http://www.websiteoutlook.com>.

WEBSTER, NOAH, *An American Dictionary of the English Language*, 2 vols. (New York: S. Converse, 1828).

WELSH, IRVING, *Trainspotting* (London: Secker & Warburg, 1993).

WENTWORTH, HAROLD AND STUART BERG FLEXNER, *Dictionary of American Slang* (New York: Crowell, 1960).

'What They Say about Slang', *University Missourian* 80, 17 Dec. 1913, 2.

WHITMAN, WALT, *Complete Prose Works* (Whitefish MT: Kessinger, 2004).

Wikipedia (English): <http://en.wikipedia.org/wiki/Main_Page>.

—— *Jazz Discussion*: <http://en.wikipedia.org/wiki/TalkJazz>.

WILLARD, JOSIAH FLYNT, *Tramping with Tramps* (London: T. Fisher Unwin, 1899).

—— *The World of Graft* (London/New York: McClure, Phillips & Co., 1901).

WOLFRAM, WALT AND BEN WARD (eds.), *American Voices: How Dialects Differ from Coast to Coast* (Oxford: Blackwell, 2006).

WOOLLEY, LISA, *American Voices of the Chicago Renaissance* (Dekalb: Northern Illinois University Press, 2000).

World of Warcraft (EU site): <http://eu.battle.net/wow/en>.

WYCHERLEY, WILLIAM, *The Country Wife* (London: Thomas Dring, 1675).

'Yankee Slang Increasing', *The Argus* (Melbourne), 19 Jul. 1913, 8.

Your Vaseline Hair Tonic Flip-Talk Contest Booklet (New York: n.p., c.1961), n.p.

YouTube: <http://www.youtube.com>.

YULE, HENRY and A. C. BURNELL, *Hobson-Jobson* (London: John Murray, 1886).

Word Index

This index links cited non-standard words sharing the same form regardless of meaning or grammatical function. The spelling of slang words varies. I have chosen the forms preferred in my main dictionary sources. References in bold are to illustrations.

Index

· ·